INTERNATIONAL REVIEW OF
HISTORY EDUCATION

Woburn Education Series
General Series Editor: Professor Peter Gordon

For over twenty years this series on the history, development and policy of education, under the distinguished editorship of Peter Gordon, has been evolving into a comprehensive and balanced survey of important trends in teaching and educational policy. The series is intended to reflect the changing nature of education in present-day society. The books are divided into four sections – educational policy studies, educational practice, the history of education and social history – and reflect the continuing interest in this area.

For a full series listing, please visit our website: www.woburnpress.com

Educational Practice
Slow Learners. A Break in the Circle: A Practical Guide for Teachers
Diane Griffin

Games and Simulations in Action
Alec Davison and Peter Gordon

Music in Education: A Guide for Parents and Teachers
Malcolm Carlton

The Education of Gifted Children
David Hopkinson

Teaching and Learning Mathematics
Peter G. Dean

Comprehending Comprehensives
Edward S. Conway

Teaching the Humanities
edited by Peter Gordon

Teaching Science
edited by Jenny Frost

The Private Schooling of Girls: Past and Present
edited by Geoffrey Walford

International Yearbook of History Education, Volume 1
edited by Alaric Dickinson, Peter Gordon, Peter Lee and John Slater

A Guide to Educational Research
edited by Peter Gordon

International Review of History Education, Volume 2:
Learning and Reasoning in History
edited by James F. Voss and Mario Carretero

INTERNATIONAL REVIEW OF HISTORY EDUCATION

Volume 3

Raising Standards in History Education

edited by

Alaric Dickinson,
Peter Gordon

and

Peter Lee
Institute of Education, University of London

WOBURN PRESS
LONDON • PORTLAND, OR

First published in 2001 in Great Britain by
WOBURN PRESS
Crown House, 47 Chase Side
London N14 5BP, England

and in the United States of America by
WOBURN PRESS
c/o ISBS
5824 N.E. Hassalo Street
Portland, Oregon 97213-3644

Website: www.woburnpress.com

British Library Cataloguing in Publication Data:

International review of history education
  Vol. 3: Raising standards in history education edited by
Alaric Dickinson, Peter Gordon and Peter Lee. – (The Woburn
education series)
  1. History – Study and teaching
I. Dickinson, A. K. (Alaric Keith), 1940 – II. Gordon, Peter
1927 – III. Lee, P. J. (Peter John), 1943 –
907

A catalogue record for this book is available
from the British Library

ISBN 0-7130-0224-7 (cloth)
ISSN 1461-4882

This series was formerly published under the title
International Yearbook of History Education
ISSN 1362-4822

Typeset by Frank Cass

Printed in Great Britain by Bookcraft, Bath

Contents

International Review of History Education
Vol. 3

Captions for Tables and Figures

Introduction: Raising Standards

'Standards'

The notion of 'standards' in history is usually treated by the press and politicians as something fairly straightforward. Students should know and understand history. Of course there is always the little matter of which passages of history they should know, and this guarantees lively, often petulant, debates whenever school history happens to be drawn to the attention of the public. But aside from content quarrels, 'knowing' and 'understanding' are taken as unproblematic; students need to know 'the facts' and understand them.

The idea that history is always more, and sometimes less, than 'the facts' does not go unrecognized, but it tends to appear as part of a self-evident distinction between 'history' and 'propaganda'. Everyone of good will and integrity knows what really happened. So 'the facts' somehow determine their interpretation and the story into which they fit.

In countries where there are overt struggles about the 'ownership' of history, it may be necessary to accept multiple perspectives, and then issues as to what history is to be taught merge with issues about which version of the past is to be ensconced in schools. Here unproblematic assumptions begin to break down, but the political difficulty can always be resolved either by marginalizing some accounts, or by stressing the liberal virtues of the existence of a variety (as if 'choice' between historical accounts were similar to consumers' decisions between shampoos or shoes).

In fact, of course, students will meet rival historical accounts outside school, however carefully they are sheltered in their encounters in classrooms or textbooks.[1] Unless they are given some tools for handling such differences, they will fall back on the everyday apparatus of 'fact' and 'propaganda', or 'opinion' and 'choice'. In the first case they will see history as given by the past, and so alternatives will be distortions or lies. In the second case they will be reduced to shoulder-shrugging helplessness, making 'personal choices' on the basis of their right to an opinion.[2]

Issues of this kind were at the root of changes of the kind that took place in the UK in the 1970s and 1980s. Similar changes were evident in some aspects of history education elsewhere (for example, in Spain and

Australia) and some tentative moves in the same direction in the USA. Interest in developments of this kind has come from history education specialists from a wide range of other countries (for example, China, Taiwan, Colombia, Portugal and Finland). But changes have often met resistance and in some countries promising early advances have been reversed by government fiat. In any case, the impact of such changes may be rather shallow. For example, although US history standards potentially offer the chance to give students an understanding of how the discipline of history works, the sheer weight of content, the influence of textbooks and the lack of teachers qualified in history all militate against the realization of that potential. Penetration seems far deeper in the UK than elsewhere, perhaps (paradoxically) as a result of the National Curriculum. (The review in this volume of *Issues in History Teaching*[3] supports such a view.) But in the UK too there are serious problems, and we will turn to these in the following section.

'Raising' standards

If 'standards' in history are not necessarily easy to agree on, or even just to pin down, it might be expected that 'raising' them might also be a complicated matter. Once again, however, for politicians, the press and their public, it looks simple. Teachers need holding to account, so targets have to be set, and teachers or trainee teachers must meet them. Everything must be monitored and inspected. Inadequate teachers – the ones who fail to meet their targets – should be 'helped' (the more liberal solution) or sacked.

This 'police' model assumes that the goals are clear and agreed, that achievement of them can be measured on at least an ordinal scale, and that it is cost-effective to carry out inspections of sufficient validity and reliability to distinguish between the good and the inadequate. None of these assumptions seems entirely secure.

It is this model that has recently prevailed in the UK. Approximately every four years inspectors (sometimes not history specialists, or even teachers) visit schools and carry out four-day assessments. Much depends on the few lessons they see in the four days, on the paperwork teachers can provide and on the visible signs (mostly also on paper) that the latter are efficiently monitoring their students. Even more turns on the grasp of the inspectors, which – judging by the language of many of the history reports – is often weak and algorithmic. In addition to inspections, schools are given places in 'league tables' according to their students' performance in all National Curriculum subjects, and, within this, history departments are judged by the examination results.

In training, beginner teachers are monitored on their achievement of 'standards'. These are discrete 'outcomes' statements that closely resemble a long-discredited behavioural objectives model, and are so numerous as to be unworkable. The danger is that a system of this kind produces mechanical, rule-bound assessment, in which monitoring against discrete statements supplants teaching towards understanding. A merely 'accounting' assessment against such standards can mean that real understanding of complex practices essential for effective teaching in the long term is discounted in favour of simplistic and low-level short-term procedures.

A very different way of thinking about improving history education is to recognize that policing may be necessary for the criminally idle or incompetent, but that for most teachers it is better to invoke their professionalism. Peter Seixas' discussion of the work of Shelly Winetraub and the teachers in Oakland offers a model more akin to the early days of the Spanish educational reforms, with their local and professional input, or the Schools History Project in the UK. History education is complex and difficult, partly because history (despite common assumptions) is counter-intuitive for youngsters: the ideas that form the basis of the discipline are not the ideas of everyday common sense. But it is also hard because the substance of history has consequences for how people see the world, and demands sensitivity and subtlety of a kind not to be found by following the rule-book. Deep understanding of particular approaches to history teaching cannot be inculcated through pressure on teachers, but grows out of the professional struggle to 'do things better'. Contrary to popular opinion, this is seldom a matter of 'methods', but more frequently of refining aims and targeting particular objectives, within a context of progression: a clear sense of the direction in which students should be moving. This in turn demands knowledge of the ideas students are likely to be working with (which sometimes means research knowledge). All too often in the absence of such knowledge, students' initial ideas are underestimated.[4]

Raising standards in history cannot sensibly be interpreted as students simply acquiring ever-increasing factual knowledge. Equally, any notion of 'understanding' that supplements 'knowing the facts' has to be spelt out so that there is some possibility of progression. This means that it should include some understanding of the basis of historical claims, a grasp of the differences between the status of singular factual statements and accounts or explanations, and an apparatus for handling rival interpretations. Development in understanding cannot be adequately characterized by facile use of words like 'describes', 'evaluates' and 'analyses' of the kind lamentably apparent in the new exemplar schemes of work for key stage 3 in the UK. Such catch-all descriptors of students' performance have to be filled out with specific ideas that mark important changes in the particular concepts that teachers are targeting.

Raising standards is no simple matter, either conceptually or empirically. If it is to happen, it must draw on research and practical experience, preferably from more than one country. The present Review makes a small initial contribution to what ought to be a sustained debate.

Perspectives on standards in history education: the 2001 Review
The first two chapters of this volume focus on work to raise standards in history initiated respectively in a district in California with very complex educational problems and in an inner-city school in New York. In 'Standards for Historical Thinking', Peter Seixas explains how early standards initiatives in North America were framed less on a notion of teaching for historical thinking than in terms of content. Those guiding recent history education reform in the Oakland District in California have addressed the problem of maintaining the state-mandated 'content standards' and at the same time building in a notion of historical thinking, of the methods and procedures by which knowledge of the past is created. Fundamental to their work is the view that historical thinking cannot sensibly be divorced from 'content' and that, as well as developing a clear statement of the fundamental concepts they are hoping to convey to all teachers and students, 'thinking standards', a successful local reform initiative also needs progammes for professional development, assessment, selection and development of materials, and research. Seixas reports in detail on the development of the first element, the standards document.

'What understandings do we really want our students to develop?' 'Why are such understandings important?' 'Is historical thinking a "relevant" aim in the development of students struggling in an inner-city area?' In 'Expecting High Standards from Inner-City Students', Veronica Boix Mansilla examines the role that disciplinary knowledge can and should play in the development of standards of less advantaged socio-economic groups. The course on autobiography and history that she taught in a school in Harlem aimed at helping students understand how people's lives are shaped by the historical times in which they live. Her case studies of three students illuminate the challenges and possibilities of expecting high disciplinary standards from 'city kids'. She argues that the need for disciplinary knowledge is particularly pressing among less privileged students because it is schooling that provides many of those students with the sole opportunity to explore the world through disciplines like history, science or literature. However, the degree to which disciplinary knowledge becomes a tool for social mobility depends less, she argues, on whether or not disciplines are emphasized in these students' curricula than on how they are represented in it. Preparing youngsters for a changing world, she claims, requires that we teach them to use disciplinary knowledge and modes of thinking as tools to engage in valuable enquiries about the world, not as ends in themselves.

Textbook narration is an important means for communicating society's accounts of events to students, and can be very influential in the achievement of standards. In Chapter 3 Dan Porat explores the nature of historical depiction in textbooks, following the changing representation of the Bar Kokhba Revolt in Israeli history textbooks over a period of five decades and showing how this changing depiction has corresponded to larger social considerations and political goals. He considers arguments for altering the nature of historical representation in textbooks, and concludes that textbooks remain primarily tools for the advancement of national identification among students. However, he also argues that history education must, through instruction, equip students with the conceptual tools for thinking historically and educate them to understand the limits of their ability to know.

Historical and international dimensions of history education can assist reflection on standards for history education. Thus argues Chara Haeussler Bohan, with particular attention to the work of the committee of Seven, a subcommittee of the American Historical Association concerned to improve the teaching of history in American secondary schools. In Chapter 4 she outlines the committee's work, including reference to its evaluation of history education in the United States, Germany, France, England and Canada. She considers the committee's recommendations and the long-term significance of their work. The work of the Committee of Seven stimulated heated debate over content and methods, echoed at the end of the twentieth century in the polarized debate that accompanied the work of those involved in the National Standards for History project in the 1990s. As Chara Haeussler Bohan emphasizes, understanding the relationship between the past and the present may help frame future deliberations regarding history curricula.

Sound empirical research can play a valuable role in the formulation and raising of standards. The next four chapters report on four recent major research studies on young people's historical thinking undertaken in Greece, England, Spain and Colombia. Irene Nakou reports on her longitudinal study of children's historical thinking within a museum environment. Her research is at the heart of the current debate on history teaching and learning in relation to working with sources, and is also related to current discussions on the changing character of museums and their educational and social role. Her longitudinal field study, based on over 1,000 responses provided by 141 pupils over a period of three years, answers questions about what pupils make of museum objects and gives a longitudinal picture of change in pupils' historical thinking on the basis of their handling of relics. Her research suggests that pupils' work with museum objects in a museum environment might be of great significance to the development of their historical thinking, especially if their work is related to carefully devised tasks that advance children's own potential in historical interpretation.

Chapter 6 reports part of the investigation and some of the findings of a project funded by the Economic and Social Research Council in England from 1991 to 1996. Project CHATA has been investigating the development of children's understanding of the second-order historical concepts of inquiry and explanation between the ages of 7 and 14 years. Among the findings reported here are that children's ideas about understanding and cause seem to be decoupled, in terms both of sophistication and progression, and that within the overall pattern of progression some 7-year-olds hold ideas about some aspects of historical explanation as sophisticated as those of most 14-year-olds. The research team suggests that insights into the development of children's ideas about history offer the prospect of basing history education on progression rather than aggregation, and of allowing history teaching objectives to be couched in terms that are discipline determined rather than content determined.

The next chapter is also concerned with the investigation of the development of children's ideas of a second-order concept. In 'Significance in History', Lis Cercadillo reports on her research, funded by the European Union, into progression in the understanding of historical significance in young people in Spain and England. Five types of historical significance are defined: contemporary, causal, pattern, symbolic and present/future. A model of progression in students' understanding was generated through a qualitative analysis considering these types of historical significance, and English and Spanish responses were compared across three age-bands: 12–13, 14–15 and 16–17 years. Cercadillo, a Marie Curie fellow, reports that the comparisons indicated several differences regarding types of significance and progression. She reports in detail on these differences.

In 'The Development of Historical Explanation in Children, Adolescents and Adults' Angela Bermúdez and Rosario Jaramillo report on their research to broaden knowledge of structural qualitative changes in students' understanding of history in order to construct a tentative model of the relationship between historical agents and their context in students' explanations of historical events. They claim that the process by which explanations become more and more complex depends not on the substitution of an intentional type of explanation for one of the structural type, but on the progressively more intricate and systematic articulation of the circumstances and the agents. They also claim that the results of their investigation suggest that the frontier between a logical, general structure of reasoning and the specific forms of reasoning of historical thought is more difficult to establish than authors such as Booth and Gardner suggest,[5] and than they had thought initially. They also report that their interviews showed students in grade 4 who had the same type of reasoning as students from grades 10 and 11. They advocate teaching that centres its attention on the careful learning of a wide range of contexts, but also warn of a need to consider carefully the relationship between 'teaching how to think' and 'teaching what to know'. Many innovative pedagogical approaches, they argue, unwisely assume that the only important aim is 'teaching how to think'.

The next two chapters focus on national efforts to raise standards in history education. In the first of these Yang Biao traces the evolution of history teaching in China in the twentieth century as a prelude to reporting initiatives in the 1990s, initiatives designed to meet the needs of a country moving from an agro-centred society to an increasingly industrialized one. He reports on the main features of the nationwide curriculum for history teaching in primary and junior high schools decreed in 1991, the curriculum for the more economically developed regions designed and implemented in Shanghai in the 1990s and the history curriculum for rural and mountainous areas designed by Zhejiang Province. During the Cultural Revolution, time for history teaching was reduced and finally obliterated. Now, in order to meet perceived economic and social needs, various history education initiatives are receiving official encouragement. Yang Biao sketches the main influences behind the new programmes.

In Chapter 10 Tony Taylor offers a brief report on current moves to raise history standards in Australia. In September 1999 the Minister of Education announced an unprecedented national inquiry into school history. Tony Taylor speculates on reasons behind this initiative and outlines the inquiry's methodology and main findings, and the recommendations submitted to the minister. These recommendations for raising standards include a national seminar to develop a coherent approach to the teaching and learning of Australian history in schools, a national centre for history education, a primary and secondary school history project and production of a handbook on the teaching and learning of history, civics and citizenship education. It is intended that this handbook will draw on national and international research and best practice.

The final chapter offers a review of *Issues in History Teaching*. As the authors stress, this review does not attempt to evaluate each paper in the book, or to discuss all the 'issues' it raises. Instead it considers the collection as evidence of the current agenda in history education and of the kinds of thinking that young teachers will meet, and hence as one indication of the condition of history education in England and Wales. History education in the United Kingdom has benefited greatly in the past three decades from the work of teachers, teacher educators and trainers, examiners, inspectors, textbook writers and curriculum developers. Nevertheless, concern about standards has been consistently and at times stridently expressed by some politicians, newspapers and parents. In their review of *Issues in History Teaching*, the authors suggest that if this book is evidence of the present state of history education in the UK then it seems that it is flourishing in many respects but that a recurrent problem, inevitably affecting standards in history education, is lack of subtlety and sophistication when it comes to conceptual analysis.

The editors hope that this volume of the *International Review of History Education* will be seen to be addressing important matters and opening up worthwhile debates. Looking ahead, they intend to seek articles and reports which will enable readers to keep in touch with the most important curriculum developments and research in history education. Unsolicited contributions will also be welcome. An authors' style sheet and general information for contributors are available on request from the publishers. We look forward to being able to provide reports and substantial articles on important developments in education from every continent in future volumes.

NOTES

1. J.V. Wertsch and M. Rozin, 'The Russian Revolution: Official and unofficial accounts', in J.F. Voss and M. Carretero (eds), *International Review of History Education: Vol. 2, Learning and Reasoning in History*, (London: Woburn Press, 1998), pp. 39–60.
2. See *CHATA* findings on student understandings of why there are differences between historical accounts. P.J. Lee, '"None of us was there": Children's ideas about why historical accounts differ', in S. Ahonen *et al.*, Historiedidaktik, Norden 6, Nordisk Konferens om Historiedidaktik, Tampere 1996. (*History Didactics: Sixth Nordic Conference on History Didactics, Tampere 1996*) (Copenhagen: Danmarks Laererhøjskle, 1997), pp. 23–58; P.J. Lee and R. Ashby, 'Progression in historical understanding 7–14', in P. Seixas, P. Stearns and S. Wineburg (eds), *Teaching, Learning and Knowing History*, (New York: New York University Press, 2000); R. Ashby and P.J. Lee, 'Information, opinion and beyond', paper given at annual meeting of AERA, San Diego, 1998.
3. James Arthur and Robert Philips (eds), *Issues in History Teaching* (London and New York: Routledge, 2000).
4. See the enormously valuable recent work of the National Research Council in the USA distilling robust principles of learning from 50 years of research: J.D. Bransford, A.L. Brown and R. C. Cocking (eds), *How People Learn: Brain, Mind, Experience and School* (Washington, DC: National Academy Press, 1999) and its shorter programmatic accompaniment, S. Donovan, J.D. Bransford and J. Pellegrino (eds), *How People Learn: Bridging Research and Practice* (Washington, DC: National Academy Press, 1999).
5. See particularly H. Gardner, *Frames of Mind* (New York: Basic Books, 1983); and M. Booth, 'Ages and concepts: A critique of the Piagetian approach to history teaching', in C. Portal (ed.), *The History Curriculum for Teachers* (Lewes: Falmer Press, 1987).

1

Standards for Historical Thinking: History Education Reform in Oakland, California

PETER SEIXAS

Much of the recent literature on pedagogical reform is built on notions of teaching for thinking or teaching for understanding.[1] Much of the recent research on history education reflects this theoretical framework, in its investigations of students, student teachers and teachers.[2] Based on a longer tradition of British work, these studies have in common a disciplinary conception of history. That is, they see knowing the past as a set of problems, the discipline of history as a set of practices with which to approach those problems, and the teaching of history as the development of children's competencies in those practices. The nature of historical thinking thus lies at the centre of the research, whether the focus is individual students or teachers, or the larger units of classrooms or departments.[3]

Early history standards initiatives in North America were framed less on this disciplinary conception of historical thinking, than on a set of history topics to be covered;[4] thus there has been a serious gap between the history standards movement and history education research. The Oakland Unified School District, in California, is one of the first North American jurisdictions to build its standards around historical thinking. As will become apparent in what follows, Oakland benefited from extraordinarily capable leadership at the district level. But the strength of that leadership was, in great measure, its ability to mobilize a committed cadre of teachers to carry the reform efforts forward. The problem those teachers faced was not only to effect changes in their own thinking and teaching, but to be able to communicate those changes – through a standards document – to other teachers in a way that was clear, powerful and persuasive. Fully understanding that they could not achieve change on the basis of a standards document alone, those who shaped the local reform programme developed initiatives on four additional fronts: an assessment programme, professional development, materials selection and development, and research.[5]

I participated in the district efforts as a highly interested outsider. Having presented several workshops to Oakland teachers, I initiated research both to document and to assist the change process, which I understood as directly aligned with reforms I had advocated over the preceding years. My role as researcher was thus both enhanced and complicated by my role as participant, consultant and advocate.[6] I observed and tape-recorded meetings, collected documents and tape-recorded individual, semi-structured interviews with district officials. I conducted semi-structured interviews with 11 (of 15) members of the District Standards Committee and collected questionnaires from 12.

It is too early to assess the impact of this programme either on teachers throughout the district or on their students. If the committee ultimately succeeds in generating a fundamental shift in how history education is conducted in Oakland – that is, in how teachers and students think about history – it will also have succeeded in providing a model for other jurisdictions hoping for similar reforms. If it does not (and this is still an open question) there is still much to learn from the process they have been through.

Historical knowledge is problematic: none of the ways in which we know the past provides a straightforward, uncontestable access to the truth.[7] Yet, in schools, historical accounts are most frequently presented as unproblematic sources of factual information. In this setting, the 'problem of historical knowledge' is too often understood simply as a problem of committing facts to memory, or, at best, separating 'biased' expressions of opinion from the true facts.[8]

Historical thinking consists of the practices necessary to confront the problem of knowledge about the past. There are many ways of conceptualizing the components of these practices. In discussing their own justification for using notions of 'evidence' and 'cause' to investigate children's historical thinking, Lee et al., note:

> We can split strands into sub-strands indefinitely, and what is a sub-strand as opposed to a strand? Why not start with children's notions of agency, rather than treat those ideas as part of their conception of cause? In the end we must accept that, just as a historical reconstruction is in fact a construction, so any hermeneutic effort can only produce something justifiable, not the only interpretation.[9]

They go on to note the limitations on the utility of any model of historical thinking. 'We can only hope to map tropisms which hold under current social, cultural and educational circumstances ... If teachers take a model seriously, its life may be even shorter.'[10] The measure of any scheme of historical thinking includes utility in not only mapping students' ideas, but also in communicating with teachers and curriculum workers who will use the scheme.[11] The teachers responsible for the Oakland School District's history standards based them on a notion of historical thinking consisting of five elements: chronology, evidence, diversity/multiple perspectives, interpretation and significance. How did they arrive at this, and what does it mean?

Setting Standards in Oakland

The Oakland Unified School District is the sixth largest in the state of California. The map of Oakland has a hole in it, where the separate, high-income, predominantly white district of Piedmont runs its own schools. Oakland has 53,000 students, 52 per cent of whom are African-American, 21 per cent Hispanic and 18 per cent Asian American. Thirty-two per cent are classified as Limited English Proficient (LEP) students. Eleven per cent of the students were suspended during the 1996/97 school year. The average grade for college preparation courses in grades 7 to 12, is D+.[12] It is the only district in California with a majority of African-American students. A five-week teachers' strike in 1996 left a legacy of mistrust. Oakland enjoyed the spotlight of the national press in 1991, for controversy over its history textbook adoption decisions, and in 1996/97 over its policy on 'ebonics'.[13] Teachers do not see it as an easy district in which to work.

In California history–social science is defined as a school subject, K-12, by the *History Social Science Framework*.[14] The framework provides both broad goals across the curriculum and course outlines for each grade level. Among the goals is a strand of 'historical literacy', which includes historical empathy, time and chronology, cause and effect, continuity and change, a recognition of 'history as common memory with political implications' and the importance of belief systems such as 'religion and philosophy'.[15] The four to ten pages of narrative for each course contain a range of kinds of statements, including substantive historical interpretation ('Jacksonian democracy should be analyzed in terms of the continuing expansion of opportunities for the common person'),[16] as well as pedagogical advice ('students should be encouraged to view historical

3

events empathetically').[17] More prescriptive state standards are currently under development.[18]

In 1991 Alice Kawazoe was recruited to establish a new Department of Curriculum and Staff Development for the district. She accepted on condition that she could appoint some key people to rethink the way school subjects were taught in Oakland. Her list included Shelly Weintraub. Weintraub had majored in history at the University of California at Berkeley, and had earned an MA in education at San Francisco State University, working on students' persuasive writing in social studies. She had taught in Oakland for 15 years, at both junior high and high school levels. As head of history–social science for Oakland, Weintraub cultivated an expanding core of history teachers between 1991 and 1996, through the development of curriculum materials and 'historiography' study groups led by local historians.[19] She was, in effect, laying the groundwork for the standards (Kawazoe interview, 16 October 1997; Weintraub interview, 8 November 1997).

In October 1996 Weintraub invited 15 teachers (K-12) to begin work on history standards for Oakland. All but three had taught in the district for more than ten years. Racially, they included African-American, European American, Japanese American and Latina teachers. Almost all of them had been involved in one or another of Weintraub's earlier projects, either the historiography groups, the development of the history kits or the Bay Area Writing Project. One of them, Stan Pesick, was in the final stages of writing a Stanford University doctoral dissertation on teaching and learning history.

The Bay Area Writing Project (BAWP) had an impact not only by forging links between English and history, but because of its attention to students' historical writing. As part of the BAWP, Renee Swayne had developed a unit around interpreting artifacts. Carole Pancho developed units on 'the forgotten heroes of history'. One unit on cowboys 'looked at black cowboys, women cowboys, and cowgirls in history and just how to develop that into units for primary students, tying in literature and writing' (Pancho interview, 16 October 1997). Grace Murozawa recalled the BAWP work as providing a framework for thinking about curriculum frameworks in general. Elizabeth Lay had a strong background in literature, writing and history, including an undergraduate degree in American Studies, and experience in both the California Literature Project and a professional development programme on the American West sponsored by the National Endowment for the Humanities. She too referred to the BAWP as a formative experience (Lay interview,

4

8 November 1997). Judy Yeager said simply: 'I tell people I've been BAWP'd' (Yeager interview, 7 November 1997).

Weintraub knew from the outset that the Oakland standards needed first to be explicit about a conception of historical thinking. Without this, teachers could follow the topics laid out in the document, but bypass the complex challenges posed by genuine historical knowledge. Secondly, the document needed to tie that conception to the substantive historical topics of the curriculum. She invited me to present a conception of historical thinking to the committee in a one-day workshop in October, 1996. Wanting the participants to understand variations in conceptions of historical thinking, I provided copies of the British National Curriculum and the US National Standards' section on historical thinking in addition to my own scheme of six elements of historical thinking.[20] The Committee met several times during 1996–97. They used my conception, those articulated in the British and US documents, as well as the framework, in order to construct a research-based conception of historical thinking which would be (a) appropriate for the Oakland School District and (b) possible to communicate to teachers who would not have been as thoroughly immersed in the discussions as had the committee. It was not a simple task.

By the beginning of a three-day work session in June 1997, as a result of extensive discussion, they had devised a set of four historical thinking standards: chronological/geographic thinking, evidence, diversity/ multiple perspectives and significance. 'Chronological thinking' enabled them to underscore the importance of contextual information as crucial for any exercise in historical thinking: here they could put the chronology of important events that would give students an overarching organizing framework when they thought about the past. 'Geographic' was added to recognize the importance of students understanding the spatial dimension of past events.

'Diversity/multiple perspectives' was a crucial addition. Politically, it was a way of signalling that history for the Oakland schools was going to build in viewpoints of those who were subjected to power as well as those who exercised it, and more specifically, that African-American viewpoints would be explicitly recognized throughout the curriculum. Under this standard, they also placed 'empathy' and 'moral judgment'. 'Analysis', 'causation' and 'interpretation' were all subsumed under the final standard, 'significance'.

As the committee members approached the construction of the document, they wanted to get across a notion of historical thinking and to tie it to curricular topics laid out in the state framework and standards at each grade level; and they wanted to approach these topics by way of large, synthesizing, thought-provoking and grade-appropriate questions which would frame individual units. Moreover, they needed to produce a manageable, usable document. Juggling all these requirements would prove extremely challenging. The committee divided into small groups, by grade level. By the end of the three days, they had made different amounts of progress, though none had finished the task. By the end of the summer, they sent their work to Weintraub, who reviewed it with Stan Pesick and Alice Kawazoe.

When the committee reconvened in mid-October, Weintraub did not mince her words: she explained that much of the work the teachers had done since the last meeting was not usable. 'I looked at [the submissions] and thought, "Shoot! If it's this hard for really good people to do, maybe we've got a problem here"' (committee meeting, 15 October 1997). She and Alice Kawazoe had identified a major difficulty the teachers were having: they had problems bringing together the topics defined by the draft state standards with the historical thinking concepts which the committee had refined over the past year (field notes, discussion with Weintraub, 14 October 1997).

Part of the difficulty was conceptualizing what they did when they taught. One teacher surmised:

> What we're trying to do here is decide first what we're talking about. And then do it. And maybe the problem is, and I would be the first to admit it, that I rarely do that. You know, I get up and I do my craft and then decide this is what I've done. Maybe it's so hard because now we're trying to get that horse back in front of the cart. (committee meeting, 15 October 1997)

The core of the difficulty, however, as many saw it, was the problem of maintaining the state-mandated 'content standards', that is, the list of historical topics defined in a draft state standards document, and at the same time build in a notion of historical thinking. 'It sounds so simple to say it now, but it's an incredibly complex operation to consider, let alone dream up and teach', said one committee member (committee meeting, 15 October 1997).

Merging the state standards with the thinking standards involved two different views of historical knowledge. As one teacher observed: 'The State document is consistent all the way through. It pretty much assumes that there's a narrative that kids have to [learn] … and they're going to

6

get information and then they have to give it back' (committee meeting, 15 October 1997). In defining the topics that students had to learn, it did not set up historical knowledge as a problem.

> It implies that there's one narrative and that what teachers have to do is to convey that narrative and students have to learn that narrative ... [At] the simplest level it would just be a question of changing verbs. You know, instead of saying 'list', you say 'compare' or 'analyze' or 'debate' ... But in the back of my head I just am suspicious that it won't be quite that simple as just changing verbs. (committee meeting, 15 October 1997)

There were two different epistemological orientations in the two documents, with the state offering an unarticulated but nevertheless quite consistent message that there was one extended historical account which was the students' task to learn. The other epistemology (that the committee was grappling with) presents historical knowledge as a problem, as a challenge. Should the committee provide teachers with two conflicting models of historical knowledge and explain the conflict? Could they include the state standards as an addendum or as an introduction?

There were also concerns about the content and 'tone' of the state standards as being Eurocentric. One teacher said: 'even though they talk about immigrants, I believe they're only really interested in European immigrants' (committee meeting, 15 October 1997). How much energy should they devote to 'translating' the state document? Beyond these concerns was another kind of problem. If it was so difficult for the teachers on the committee – with all of their background and discussions – to write up units embodying the standards for historical thinking, how likely would it be that teachers beyond the committee would be able to use these ideas to create lessons of their own?

Throughout the meeting, the teachers remained firm on three points. First, the document had to pose historical thinking as a challenge for teachers. That is, it had to be presented in a form whereby an explicit conception of thinking could not be bypassed. Second, historical thinking was not something that could be divorced from 'content'; it only made sense in relation to topics of historical inquiry, which the document also had to define in relation to the state curriculum. Third, teachers needed examples to show them what this looked like for the purposes of teaching.

The participants refused to be deterred from these principles. When

7

shown serious problems with some of their sample units at one point, they insisted on trying again, rather than deleting the exercise. If their work had not been right, they argued, Weintraub should give them a short workshop showing them what was wrong, and what a good unit for the document would look like (committee meeting, 15 October 1997). This resolution was a measure of their commitment to constructing workable standards that would convey to other teachers what they felt to be important.

By their next meeting in November, a teacher shortage in the district had led to restrictions on the committee's use of substitute teachers. So, on a Saturday, Weintraub provided the mini-workshop that they had asked for: a critique of one of their units – 'World War I and its consequences' – and the construction of a new unit on the constitution (committee meeting transcript and field notes, 8 November 1997). Their discussion about a culminating exercise for the latter showed that, even at this point, with all their commitment and experience, there were still gaps and disagreements on their common understanding of the fundamental concepts they were hoping to convey to a broader audience of teachers:

> Teacher A: We could almost all sort of aim for that being a culminating writing … Kind of make that interpretation. Kind of pulling together … teachers would say oh, this is like the end of the unit, the piece of writing that will pull it together …

> Teacher A: [I]t would show the teacher that these other things are building blocks, towards the writing exercise, whether it's a story. If we made interpretation like the writing exercise, we'd have some unity all through the entire document.

> Teacher B: I think there needs to be a real important distinction, however, between interpretation and significance. Because when you get into significance, you could do the same assignment there. I think it's important to make a distinction between seeking interpretation and stating an opinion.

There had not been any discussion, in my presence, about the relationship between 'opinion' and 'interpretation', nor, clearly, was there consensus. The discussion continued:

> Teacher A: I think interpretation could be a place that is more

reflective. Significance could be a place where it is more diverse or more argumentative.

Teacher B: I would take just the opposite. Just in the kinds of essay assignments that I give as an English teacher. Interpretation is the most common kind of critical analysis. What is your interpretation of blah blah blah, where you actually gather evidence and make of that but the significance is more an evaluation than a statement of opinion.

This exchange was an attempt to define and clarify the distinction between 'interpretation' and 'significance'; with a few more twists and turns and Weintraub's timely intervention, things did get somewhat clearer. The question remained how well other teachers beyond the committee were going to be able to sort these things out.

For the remainder of the day, the teachers worked on units for their grade levels. Again, they did not finish by the end of the day. Again, they sent their work in to Weintraub. And again, she and Kawazoe knew that it would need editing, abbreviation and supplements. She and Pesick had a draft document, with one unit per grade (as she had suggested back in October) ready for the committee by January 1998. After a day of discussion and relatively minor adjustments, the document was complete.

No piece of this was straightforward. The document developed in fits and starts, bouncing back and forth between Alice Kawazoe, Shelly Weintraub and the committee members over a period of a year and a half. The conceptual framework, the format, the level of prescription, the depth of the pedagogical challenge were all refined, but not without many wrong turns and much backtracking.

Thinking about Historical Thinking

The committee was united in a commitment to conveying a notion of historical thinking: that was its achievement and that was its problem. Joan Wilcox, committee member and grade 4/5 teacher, said she thought the thinking standards were 'brilliant', 'I think this is a whole new way of looking at history, one that most of us, you know, never really considered … until we set out to do this work' (Wilcox interview, 16 October 1997). Jonas Zuckerman, who taught grade 3 students, concurred: 'they made me reanalyze how I think about history'

(Zuckerman interview, 16 October 1997). Renee Swayne had been introduced to a black perspective in the study of history as an undergraduate at the University of California at Santa Barbara in the 1960s: 'It was the first time I'd ever seen history with a black spin and before that all of that had been left out.' But, prior to her work with the committee, she still had a more traditional approach in much of her teaching: 'so if we did Martin Luther King then I would often talk about him ... but I didn't really do a lot for the kids to, well there was more lecturing than it was involvement for students' (Swayne interview, 16 October 1997). Others sensed that the changes had started earlier.

> Using artifacts, using primary documents, having them ask questions, inquiry questions, having them set up museums in the classroom, having them go on field trips and look at a place and try and determine what went on here historically ... looking at photographs and saying, 'Well, what does this picture tell us?': all that kind of teaching which was going on already but we just tied it together and we talked to each other and we heard what elementary school teachers were doing and what we were doing ... We started from that point and we have this common vocabulary and this common mission ... And that's why those standards are in there, those five areas because we've been talking about those five areas for five years. So that's a strength. You've got a group of people that are already sort of on the same page. (Yeager interview, 7 November 1997)

But the committee process had consolidated and helped to define their thinking:

> I knew my narrative ... stories that I had the kids write ... would meet these different thinking standards in history. I just didn't have words for that, I didn't have labels, I didn't have the language to go along with that. And as I progressed through the year with the Committee, of course, I began to attach the language. And once I attached the language, then I was able to create new assignments in my classroom. And that's of course the transfer process. (Lay interview, 8 November 1997)

Zuckerman recalled changes in the committee's attitudes:

> I guess last year and then in the summer we started to work on them ... I don't think the committee was sold that we liked the

historical thinking standards. But now I think we absolutely are. ... because we kept coming back to ... what I heard over and over was, we're not emphasizing the historical thinking standards enough ... And I don't think that was the case at the beginning. (Zuckerman interview, 16 October 1997)

Sue Scott, a fifth-grade teacher, reiterated: 'If we want to make some real changes in history, in the teaching of history, then we need to stick to that [idea of historical thinking]' (Scott interview, 7 November 1997).

Asked what she had taken from the committee's work to her own teaching, Carole Pancho, currently a district science support teacher, gave this example:

I try to test out whether these third graders or second graders can get the idea of point of view – 'Do you see why [Christopher Columbus] did this?' or 'Is he always a bad guy?' ... I think I wanted to test out significance and point of view and can kids see a different point of view based on what they already come ... with or based on what I'm saying. (Pancho interview, 16 October 1997)

Anita Bowers was impressed with what other committee members were able to do with their students, but noted her own LEP students' extra problems: 'For my students they have to just kind of get the nitty gritty, get the facts, it's very hard for them to give different interpretations. I mean I hear all these wonderful ideas. I try to bring in [as] simplified things as I can, but sometimes just the language is so, it's so tough' (Bowers interview, 7 November, 1997). Mel Stenger, a seventh-grade teacher, affirmed: 'I hated history all through school and I love it now. And part of it, not part of it, most of it's because I love the way I teach it' (Stenger interview, 7 November 1997).

Having spent a year and a half struggling to define the concepts, clarify them, tie them to historical topics and teaching activities and present them in a form which would be understandable by teachers, committee members were still forthright about their difficulty. Carole Pancho admitted: 'There will have to be ... ongoing staff development about what that means ... I'm still grappling ... Can I really show evidence or significance or really do an activity that shows interpretation?' (Pancho interview, 16 October 1997).

Indeed, despite the written standards document there was still a question of how much consensus there was among individual members around the definitions of the historical thinking standards. I asked each

11

of the interviewees how they would present the concepts of evidence and multiple perspectives to a group of teachers who had not been involved in developing the standards. Elizabeth Lay's fair response was: 'I think the first thing that I would probably do is think about this a great deal … I would certainly not do this off the top of my head' (Lay interview, 8 November 1997). The discussion below is based entirely on their thoughts 'off the top of their heads'. And yet the persisting variation among their spontaneous responses is at least an indication of the challenging task they had undertaken.

Many of the committee members spoke of the use of evidence as based in the use of primary sources, both artifactual and documentary, to raise questions and stimulate thinking. For example, Carole Pancho suggested:

> I'd first start with their own schools, look at photos and look at newspaper articles about what do photos tell you about the school. I mean an old picture of the school or a modern picture … what does this tell you, what does this article or this photograph tell you about the way they dress, what can you say about, you know, what's happening here? (Pancho interview, 16 October 1997)

Jonas Zuckerman proposed a comparable exercise:

> If we're dealing with third grade, Oakland history, I would bring maps. We do have maps of Oakland at different years. You know, we have a map in 1850, a map in 1876 … You can actually see the streets develop and the streets are the same today, it's just that they were only five blocks long in 1850 … so you can see how the streets developed and how that transportation led to the growth of the city. (Zuckerman interview, 16 October 1997)

Another teacher said: 'I would suggest to them that evidence cannot be obtained from a textbook alone. That it must be obtained from varied sources and as much as is possible from primary sources.' Given the symmetry of textbooks and primary sources as types of texts in this statement, it might convey to other teachers only that there are different places to obtain information, not that work with primary sources as evidence demands the construction of inference and argument.

On the other hand, another teacher made the inferences and arguments central to the presentation of the meaning of evidence, and did not discuss primary sources at all:

I've seen second grade math sheets, for example, that say name three different ways that you can total two numbers and get 8. And then it says, explain how you know? That's evidence. I mean ... that's challenging a child to go back to what they did and account for it. It's cognitive accountability ... Or in book discussions or story discussions from kindergarten on up, you know, 'Well is the froggie happy?' 'Yes, the froggie is happy.' 'How do you know the froggie is happy?' The little kindergarten says, 'Cause the froggie is smiling.' Right. Well there you have, I mean it's very simplistic but it's, that's the basic central issue of having a child make a statement and then using evidence to back up their statement ... [Y]ou don't just blurt out these things just out of the blue: 'Lincoln was a criminal.' 'Well how do you know?' 'Why are you saying that Abraham Lincoln was a criminal?' 'Well because da da da da.' ... And that's the same ... kind of thinking that we're asking kids to do on every level, kindergarten through 12. It just gets more complex as the child progresses through the grades, as we hope their thinking gets more complex. (Stenger interview, 7 November 1997)

This notion of evidence as the grounds for a claim potentially fits with the notion of evidence as use of primary sources, but has a different emphasis. In presentations to other teachers, the committee members will need to consider both notions.

One teacher liked the idea of documents, but decoupled such texts entirely from the notion of evidence and inference:

A: I'd tell them how I do the review unit in history. The kids teach it and they work in work groups, panels, and they make primary sources ...

Q: They make primary sources?

A: They recreate.

Q: Okay.

A: They have to really look at these documents to understand them, and then they rewrite them and then they burn them and make them old and recreate them and the kids see them. I mean it just took off and it started with finding an original document ...

[Then, they] find out everything they could about that document to share with the class.

While this sounds like a productive exercise, it did not really rest on any clarification or confrontation with the problems of evidence. Perhaps not surpisingly, the committee's first thoughts on how to present the concept of 'evidence' to other teachers formed a loose constellation of ideas about primary sources, inference and historical argument. They lacked, however, the kind of coherence and unanimity that may be necessary as they reach out to the larger body of Oakland teachers.

Similar variation emerged in relation to the concept of 'multiple perspectives'. Again, in considering how they would present these to other teachers, committee members articulated ideas with potentially contradictory pedagogical implications. 'Multiple perspectives' may refer to the perspectives of historical actors, and thus the standard may refer to something like 'historical empathy' or Downey's 'perspective taking'.[21] Alternatively, it may refer to the problem of historical interpretation, that is, different historians construct different interpretations of the same events.

Several elementary school teachers started their hypothetical explanations for other teachers with examples from daily life: 'my viewpoint would be different from yours and just sort of looking at why is it different based on our experiences, our backgrounds and so forth ... just take something common like that' (Pancho interview, 16 October 1997).

Built into this explanation was the assumption that 'your values or your family background, your ethnicity' would shape those views (Pancho interview, 16 October 1997). Or, as Sue Scott suggested: 'You could probably pick an issue and find two multiple perspectives, you know very different views taken from very different cultural groups on a particular event.'

Jonas Zuckerman built this notion of multiple perspectives (the different views of participants in an event) into a specifically historical case:

> We always sail with Columbus to the new world. We never are in the new world watching Columbus sail in ... Multiple perspectives means take yourself up, take yourself off the ship, put yourself in ... San Salvador. Start with the island ... and be there as he arrived and think about what that means to you. (Zuckerman interview, 16 October 1997)

14

A problem with this approach, as he saw it, was 'there's very little evidence, in some cases no evidence of the other perspectives' (Zuckerman interview, 16 October 1997).

Grace Murozawa asserted that K-3 teachers 'already ... talk about [multiple perspectives] in a lot of different ways', not only in interpersonal conflict resolution among students, but in relation to literature (Murozawa interview, 7 November 1997). Mel Stenger expanded:

> You can take a story like The Three Little Pigs, and this has already been done, where the three little pigs story is retold by the wolf. Then you can also then turn around and have the children take another story and rewrite it. That would demand that a child look at the story, retain the basic elements of the story and yet shift her point of view to someone else. And therefore shift the way all the details of the story are viewed and thought about. (Stenger interview, 7 November 1997)

Turning to literature moves the problem from multiple perspectives in daily interaction to the multiple ways of constructing a story about a whole event. In some ways this is helpful (in so far as the historian's task is one of constructing a narrative). But, unlike Stenger's wolf or any fictional narrator, the historian must see the past from a viewpoint beyond that of any one group of historical actors.

In order to see the problem, let us return to Murozawa's reference to classroom conflict. Presumably, in constructing an account of classroom conflict, the teacher attempts to arrive at an overarching explanation that incorporates the multiple perspectives of the participants. If the teacher can arrive at no more than 'just another story', no different in kind from those of the feuding students, then he/she has no tools for dealing with the dispute. Similarly, the tools of historians enable (indeed command) them to go beyond the perspectives of any particular historical actors.

Our teaching 'multiple perspectives' in history thus conveys to students one of two very basic (and incompatible) lessons about the nature of historical writing. Either it tells them that, in looking back over the past, the historical account must build in – as far as possible – the perspectives of all the relevant actors, and this is what makes it better history than more partial views. Or it tells them that every historical account is shaped by the 'background, ethnicity or cultural group' of the historian, and thus that historians are really in no better a position to construct historical accounts than the historical actors (or the fiction writers or myth-makers).

Joan Wilcox articulated clearly what most of the teachers seemed to believe, that 'multiple perspectives' meant both of these things. First, the perspectives of all the relevant groups must be included so that we can 'tie together' a historical account:

> For instance, when the United States was first being colonized, the Indians perceived this colonization quite differently from the Europeans and the different groups of Europeans perceived their own efforts at colonization different from other groups ... And the people who came over as slaves saw colonization from a different perspective ... As we understand all of these perspectives, then we can begin to, I guess, tie together our own versions of American history. (Wilcox interview, 16 October 1997)

But 'history is also a matter of interpretation and each group within our culture has its own take on history' (Wilcox interview, 16 October 1997). Similarly, Anita Bowers spoke of the perspectives of people in history (slave owners and slaves, Nazis, Jews and Gypsies) as well as different interpretations about the dropping of the atomic bomb.

There are two ways of seeing the lack of resolution about some of the basic concepts of Oakland's historical thinking standards. On the one hand, it may make communication of the concepts to other teachers more difficult. On the other, it is probably preferable to a formulaic and unthoughtful recitation of a uniform definition. Each of these teachers' hypothetical presentations of complex concepts was based not only on the discussions of the committee, but also on their own teaching experiences. If the persisting problems are clearly articulated, they may provide material for important discussions and further development among teachers beyond the committee.

Conclusion

The schools of Oakland pose many challenges: students achieve low scores on state assessments, their grade point averages are low, the drop-out rate is high. Demographically, there are high rates of poverty. The city is racially divided. School politics have been heated and acrimonious in recent years. And, despite all of these contextual challenges, the district embarked on an ambitious programme in history education reform. Weintraub herself was the key person in this process. Located in a central position, her familiarity with the discipline of history, the Oakland schools and the challenges of the classroom enabled her to fulfil this role. She built a cadre of highly committed, active, informed and articulate teachers. They ensured competent negotiation between teaching practice on the one hand, and the codification and articulation of essential elements of that practice on the other.

As the committee well understood, the standards document alone would not change anything in the district. And yet the standards were worth getting right. Clearly articulated standards would help the implementation of each of the other components in the reform programme – assessment, materials development, professional development and research (Weintraub interview, 8 November 1997, pp. 13–14). Activities took place in each of these areas in 1997/98. A district-wide assessment in history–social science at the middle school level was piloted, bringing teachers together to discuss and evaluate students' responses. Development of curriculum materials continued with a new project for third grade using materials from an archeological dig in West Oakland.[22] Teachers from five elementary schools conducted research on their own history teaching. And Stan Pesick (now as one of three 'cluster leaders') led monthly sessions for middle school teachers, informed by his own work on students' historical thinking.[23] Perhaps most significantly, 200 teachers took part in a series of study sessions, where they examined the nature of history and the problems of teaching it. These teachers became a broadly constituted committee for the selection of textbooks in 1999/2000.

The decision to shape the standards around historical thinking had implications for the questions of race, multiculturalism and historical interpretation which loomed so large not only in earlier Oakland district curriculum debates, but also in the controversy over the US National History Standards. Concern with the kinds of representations that would be promoted by the standards led the committee to build 'multiple perspectives' into the core of the historical thinking standards: they demanded an inclusive history. But, through their focus on historical thinking, the central question became something other than 'Which historical interpretation are we going to teach our young people?' Students would learn, over the course of the K-12 curriculum, about the nature and problems of historical interpretation. Or that, anyway, would be the goal of history education in Oakland, rather than the inculcation of any one particular historical account. How such a relatively complex approach to teaching and learning history would work – if at all – in a broader public arena remained to be seen.

NOTES

1. See, for example, L.B. Resnick and L.E. Klopfer (eds), *Toward the Thinking Curriculum: Current Cognitive Research* (Washington, DC: Association for Supervision and Curriculum Development, 1989); D. Perkins, *Smart Schools: From Training Memories to Educating Minds* (New York: Free Press, 1992); H. Gardner and V. Boix-Mansilla, 'Teaching for understanding in the disciplines and beyond', *Teachers College Record*, 96, 2 (1994), pp. 198–218; B.S. Nelson and J.K. Hammerman, 'Reconceptualizing teaching: Moving toward the creation of intellectual communities of students, teachers, and teacher educators', in M.W. McLaughlin and I. Oberman (eds) *Teacher Learning: New Policies, New Practices* (New York: Teachers College Press, 1996) pp. 3–21; and M.S. Wiske (ed.), *Teaching for Understanding: A Practical Framework* (San Francisco, CA: Jossey-Bass, 1998).
2. For surveys, see S. Wineburg, 'The psychology of learning and teaching history', in D.C. Berliner and R.C. Calfee (eds), *Handbook of Educational Psychology* (New York: Macmillan, 1996), pp. 423–37; and P. Stearns, P. Seixas and S. Wineburg (eds), *Teaching, Learning and Knowing History: National and International Perspectives* (New York: New York University Press, 2000).
3. Historical thinking is increasingly recognized as an explicit goal for history education. See American Historical Association, 'AHA statement on excellent classroom teaching of history', *Perspectives*, 36, 4 (1998), pp.11–12.
4. See, for example, National Center for History in the Schools, *National Standards for United States History* (Los Angeles, CA: 1994).
5. J.W. Little, 'District policy choices and teachers' professional development opportunities', *Educational Evaluation and Policy Analysis*, 11, 2 (1989), pp. 165–79.
6. Y. Lincoln, 'From understanding to action: New imperatives, new criteria, new methods for interpretive researchers', *Theory and Research in Social Education*, 26, 1 (1998), pp. 12–29.
7. The conceptualization that follows is drawn from my own work (e.g., Seixas, 1996, 1997; details in note 20 below). I presented this conception to the Oakland Standards Committee in October 1996, as the committee started its work. My invitation was a signal that a direction had already been set; that historical thinking would lie at the core of the work that the committee would undertake.
8. L. Cuban, 'History of teaching in social studies', in J.P. Shaver (ed.), *Handbook of Research on Social Studies Teaching and Learning* (New York: Macmillan, 1991), pp. 197–209.
9. P.J. Lee, A.K. Dickinson and R. Ashby, 'Some aspects of children's understanding of historical explanation', paper presented at the American Educational Research Association annual meeting, San Francisco, 1995, p. 7.
10. Ibid., p. 8.
11. Other conceptions of historical thinking provide frameworks for various other efforts to promote a more rigorous programme of history teaching. In England, the National Curriculum divides the discipline into change and continuity, causes and consequences, key features of past situations, interpretations, and the use of sources: Department for Education and Science, (*History in the National Curriculum* London HMSO, 1991). The National History Standards (National Center for History in the Schools, 1995) in the United States include a short section defining historical thinking (p.7) listing chronological thinking, historical comprehension, historical analysis and interpretation, historical research, and historical issues analysis and decision making. There is little use in comparing these schemes in the abstract. The question is rather how useful they are in serving the purposes for which they were constructed.
12. Oakland Unified School District, *Annual Report to the Community on Oakland Public Schools* (Oakland, CA: 1997).

13. T. Gitlin, 'Rewriting history', *Teacher Magazine* (November–December 1995), pp. 43–53; T. Perry and L. Delpit (eds), *The Real Ebonics Debate: Special Issue of Rethinking Schools*, 12, 1 (1997).
14. History–Social Science Curriculum Framework and Criteria Committee, *History Social Science Framework* (Sacramento, CA: California State Department of Education, 1988).
15. Ibid., pp. 12–13.
16 Ibid., p. 71.
17. Ibid., p. 70.
18. California State Board of Education, *History–social science content standards: Grades K-12* (2000). http://www.cde.ca.gov/board/historya.html
19. These materials and studies included two unpublished volumes by S. Weintraub for a planned historiography inservice series, *Students Writing History* (vol. 1, 1991/92) and *Emergent Historians* (vol. 2, 1992/93). See also A. Kawazoe, 'Historiography? What's that?', *Quarterly of the National Writing Project and Center for the Study of Writing and Literacy*, 16, 2–3 (1994), pp. 1–4.
20. P. Seixas, 'Conceptualizing growth in historical understanding', in D. Olson and N. Torrance (eds), *The Handbook of Education and Human Development* (Cambridge, MA and London: Blackwell, 1996), pp. 765–83; P. Seixas, 'The place of the disciplines within social studies: The case of history', in I. Wright and A. Sears (eds), *Trends and Issues in Canadian Social Studies* (Vancouver, BC: Pacific Educational Press, 1997).
21. M. Downey, 'Perspective-taking and historical thinking: Doing history in a fifth grade classroom', paper presented at the American Educational Research Association annual meeting, San Francisco, 1995.
22. S. Steward and M. Praetzellis (eds), *Sights and Sounds: Essays in Celebration of West Oakland* (Oakland, CA: CALTRANS, District 4, 1997).
23. S. Pesick, 'Reading, writing and history: Teaching for historical thinking and understanding', PhD dissertation (Stanford University, 1998).

2

Expecting High Standards from Inner-City Students: Challenges and Possibilities

VERONICA BOIX MANSILLA

Being There: Harlem, NYC, January 1997

I get off the subway at 103rd Street. As usual the streets are full of colour and hardship. It is a typical cold and sunny winter afternoon in East Harlem. Painted on a wall, the memorial of a young man shot a few months ago serves as a background to the lively laughter and paced conversation among three women. Portuguese and Puerto Rican Spanish intermingle in the air as I walk by fast. I follow my usual Monday path along 106th, through the smelly tunnel under the railroad, down to Madison, to the corner of the school. My mind is full of small tasks for the day. 'I'll have a conversation with Makeka.[1] She might not like to have to do a fourth revision of her paper. Will Yasef have time to help Erin with his research? I can't forget to give Wuan last week's *Atlantic Monthly* article on immigration.' As usual I cross paths with JT, Rose and Julia who are rushing out for lunch. Hi Veronica! Hi guys, we are starting soon! Hurry up!

In the fall of 1996 I taught a course on autobiography and history to 19 students at Central Park East Secondary School (CPESS), a public school located in East Harlem with a population of about 450 students mostly of African-American and Latino descent. The course aimed to help students understand how people's lives are shaped by the historical times in which they live. Students were expected to use the narratives and modes of inquiry that are central to the discipline of history (natural components of advanced placement or academically demanding courses) to revisit and expand their personal experience. Most ambitiously, they were expected to place aspects of their own lives in historical context. To me, 'Autobiography and History' – as the course came to be called –

20

entailed an exploration of the challenges and possibilities of expecting high disciplinary standards from able inner-city kids.

By bringing a disciplinary emphasis to the lives of youngsters in the inner city, my course stood at the centre of the sociological debate about school knowledge.[2] Was historical thinking a 'relevant' aim in the development of students who are struggling in the streets of Manhattan? Was my agenda actually one of ensuring the hegemony of disciplinary knowledge in the symbolic market place of our culture? Or was I, on the contrary, giving students access to socially valued tools to reinterpret who they are and what they could become? Beyond scholastic queries and political debates, questions of this sort lie tacitly at the heart of the decisions that teachers make every day as they distribute knowledge in their classrooms.

This chapter examines the role that disciplinary knowledge could or should play in the development of students of less advantaged socio-economic groups. I propose that enhancing all students' understanding of themselves, and of the natural, social and cultural worlds in which they live, calls for a reconceptualization of the epistemological status of school knowledge – one in which principles of scientific research, aesthetic decisions behind Picasso's *Guernica*, or historical accounts of the Industrial Revolution cease to be transmitted as information. Instead, they become flexible frameworks with which youngsters can engage in culturally relevant tasks such as testing a broadly held belief, interpreting the drama of a civil war or examining social inequalities stemming from rapid technological change.[3] Among less privileged students, I will argue that the need for such reconceptualization is ever more pressing. It is schooling – rather than after dinner conversations – that provides many of these students with the sole opportunity to explore the world through disciplines like history, science or literature. The degree to which disciplinary knowledge tacitly perpetuates the social order in which these students live or becomes a tool for social mobility depends less on whether or not disciplines are emphasized in these students' curricula than on how they are represented in it.

Autobiography and History at CPESS

CPESS was a privileged intellectual home for my 'Autobiography and History' course. The school community shares a commitment to knowing students well, building on their natural curiosity, and challenging them to develop sophisticated habits of mind and work (for example, from considering multiple perspectives on a problem to providing constructive peer feedback).[4] Such commitment offered a fertile ground for a course defined by its attempt to bridge the personal with the historical. I found that students at CPESS were remarkably ready to discuss aspects of their lives and to expect respect and care for their experiences.

To enable concentrated work, the school brings together students from grades 11 and 12 in small classes and long-time blocks dedicated to the humanities and math–sciences. Graduation requires the public presentation of 14 portfolio exhibitions. To build each portfolio, students enlist the help of their advisers to select and analyze their best pieces of work in a domain. They present their work to a committee composed of other teachers, a peer student and a disciplinary specialist and/or a member of the community. Because autobiography and history are the topics of two of the mandatory portfolios, the course gave students an opportunity to prepare pieces of work that would contribute to their graduation.

'Autobiography and History' was a semester-long course, structured in three units. Its goal was to help students place their personal life stories in the larger context of the social, political and cultural changes in America during the 1980s and early 1990s. Understanding this recent portion of American history entails more than remembering key occurrences. Reagan's ascension to power, the fiscal conservative economic adjustments and the Gulf War are not isolated facts. Rather, they are embedded in multiple, often conflicting, historical interpretations of the period that give them meaning. Narratives about this period are driven by different questions and interpretive frameworks and establish distinct bodies of evidence to explain, for example, how and why American life shifted toward conservative values during those years. Trained historians build and validate such accounts through the use of disciplinary modes of thinking (for example, understanding historical actors' points of view, analyzing continuity and change over time, building multi-causal explanations). Understanding history in depth requires that students embody such modes of thinking as they make sense of the past.

Understanding recent history and placing family experience in it presented students with an additional challenge. The lack of temporal distance between the past under study and the present makes judging the potential implications of known events impossible. Accounts of the recent past stand at the crossroads where memory becomes history, rendering such accounts ever more provisional and subject to debate.

Left to their 'unschooled minds', students would read historical accounts as fixed representations of the past and fail to historicize their family experience. They would draw on family anecdotes and myths (the epistemological tools of memory) as their main source of understanding. They would fail to place family events in the broader context of the times, to render the familiar unfamiliar.

Unit One was dedicated to understanding the making of narratives with an emphasis on autobiographies. Through analysis of Maya Angelou's autobiography,[5] students explored the spirit of various types of prose. They identified portions of 'celebratory', 'confessional', 'revisionist' and 'objectivist' prose and explained how Angelou's language and ideas in them worked to convey such spirits.[6] Creating a chronology of their lives and that of their families allowed students to discuss the criteria for inclusion or exclusion of events in the list, the subjective nature of chronological arrangements and the multiple narrative paths emerging from single chronologies. Students' chronologies also allowed us to identify potential points of intersection between macrocultural, social and political forces that dominated the Reagan/Bush years and students' personal lives (for instance, a parent losing his/her job or immigrating to America, a family losing health care).

In the second unit, students briefly revisited world-views and tensions that dominated the 1960s and 1970s (for example, the Civil Rights Movement, Vietnam and Nixon's resignation) as a point of contrast to the conservative turn experienced by many Americans in the 1980s and 1990s. Students worked in groups composing visual portraits of the 1960s and 1970s where images, documents and explanation intertwined. They presented their posters to the class and to visiting faculty.

Most of the course was dedicated to Unit Three – 'The conservative turn in the 80s and early 90s'. Students analyzed Reagan's inaugural speech of 1981 as well as *New York Times* clips describing controversies around the conservative values dominating the decade. They also compared and contrasted a variety of historians' accounts of the Reagan years.[7] Writing an essay entitled 'The Reagan Revolution?' allowed them to integrate readings into a personal position about the impact of the Reagan years on American life. During this portion of the course, students also crafted their final project: a paper in which they linked a particular aspect of their life-story with the larger changes taking place in America during the 1980s.

Establishing meaningful links between the autobiography and the history agendas in the course proved challenging in two major ways.

First, using academic history to revisit their personal lives placed students' efforts at the crossroads between memory and history – two rather distinct interpretations of the past. Typically crafted from idiosyncratic family anecdotes and recollection of experience in time, and exempt from systematic epistemological scrutiny, memory has a strong cognitive and emotional hold on personal identity. On the other hand, history attempts to contextualize human experience along a spectrum of social, political, cultural and economic forces over time. Unlike memory, historical narratives are subjected to disciplinary standards of evidence, multi-causality and consistency with interpretations held as acceptable by a society at a particular moment in time. Throughout the course, students' subjectivities were often at odds with the disciplines' inter-subjectivities.

The second challenge that my students and I confronted stemmed from the fact that, while most students seemed clear about the importance of developing sophisticated modes of thinking (for example, 'taking perspective' or 'providing supporting evidence'), they were less likely to appreciate the particular ways in which 'perspective' or 'evidence' play out in the discipline of history. For example, when I asked students to provide historical evidence for their claims about the conservative turn in the early 1980s, I often found that they interpreted my request as a call for 'fors' and 'againsts' the position proposed in their writings. Considerations of how we know that certain things did in fact happen or what they might have meant for people at that time initially seemed superfluous to most of the students with whom I worked. For many students, narratives about the past seemed to transparently reflect the past; they viewed their challenge as one of developing a personal position about an issue ('reaganomics', unemployment) rather than providing ground for their claims about how and why things happened in the ways expressed in their narratives.

Students Engaging in Disciplinary Thinking

The final project design allowed students to pursue idiosyncratic sorties into recent American history. Foci ranged from civil rights movements to media, from drug traffic to education, and yet students' efforts seemed to concentrate on three major challenges. Some struggled with the process of refining their budding ability to think historically. Others concentrated on resolving the clash between memory and history as they tried to reinterpret their family's past through the lens of history. Still others struggled to understand the very appropriateness of historicizing a problem to understand it. In what follows I draw on illustrative cases to shed light on these three struggles.

Wuan, refining the ability to think historically
Wuan's narrative was an exercise in multi-causality – a central intellectual stance in the discipline of history. Wuan, a committed 17-year-old of Chinese descent, inquired about the reasons that led thousands of Chinese families like his to migrate to the United States in the early 1980s. A journal entry reflecting on his chronology led us to his final project investigation. He had written: 'American's [*sic*] think that the Chinese came here for the money but I don't think so. I really don't know why people from China came but it was not only for the money or to take other people's jobs.'

The richness of Wuan's final account lay in his consideration of various historical actors' reasons to migrate, and his attention to some unintentional consequences of their actions (such as, overcrowding, resentment from old-timers in the USA). He opens his narrative in the following way:

> The reasons for Chinese immigrants to come to the United States were as varied as their social and economic backgrounds themselves. Some people came to the US because their relatives were here and wanted to live together. Some people came to work. China had very competitive farmers. In the 80s, United States were interested in bringing peasants from China to United States for farm work. Another reason people came to United States was to live in a capitalist society as opposed to a communist one. Politicians and students were most commonly in this group. Students sometimes came to study so they could get a better study environment. In some cases there were Chinese criminals who also wanted to escape their country's punishment so they moved to another country for hiding.

In explaining why people from China migrated to the USA, Wuan moved beyond the single, overall, causal attribution typical of naive history thinkers. Instead, he proposed a spectrum of causes that are directly linked to people's decisions to migrate. As he continues to develop in his ability to explain past events, Wuan will face the challenge of placing events like immigration in a network of causal relationships where causes are directly and indirectly associated with people's decisions to leave. Ideally, Wuan will become able to distinguish the long-term enabling conditions that allowed a process to take place (e.g. long years of economic hardship and declining standards of living in rural areas) from the specific events that precipitated it (e.g., a particular drought, Tianamen Square).[8]

Reflecting on the course, he expresses how history informed him in ways that his family memory had not quite done: 'My parents really don't like to talk about the trip they made to come to this country. They say it is not for me to know. But this paper helped me figure out what it was like to be there, why people risked their lives to come to this country and what happened then.'

JT's journey at the crossroads: resolving the clash between memory and history

During the first two units of the course JT sat for long periods of time with his head on the desk and his eyes closed, rather apathetic among his dynamic classmates. A sketch of his family life in the early 1980s allowed me to understand him better and find an entry point to make history meaningful to him without losing sight of the rigour of disciplinary understanding.

> I was four years old and I started Head Start, later that year we went to Puerto Rico to my grandfather. My mother was in and out of the hospital with my sister through out the years. My sister passed away, she was only 17 years old ... My father lost his job, everything took a down fall after my sister's death ... after school I would go home and see nothing but terror, my father used to cook drugs, do them and try to beat on my mother. My father started to sell drugs. Got arrested. Came out and ended up right back in. For some time we didn't have health care. We were struggling ...

His father's story served as an entry point to study the 1980s. Was his father's experience unique at the time? What was it like to live without a job in the early 1980s? How did the social safety net operate once federal social spending was drastically reduced? To what degree was JT's father's behaviour a result of his personality, personal circumstances and broader economic and social forces such as waves of unemployment, the stock market crisis of 1987 and social spending cuts? Questions of this sort and the invitation to explore them in his research project piqued JT's interest. He started to stay after class to discuss aspects of his work.

JT inquired about unemployment and drug trafficking during the early 1980s. He asked the school librarian for help learning how to use microfiches to explore 1980 to 1988 *New York Times* articles on the DARE programme and economics. He reviewed a couple of economics reports and general publications produced in the late 1980s on economic polarization. Not without effort JT analysed historian Arthur Schlessinger Jr's accounts on 'Reaganomics'. An interview with his mother revealed, to his surprise, that she was not particularly aware of the economic changes of the 1980s. JT submitted particular sections of the paper one at a time for feedback. Helping JT pace his work so that he would keep momentum and not be overwhelmed by the complexity of readings or the personal weight of his project became important. His opening paragraph captures the nature of his goals and personal involvement.

> How did Reagan economic ideas affect the job opportunities for Americans in the early 1980s? How did they affect my family? These questions are of great significance for me personally as well as for society. The mid 1980s were years in which it was hard to get a good job and sustain it. Jobs are crucial to raise a family. If you didn't have a job and you were trying to raise a family life wasn't easy. In this paper I will first describe Reagan's economic ideas and the effects they had on jobs for Americans during the early and mid 1980s. Then I will explain how these economic changes affected my family.

In this project JT faced the challenge of understanding his father as a historical actor. He needed to place individual actions and intentions in the broader socio-economic contexts that define the range of options available to an individual at a particular moment in time. Research in historical cognition suggests that, early in their development, children tend to believe that historical events are solely determined by their actors' intentions.[9] As they learn about broader socio-economic forces within which actors existed, they often adopt a social deterministic position that is equally oversimplified. The greatest challenge for students like JT is to see the relationship between individual intention and the socio-economic forces that contribute to shape an event.

JT's paper constituted a first step toward integrating idiosyncratic and societal experiences of unemployment and economic polarization in the early 1980s. He addressed central aspects of Reagan's economic programme and moved quite flexibly between examples and generalizations. He included spontaneous attempts to put himself in the position of an adult at the time:

27

Reagan had many ideas for our economy when he took power in 1981. Tax cuts were one of his ideas. He thought they would help the economy grow. The cuts that he proposed were especially for the wealthy people and for businesses. For example the taxes on the highest incomes went from 48% to 28%. Reagan hoped that by cutting taxes for business leaders they would re-invest in their companies and generate more and better jobs. He thought that the country would be more successful and prosperous.

A concern that Reagan had was that America needed to create new jobs. He actually succeeded on this partially. Most of the jobs that appeared in the 1980s were very low paying jobs meaning you still would probably have to get a second job if you were thinking about raising a wife and kids.

Ronald also believed in small government. That is he thought the government should have a very small role in taking care of people, their health, their education or well being. Only in the early 1980s, thirty eight billion dollars were cut from government social programs – programs such as Medicare Medicaid and unemployment compensation, ADC Aid to Dependent Children, and food stamps. Let's say you needed unemployment compensation or medical aid what would you do? The cuts affected many families at the time.

Throughout the 80s, there was an increase in poverty, hunger, and homelessness. After the Reagan's administration the rich were richer and the poor were poorer. The middle class which was not used to struggling had to work much harder in order to maintain a good living. People at the time also began major debts.

JT's macroeconomic portrait was followed by his family's experience. He began by portraying his family's transition 'from the middle class to the lower class', but soon his prose lost the broad socio-political perspective with which he had begun.

In the beginning of the 80s, my family moved from being part of the middle class to being part of the lower class. My father lost his job as an x-ray technician at Mt. Sinai hospital. My mother also had lost her job a few months before and had decided to get on welfare.

> My father began to sell drugs. At my young age I used to believe it was good since I used to get everything I wanted. It was late September when he got arrested. Since then he came out of jail to end up right back in. Till this day he's still in jail.

JT's uneven written expression (sometimes clearly colloquial, sometimes deeply scaffolded by his readings) illustrated more than his efforts as a student who is only partially familiar with academic writing did. His language captured the struggle between two distinct representations of the past, which he was now attempting to integrate: memory and history. JT's family's memory was simply scripted. It commemorated his mother's strength as a single mother who remained distant from the world of drugs that enslaved her husband. The story denounced the weak man of the house – JT's father. Some phrases like 'he came out of jail to end up right back in' seemed ritualistically coded. They were repeated almost verbatim as part of a story told many times, always ratifying family roles and emotional allegiances.

History, on the other hand, confronted JT with an intellectual approach constrained by what can and cannot be reasonably said about the past, where historical actors behave within a complex network of forces. JT's initial understanding of the relationship between intentional and broader socio-economic forces that intervene in individuals' decisions was particularly evident toward the end of his paper. His depiction of his father allowed for a complexity that was absent in his initial family story. JT's effort to take a different standpoint to understand (though not to justify) his father's actions entailed a deviation from the memory script. Perhaps that explains his impetus to remain faithful to his family story in his closing sentence of his paper.

> My father had not that many options in the late 80s. He had a high school diploma and a couple of years in college but at that time you needed more than that if you wanted a well paying job. I know my father wasn't the only one who had gotten fired or laid off. At the time unemployment was high and unemployed parents didn't have many opportunities. I can see why people turn to drugs or selling them because it would be stressful to know you have a family waiting at home and you can't feed them or please them. It was very hard for my mother and I. We had to depend on welfare for everything and even that was not going well at the time. Maybe my father was a lost case but my mother was strong and I love her for that.

Makeka: between voicefulness and historization

If Wuan's paper exemplified genuine engagement in historical thinking, and JT's illustrated ambivalence at the crossroads of memory and history, Makeka represented voiceful resistance to historization. Makeka was a talented and lively African-American 17-year-old who brought creativity and independence to her inquiry on the death penalty. She justified her choice of topic, saying: 'I have witnessed too much crime in my short life and I believe that the death penalty is a way to stop crime'. To satisfy the expectations of this course, Makeka was asked to trace the recent history of capital punishment and see how her and others' views were informed by the broader cultural changes that took place in America during the 1980s. Historicizing capital punishment entailed examining the evolution of capital punishment (its rationales, patterns and debates) over time, and placing it in the larger context of social, political and economic forces dominating the decade. I hoped, for example, that Makeka would use what she had learnt about the cultural shift toward conservative values in the 1980s to interpret reports on fluctuating crime rates and capital punishment decisions.

Makeka wrote six drafts prior to her final paper. In the first four she demonstrated her ability to propose and sustain a polemic position. However, the debate about the death penalty remained a-historical. No empirical reference to specific cases or trends in crime and capital punishment supported her claims. The goals of the course were not being met. 'I spoke my mind and I gave lots of evidence to support my points … so that's the paper. It's done!!', she explained with frustration when I brought a series of reports published in the late 1980s to inform her analysis.

Makeka clearly did not see the worthiness of a historical approach to the problem. 'Looking at the 80s won't make me change my mind', she explained. In her mind, providing 'evidence' was a matter of proposing specific opinion claims. She viewed having a personal position about the topic as an achievement and was not ready to be questioned. She seemed to view history as a rather straightforward collection of facts about the past disconnected from our current thinking about issues like capital punishment.

Producing her last two drafts entailed a demanding effort of historization for Makeka. Initially, she incorporated information about the relationship between death sentences and crime rates between 1957 and 1985 without challenging the major tenets of her initial prose. Her interpretation of historical data remained oversimplified and isolated from the broader societal and economic shifts of the times. She proposed a linear causal relationship between punishment by executions and crime reduction.

> The relationship between the death penalty and murder are when more criminals are given the death penalty fewer murders are committed. For example in 1957 there were 65 executions and 9,060 murders in the US. In 1966 there was one execution and 10,920 murders and in 1980 there were no executions and 23,040 murders. Then again in 1985 an article in the *New York Times* shows the death rows grew 16% from 1984 to 1985. However how many murders occurred during the same time is not known.

It was only in a written reflection produced toward the last days of the course that Makeka indicated an incipient ability to move beyond the linear consideration of number of crimes and executions presented in her paper, to embrace a broader range of factors associated with crime rates and punishment choices. She writes:

> The part that society played with Capital Punishment in the eighties was that many people were committing crimes in order to survive. Since many people were unemployed, many were in a way forced to go into the life of crime. Also more people of color were believed to commit crimes and put in death row. I am not really blaming these problems on the economy but if there was equal opportunity meaning good jobs for everybody then there would not be as much crime and there would be no need for capital punishment.

To Conclude:
Disciplinary Understanding among Youngsters in the Inner City

My experience at Central Park East Secondary School revealed to me the importance of re-focusing our attention on the substantive aspects of our educational tasks (that is, the kinds of understandings that we would like our students to develop and the rationales underlying our choices). All too often our pedagogical discourse is distracted by questions of methods, logistics, school structures or motivational techniques.[10] We spend a great deal of effort (and ink) devising reliable items for a test, designing creative portfolio assessment, pondering the importance of slack time for teachers or the power of collaborative work. We do so in the hope that, in the end, we will be able to support students' understandings of the world around them. And yet, as new terms enter and exit our professional discourse, two educational questions remain unaddressed: 'What understandings do we really want our students to develop?' and 'Why are such understandings important?'

'Autobiography and History' stood on the premise that preparing youngsters for a changing world requires that we teach them to use disciplinary knowledge and modes of thinking, not as ends in themselves simply justified by the rituals of schooling, but as tools to engage in valuable inquiries about the world.[11] For those students who are sceptical of what looks to them like a dry and distant academic pursuit, the burden of proving that history furnishes their mind with sophisticated lenses into their world rests upon us, their teachers. Our challenge is to help students see that, by putting rich disciplinary knowledge and careful modes of thinking to the service of a deeper understanding of aspects of the world that they care about, both their integrity as able intellectual inquirers and the integrity of the discipline as our best epistemological tool for making sound claims about the world are preserved.

To succeed in such a challenge, teachers need not only to count a broad and flexible repertoire of historical knowledge (for example, fluctuating patterns of unemployment during the early 1980s) and modes of thinking (for example, handling multiple causality or moving between history and memory). We also need to understand the questions that students and societies deem relevant ('How can one challenge broadly held stereotypes about particular immigrant groups?'; 'How can one make sense of a conflicting portion of one's past?'; 'Under what conditions can a society support the death penalty?').[12] Perhaps my greatest challenge as a teacher was to help students select the particular pieces of knowledge and modes of thinking that could best inform the questions that they had about their world. Personalizing their learning experience in this way allowed Wuan to work on multi-causality, JT to understand how history revises memory and Makeka to struggle with historization.

When we transform our conception of history, science or any other discipline from 'ends in themselves' to powerful 'tools for action', the question of whether disciplinary knowledge per se is contributing to or challenging the social status quo gains new meaning. No longer is history a collection of empowered versions of the world to be assimilated by students of any group or social class solely (because-they-are-good-for-them-period). Nor is history as a disciplinary endeavour proposed as 'too rigorous' or 'too abstract' for the least advantaged of our fellow citizens. Instead, history becomes a conceptual tool to understand complex problems in depth – to determine what can and cannot be confidently said about how events unfolded in the past. It will be up to the students to decide whether they use what they learn about the past to justify the death penalty or to criticize it, to support or reject a less restrictive immigration policy.

Critical theorists have frequently called educators' attention to the ways in which school practice impels underserved youngsters to develop a critical view of what they learn in schools.[13] In their view, schools present (or 'impose') 'professional middle class' interpretations of the world on students through mechanisms such as textbook-based tests or memorization quizzes.[14] In part, the alienating power of such transmission is rooted in the fact that the bodies of knowledge taught are detached from the methods and procedures by which they were created. When we help students understand the procedures and modes of thinking that lead to what we know about the past, we invite them to see the humanly constructed and provisional nature of our current knowledge. In so doing we invite them to develop a healthy scepticism about what they learn.[15] At best, we enable them to discern among conflicting accounts and theories about the world, and explore new problems by themselves. As one of the students stated in an informal conversation about the course: 'It was important to learn that there are methods that you can use to find out about the past – like you look at the sources they [historians] used and you check the time [when they were written] – and that you can say what stories you believe more.'

Perhaps the most important challenge involved in differentiating knowledge according to the needs of particular students without discriminating against those coming from underserved social groups is to distinguish 'entry points' from 'exit points' when teaching valuable content. Writing a voiceful paragraph about the death penalty or a brief account of personal life proved to be powerful ways for Makeka and JT to engage in the work. However, reaching students and gaining their genuine commitment is not enough to enhance their understanding of the world and themselves nor to open their access to the knowledge and modes of thinking valued by contemporary post-industrial societies. As a teacher, I faced the challenge of setting standards for my students' final performance. I set standards that, being closely informed by a rich view of history, would require students to demonstrate a deepened understanding of the period we studied. I expected students like Makeka and JT to think about information on the 1980s' crime rates or unemployment. I also expected them to interpret primary sources and to put themselves in the position of an historical actor. These standards served as the parameters against which I assessed partial achievements and failures in this project. In Makeka's case, particularly, embracing her resistance to demonstrate an historical understanding of the death penalty in order to celebrate her voiceful prose would have entailed compromising the possibility of long-term empowerment for an immediate satisfaction of her self-esteem.

While typically difficult, the complex lives of youngsters in the inner city hold an important promise for teachers working in various educational levels and socio-economic contexts. Pressing conditions do not give us time for distractions. On the contrary, they force us to make hard curriculum decisions and reflect on what matters more: what understandings would we like our students to develop and why do these really matter? Addressing these questions invites a deeper reflection about the very purpose of our teaching profession and our role in making a better society.

Acknowledgements

This chapter was written with the generous support of Thomas H. Lee and the Spencer Research Training Grant Program. I would like to thank Theodore Sizer and Paul Schwarz for their provocative invitation to explore students' engagement with historical modes of thinking 'from within', as a Central Park East Secondary School visiting faculty. My special gratitude goes to the 19 students whose life stories and intellectual adventurousness continue to inspire me; to Julian Cohen, my friendly guide into the school's ethos; and to Lisa Bromer, Howard Gardner and David Smith for their comments on previous drafts.

NOTES

1. All names are pseudonyms.
2. J. Oakes, *Keeping Track of How Schools Structure Inequalities* (New Haven, CT: Yale University Press, 1985); R. Page, *Lower Track Classrooms: A Curricular and Cultural Perspective* (New York: Teachers College Press, 1991).
3. V. Boix Mansilla and H. Gardner, 'What are the qualities of deep disciplinary understanding?', in Stone Wiske (ed.), *Teaching for Understanding: A Practical Framework* (San Francisco, CA: Jossey-Bass, 1998).
4. D. Meier, *The Power of Their Ideas* (Boston, MA: Beacon Press, 1995).
5. M. Angelou, *Gather Together in My Name* (New York: Random House, 1974).
6. J. Van Maanen, *Tales of the Field : On Writing Ethnography* (Chicago, IL: University of Chicago Press, 1988).
7. B. Bailyn *et al.*, *The Great Republic: A History of the American People* (Lexington, MA: D.C. Heath, 1992); B.B. Kymlicka and J.V. Matthews, *The Reagan Revolution?* (Chicago, IL: Dorsey Press, 1995).
8. P.J. Lee, A.K. Dickinson and R. Ashby, 'Some aspects of children's understanding of historical explanation', paper presented at the annual meeting of the American Educational Research Association, San Francisco, 1995; M. Carretero, M. Asensio and J. Pozo, 'Cognitive development, historical time representation and causal explanations in adolescence', in M. Carretero, P. Pope, R.J. Simons and J. Pozo (eds), *Learning and Instruction: Vol. 3, European Research in an International Context*, (Oxford: Pergamon Press, 1991), pp. 27–48; and M. Carretero and L. Jacott, 'Reasoning and causal explanations in history', paper presented at the Conference on Psychological and Educational Foundations of Technology-based Learning Environments, Crete, 26 July–3 August 1992.
9. See P.J. Lee, A.K. Dickinson and R. Ashby, '"Just another emperor": Understanding action in the past', *International Journal of Educational Research*, 27, 3 (1997), pp. 233–44; and Lee, Dickinson and Ashby, 'Some aspects of children's understanding'.
10. S. Aronowitz and H. Giroux, *Postmodern Education: Politics, culture and social criticism* (Minneapolis, MN: University of Minnesota Press, 1991).
11. H. Gardner and V. Boix Mansilla, 'Teaching for understanding in the disciplines and beyond', *Teachers College Record*, 96, 2 (1994), pp. 198–218; H. Gardner, *The Unschooled Mind: How Children Think and How Schools Should Teach* (New York: Basic Books, 1991), and *The Disciplined Mind: What All Students Should Understand* (New York: Simon & Schuster, 1999).
12. T. Sizer, *Horace's Compromise: The Dilemma of the American High School* (Boston, MA: Houghton Mifflin, 1992), and *Horace's Hope: What Works for the American High School* (Boston, MA: Houghton Mifflin, 1996).
13. P. Bourdieu and J.C. Passeron, *Reproduction in Education, Society and Culture* (Bristol: J.W. Arrowsmith, 1990); and Aronowitz and Giroux, *Postmodern Education*.
14. M.W. Apple, *Official Knowledge: Democratic Education in a Conservative Age* (London and New York: Routledge, 1993).
15. T. Becher, *Academic Tribes and Territories: Intellectual Enquiry and the Culture of Disciplines* (Buckingham: Open University Press, 1989); J. Schwab, *Science Curriculum and Liberal Education: Selected Essays* (Chicago, IL: University of Chicago Press, 1978).

3

A Contemporary Past:
History Textbooks as Sites of
National Memory

DAN PORAT

In *1984* George Orwell describes Winston Smith's arrival one morning in the Ministry of Truth of Oceania to face the task of rewriting history. Smith reflects on the ministry's altering of history so it matches the changing politics of The Party. The propaganda machine of Oceania, Smith thought to himself, communicated

> that people today had more food, more clothes, better houses, better recreations – that they lived longer, worked shorter hours, were bigger, healthier, stronger, happier, more intelligent, better educated, than the people of fifty years ago. Not a word of it could ever be proved or disproved ... It was like a single equation with two unknowns. It might very well be that literally every word in the history books, even the things that one accepted without question, was pure fantasy. For all he knew there might never have been any such law as the *jus primae noctis*, or any such creature as a capitalist, or any such garment as a top hat ... The past not only changed, but changed continuously.[1]

For the Oceania Ministry of Truth, history is a tool to recreate continuously the state's image. The past is altered to portray the nation in the most enlightened and progressive light. For all Smith knows, this history might be completely illusory, but fidelity with the past is not the goal of the state: patriotism is. Smith himself has broken loose from the confining historical framework imposed by the Ministry of Truth. He questions the role of history as an instrument, and he expects congruence between events and their depiction.

The different conceptions of history have deeper epistemological roots. One goal is the perpetuation of an understanding of the past that will enforce the national memory. Early in the twentieth century the French sociologist Maurice Halbwachs was one of the first to use the term 'collective memory' to refer to a reconstruction of the past that 'provides the group with a self-portrait that unfolds through time'.[2] Through education, social interaction, media and other forms of communication, the past is constructed and reconstructed to pass on a commonly meaningful past to the citizenry. This historical story helps the group understand its present situation and endure over time as a cohesive and united group.

Historians have a different approach to the past; that is, they centre their efforts on a better understanding of the past through analysis and interpretation of sources and social circumstances. The prominent Jewish historian Yosef Haim Yerushalmi points out that the historian's interest in the past is distinct from that of memory:

> Memory and modern historiography stand, by their very nature, in radically different relations to the past. The latter represents, not an attempt at a restoration of memory, but a truly new recollection ... With unprecedented energy it continually recreates an ever more detailed past whose shapes and textures memory does not recognize. But that is not all. The historian does not simply come in to replenish the gaps of memory. He constantly challenges even those memories that have survived intact. Moreover, in common with historians in all fields of inquiry, he seeks ultimately to recover a total past ... even if he is directly concerned with only a segment of it. No subject is potentially unworthy of his interest, no document, no artifact, beneath his attention ... The point is that all these features cut against the grain of collective memory which ... is drastically selective. Certain memories live on; the rest are winnowed out, repressed, or simply discarded by a process of natural selection which the historian, uninvited, disturbs and reverses.[3]

While memory sees events from a single vantage-point, history exposes multiple perspectives. History empathizes with protagonists' dilemmas while memory centres on results. History contextualizes while memory disregards context. While history embraces complexity and ambiguity, memory stands for a simplicity and straightforwardness. For history, the past is distinct from the present; while for memory, the only significance of the past is in the present.

While it may seem that history and memory stand as opposites, as enemies which 'stalk each other across the fields of the past', one should remember that they overlap in some ways.[4] David Lowenthal, for one, states that '"memory" includes second-hand accounts of the past – that is, history; "history" relies on eyewitness and other recollections – that is, memory ... history and memory are distinguishable less as types of knowledge than in attitudes toward that knowledge'.[5] Historical work emphasizes contextualization within the past, and memory also uses materials from the past; just like memory, history is affected by changing conceptions of the present. Any distinction between the two constructs is therefore blurry.

This study explores the way textbook authors have negotiated the tension between collective memory and critical history; how authors have walked the tight-rope between depicting an event in a form which will enhance national identification and one which will promote historical thinking. In analyzing textbooks, many researchers have centred on how 'objective' and accurate the depiction in the textbook appears. The basic assumption guiding these studies is that textbooks communicate 'facts', as though these can be separated from interpretation. As Jane White cautions in her review of research done on textbooks:

> We must be careful not to adopt a 'conduit' metaphor of knowledge transmission for textbooks – the notion that purely objective forms of knowledge can be constructed in textbooks that is not constrained by time or place nor by values or beliefs of the culture within which it is written. Textbooks are not neutral pipelines across the ages that link present-day students with events as they 'really' happened.[6]

A more fundamental question than whether or not textbooks are objective is 'What are textbooks?' What role do history textbooks play in the national arena?[7] Do inaccuracies and one-sided accounts serve a larger social goal?

In this chapter I follow the changing depiction of one historical event in Israeli textbooks over five decades and identify the causes for change.[8] In my analysis I will show the social and political goals which the changing account serves. After analyzing the textbooks, I will discuss the social role of textbooks and their implications for education.

The event I studied was a second-century revolt against the Roman rule in the Land of Israel – the Bar Kokhba Revolt. The revolt, named after its leader, Simon Bar Kokhba, was successful in its first stage: the rebels liberated parts of the country and nominated Simon Bar Kokhba as leader (*nasi*).[9] However, the Roman Empire advanced several battalions to overcome the rebels, and, in AD 135, they reclaimed the land and suppressed the Jewish settlement. The Romans killed hundreds of thousands and sold many more into slavery, while those who remained suffered from harsh decrees.[10]

A Mesmerizing Past: Textbooks in the 1950s and 1960s

Three years after the 1948 establishment of Israel, the Israeli Prime Minister, David Ben-Gurion, wrote in his personal diary: 'there is no doubt [that] schools in general and elementary schools especially, determine to a large extent, and possibly in a decisive manner, the spiritual countenance of the youth and thereby the nation'.[11] Political figures such as Ben-Gurion viewed the educational system as essential for the formation of the new nation. Furthermore, Ben-Gurion saw the educated students as messengers of national ideals to their families and the community at large.

One way to intensify students' identification with the nation was through an obligatory history curriculum for state (*mamlachti*) elementary schools published by the Ministry of Education in 1956. This curriculum, which was designed under the personal supervision of the Minister of Education, Ben-Zion Dinur, a professional historian himself, presented a national overarching narrative of Jewish history in the land and in exile. It was an extensive historical story which covered 3,000 years of Jewish history. The curriculum attempted 'to give the student the knowledge that our nation ... maintained its religion, customs and beliefs over two thousand years of exile ... and did not cease to exist as one nation in all its Diaspora'. Jews continued to have 'a constant connection to their homeland and dream of redemption'. The aspirations of Jews to their homeland, pointed out the curriculum, 'helped the nation stand against all enemies and maintain its independence, which finally led to the gathering of exiles and the rebuilding of the State of Israel'.[12] Clearly this curriculum was centred on promoting students' national identification through exposure to the past.

In a 1961 educational conference, an official in the Ministry of Education, Yochanan Ginat, pointed out that 'we dedicate a large portion of our education to teaching the ancient history of our nation and there are reasons for this. Our life in the land connects to the ancient era ... [to the] Biblical and Bar Kokhba eras'.[13] To advance its political goals of establishing a Jewish homeland in the Land of Israel, Zionism created an historical link between the ancient past of the Jews in the land and their modern return to the land. Drawing on this ancient and common past served to establish a common historical frame of reference for the Jews assembled in modern Israel from the four corners of the globe.[14]

Indeed, the 1950s and 1960s textbooks centred on demonstrating the common tradition which united the Jews assembled in Israel. One important means of demonstrating this was the selection of sources cited in textbooks. Authors chose to highlight Jewish sources in their depiction and ignore those which professional historians considered most credible. In the case of the Bar Kokhba Revolt, the account of a Greek historian Dio Cassius, which 'all researchers' described as 'the sole consistent survey of the revolt', was absent from textbooks.[15] From a total of 14 citations which appeared in five textbooks, 12 were from Jewish sources and only one citation was from Dio Cassius.[16]

Instead of the credible source, textbooks cited legends from the Jewish Talmud – a collection of discussions and contemplation on Jewish tradition and law. A typical Talmudic account which appeared in three textbooks was the following:

> Ben Kozebah was there, and he had 200,000 troops who had cut off their little fingers. Sages sent word to him, 'How long are you going to turn Israel into a maimed people?' He said to them, 'How otherwise is it possible to test them?' They replied to him, 'Whoever cannot uproot a cedar of Lebanon while riding on his horse will not be registered in your army'. So there were 200,000 who qualified in one way, and another 200,000 who qualified in another way. When he would go forth to battle, he would say, 'Lord of the world! Do not help and do not hinder us! "Hast thou not rejected us, O God? Thou dost not go forth, O God, with our armies."' (Psalms 60:12)[17]

The difficulty of deciphering between credible and legendary historical information in such a source is self-evident. As two scholars point out, 'the evaluation of the Talmud as an historical source is problematic in general, and this is particularly true of evidence relating to the revolt'. They add that 'the character of the Talmudic literature is such that historical facts are mentioned only incidentally'.[18] But, inspired by the national history curriculum, authors of history textbooks in the early years of the modern Jewish state incorporated them into their account, hoping to create a common image of the nation in the minds of students.

The legendary sources also provoke students' imaginations. This is reflected in the way the authors depict the leaders of the revolt. Simon Bar Kokhba's appearance and ascent to power came in textbooks with no historical background or explanation. In the most popular textbook for national schools, the authors described Simon as follows:

> On the side of Rabbi Akiva [in organizing the revolt] stood a previously unknown man of wonder [*peley*], named Simon [Bar Kokhba], from the village of Kuziva in the Galilee (Bar-Kuziva). Researchers believe he was a descendent of Yishai from his father's side and an offspring of the Hasmoneans from his mother's side.[19]

Simon is backed by a leading religious figure, Rabbi Akiva, and is a descendant of King David and of the second-century BC Hasmonean Dynasty which have heroic associations within Jewish history – hinting that Simon is also destined for great national deeds.

While Simon Bar Kokhba probably enjoyed widespread support, some known opposition existed particularly among rabbinic sages.[20] Except for one textbook, to which I will return soon, all other textbooks omitted from their accounts any mention of opposition to Simon.

But how could textbooks portray a disastrous event as a heroic victory? Textbook authors attempted to refocus the readers' attention from the defeat to the fighting. Many books portrayed the Roman conquest as one which almost failed due to the relentless opposition of the Jews. There was great disparity between the descriptions of the Jewish defeat and the Jewish conquest:

> 'Victory', 'Defeat'. The legions of Bar Kokhba stormed over the Roman fortresses like a great wave, and the Roman legions fled from them in fear. Within *one year* the Jews captured ninety fortified cities and about *one thousand cities and villages* in Judeah, the Galilee, and Samaria, among them also Jerusalem. For over *three years* Bar Kokhba stood in front of the Roman fierce armies, but, the many [Roman] legions finally succeeded in weakening the resistance of the Jews. *Slowly, slowly*, after a long siege and many bloody battles, the fortresses fell *one by one* to the enemy hands. (emphasis added)[21]

When describing the Jewish defeat, the authors mentioned the entire three years from the beginning of the revolt to its end (AD 132–35); in describing the Jewish conquest, they only referred to one year of fighting. In the case of the victory, they used the metaphor of water to describe the quick conquest by the Jewish army; in contrast, in the case of defeat, they

41

used the words 'slowly, slowly' to emphasize the difficulty the Romans experienced in overcoming the Jews. Finally, in victory, they referred to the entire number of cities captured simultaneously (90 fortresses and 1,000 cities and villages), giving the impression that it was a quick and easy conquest; in defeat, they pointed out that 'one by one the cities surrendered'. While the historical facts in these excerpts were all accurate, it was the presentation which communicated the difference in significance of the two battles. By slowing down the text in one instance and speeding it up in another, the authors created a contrast between the effort that each group had put into its victory, highlighting the Jewish achievements over those of the Romans.

The authors downplayed the defeat due to the present-time meaningfulness of the past in Israeli society. The goal was to create symbolic connections between the new Jewish State and the second-century Jewish kingdom. In summarizing the revolt, the authors of a popular book contended:

> In spite of these attempts to persecute and oppress the nation the great Roman Empire could not succeed in breaking the spirit of the nation. On the contrary: all these persecutions united the nation and fortified it. In the end, the great Roman Empire disintegrated and vanished from the world, while the weak and persecuted nation continued to weave its life and finally succeeded in rebuilding its land.[22]

The text located the end of the revolt not in AD 135 but in 1948. By leaping some 1,800 years ahead from the second century to the twentieth century, the authors pointed to the establishment of the State of Israel in 1948 as the final episode and victory in the battle against Rome.

Only a handful of people questioned the nature of the Israeli history curriculum in the 1950s and 1960s. Jacob Katz – who was to become one of the most prominent historians of modern Jewish history – pointed out that Israeli textbooks of Jewish history were simplistic and dull as well as inflated in their narrative style.[23] A few years earlier, Katz had written a series of textbooks for the national-religious trend. In his autobiography he testified that 'I could not bring myself to write a history, even for beginners, that depended on secondary and tertiary sources. I therefore felt obligated to examine the pertinent sources before writing each chapter.'[24]

In fact, in its historical accuracy and style this textbook was visibly distinct from any other textbook of the era. Unlike other textbook accounts of the 1950s, in Katz's book Bar Kokhba's leadership stemmed not from his miraculous appearance, nor from his famous genealogy, nor from his physical power. Consistent with his professional pursuit as an historian, and his views about textbook writing, Katz presented Bar Kokhba's image in political terms as someone who 'conversed with all the rebels and became their leader'.[25]

Katz referred also to those who opposed the revolt. He cited one sage who argued that 'there will be no benefit in an armed revolt, because the Roman kingdom for the time being ruled the world and the nation of Israel must wait until God has mercy for his nation'. Moreover, Katz did not divert attention from the result of the revolt to the process. He explicitly pointed out that 'the war did not benefit Israel, indeed it enlarged the destruction of the land. Whole districts in Judea were desolated because their inhabitants were killed by the Romans'.[26]

Although Katz wanted the historical narrative to represent a viable historical account, he saw no point in presenting the students with the intricacies of historical research. Katz firmly believed that 'history is not anything but the story of past occurrences which is passed down to the next generation orally or in writing. The process of transmitting a tradition means an active giving of the story teller and a passive role for the listener.'[27] Indeed, he chose to present the past as factual and complete, as though one had a precise knowledge of past occurrences. The text concealed from the students any controversy among historians in interpreting the past. For example, Katz states that the motivation for the revolt was the belief among Jews that Hadrian would build a temple for them in Jerusalem; but, continues Katz, 'Hadrian did not actually ever intend to build a Temple for God in Jerusalem. He wanted to build the city and a Temple for Jupiter in it.'[28] Although some historians do hold this view, others disagree and argue that a 'ban on circumcision' caused the revolt.[29] Katz concealed any disputes or disagreements in the interpretation of the past.

Textbooks in Israel of the 1950s and 1960s assisted in the formation of the new Jewish nation. One senior official in the Ministry of Education, Michael Ziv, pointed out in 1957 that 'there will not be an "official" history textbook – that is the meaning of a democratic state'. However,

> It is obvious that [history textbooks] bear a responsibility not to endanger the security of our lives – over this there is no debate. It is not a sign of health when a person asks what the role of a certain

part of his body is; it is not a sign of spiritual health if a person asks what the role of his mother and father is. Such a question is itself a sign of crisis.[30]

The state guided students as parents guide infants. Questions and criticism about state actions symbolized the failure of history education. Students should regard the state as beyond reproach, just as infants view their parents with admiring eyes. The emphasis of the national curriculum and textbooks was on creating a national collective memory, not on developing critical capabilities.

An 'Objective' Past – Textbooks in the 1970s and 1980s

The Israeli Ministry of Education published a revised national history curriculum in 1970. The new curriculum strongly drew upon the ideas of American researchers such as Benjamin Bloom, David Krathwohl and Jerome Bruner, who argued that many of the educational objectives up to that point centred on simple educational tasks such as recall.[31] Instead, these educational researchers called for a shift to an approach that included application of theories and concepts, detailed analysis of material and the synthesis and evaluation of evidence. The goal was to emulate scientific disciplines, since 'any subject can be taught in some intellectually honest form to any child at any stage of development'.[32]

The 1970 history curriculum pursued students' attainment of academic conceptions as one primary goal. From eight curriculum principles, the majority focused on cognitive goals such as 'comprehension ... of historical concepts' and 'development of historical thought'.[33] Furthermore, students would develop their own 'assumptions to explain historical events', increase their historical empathy through 'entering the web of life embedded in the relics and documents in our hands', as well as 'seek, in a systematic manner, the different causes and results which may serve as possible explanations for historical events'.[34] The final goal, however, continued to focus on forming a national collective memory requiring that history education 'foster [among students] a sense of identification with the nation and the state'.[35]

As a result of the new curriculum, historians became an integral part of the curricular development teams. This change showed up immediately in the new textbooks. While textbooks of the previous generation cited solely Jewish sources, the four new books published during the 1970s and 1980s had a diverse collection of citations: seven from rabbinic sources, six from Dio Cassius and eight from archaeological findings (especially from scrolls written by Simon Bar Kokhba himself found in the 1960s in archaeological digs).

The manner in which the authors used the traditional Jewish sources also differed significantly from their use in earlier books. While early textbooks used legends to illuminate the historical protagonists, the new books focused mostly on informative citations. For example, in three of the books the authors cited a Jewish prayer written after the destruction of the Second Temple: 'May our eyes behold thy return in mercy to Zion.'[36] This and similar prayers pointed out the social unrest in Second Temple Jewish society which resulted ultimately in the Bar Kokhba Revolt.

While the 1950s and 1960s textbooks attempted to depict Simon himself as an unearthly figure, post-1970s textbooks avoided such heroic depictions. Instead, authors of a text for secular schools stated that 'Simon Bar Kokhba, supported by Rabbi Akiva and the majority of sages, supervised the preparations for the revolt.'[37] Simon prepared for the revolt and became the leader only after the unrest began and after he had gained political support from prominent religious figures. The defeat as well became vivid and harsh. One book concluded that 'Bar Kokhba was killed. The revolt was suppressed. The last attempt to redeem the Land of Israel by force had failed. The fight had lasted for three years, bringing terrible destruction and disaster to the land.'[38]

Yet, although they avoided a glorious account, the new textbooks failed to achieve the ambitious cognitive goals stated in the 1970 curriculum. Contrary to the goals of the curriculum, the authors did not allow students to participate in the process of reconstructing a historical event, in developing historical hypotheses or in analysing sources.[39] In the textbooks historical material appeared as part of a narrative, as a testimony. The sources validated the authors 'true' account of the past. For example, on the face of coins of the era appeared symbols associated with the temple in Jerusalem. The authors presented these coins, stating that the 'coins were minted in free Jerusalem'.[40] However, the authors ignore an alternative explanation: the illustration on the coins expressed only the rebels' aspirations to rebuild the temple. The authors frame the historical event from one vantage point, one that, because of its monolithic nature, could help create a shared memory in students' minds.

Although the new textbooks for seventh graders avoided explicit use of history for national interests, at times political issues still coloured their depiction. These cases related to acute issues in the contemporary

Israeli political agenda, such as the status of Jerusalem. 'It is not clear whether Jerusalem was captured by the Jews in the revolt of Bar Kokhba', state Isaac and Oppenheimer in their review of the research.[41] All textbooks from the 1950s to the early 1990s, however, were conclusive: 'Jerusalem was freed, and again there was a high priest and the preparations for building the Third Temple began.'[42] As is evident from this excerpt, many textbooks argued that not only was Jerusalem captured by the rebels, but that they renewed work at the temple, a view with almost no support among scholars.[43]

An explanation of the consensus among textbooks about the capturing of Jerusalem relates to the present-day status of the city in the minds of Israelis. In their depiction of Jerusalem during the revolt, the authors were influenced by a long-standing belief among Israelis about their right over the entire city.[44] The present political disagreements between Jews and Arabs on the status of Jerusalem caused textbook authors, perhaps inadvertently, to argue that Jerusalem was captured in the second century as well. Establishing Jewish control over Jerusalem just before Jews were sent to exile perhaps enhanced their argument for Jewish control over the city when they returned in modern times. Textbook authors reflected here, and were influenced by, a widespread belief in the Israeli public domain.

In sum, the textbooks of the 1970s presented a canonical account of the revolt. Consequently, they avoid the central goal of the new history curriculum published in the 1970s of promoting critical historical skills. Although they avoid the missionary goal of earlier textbooks, these newer textbooks focus on communicating a predominant narrative to the future Israeli citizenry.

A Universal Past – Textbooks in the 1990s

A new edition of the national history curriculum was published in 1995. This edition signalled a shift away from the national focus of the two previous curricula and highlighted instead social and cultural perspectives. 'National history is one component within [history], just as other parts of history make up other components of it: the history of women or the history of sports or modern history. Each one is a frame within the larger frame [of history]', emphasized Moshe Zimmerman, the head of the curriculum committee and professor of German history at the Hebrew University.[45]

The curriculum reiterated the entire list of introductory goals which appeared in the 1975 curriculum, including the one that required that students 'acknowledge the uniqueness of the people of Israel among the nations, in their essence and destiny'.[46] But the new syllabus presented Jewish history as a sub-topic, albeit a recurring one, of a greater global historical framework. For example, Zionism – the ideological foundation of Israel – surfaced only as a sub-topic of nationalism. Similarly, the establishment of the state surfaced only as a sub-topic of the Cold War.[47] Finally, the Holocaust, an event of great magnitude for the Jewish people and a central event in Israelis' identity, emanated as a sub-topic of the Second World War. In fact, with only moderate changes, this syllabus would be fitting for any Western country.

In a textbook published in light of the new curriculum, the shift away from a national focus was noticeable. In the introduction to the textbook, the author told students that learning history was not 'only about the story of kings, conquests and wars. We want to know how people lived … what they thought about themselves, and what they believed.' The author expected students to develop their own independent views of events, since history is basically 'a story of the events that occurred in the past, based on different sources'. Students were required to 'ask the right questions, and develop an independent view' of events.[48] As we will soon see, the textbook did not stand up to the author's own criteria.

In her reconstruction of the Bar Kokhba Revolt, author Bruria Ben Baruch cited only the Greek source of Dio Cassius regarding the revolt. The traditional Jewish sources were completely absent. This shift away from Jewish elements was also reflected in the Hebrew title of the textbook *In Greek and Roman Times*, with no reference to the Jewish past.[49]

The textbook author also cited a modern critic who said about the Bar Kokhba Revolt:

> With the exception of the Holocaust of European Jewry, it would seem that there was never such a catastrophe like that of Bar Kokhba, one in which so many Jews were killed at once. Jerusalem was entirely in ruins. In Judea, the Romans destroyed almost every settlement … The name 'Carthage' connotes total ruin. Yet the number killed in Judea was more than twice, and perhaps three times the number of victims among the Carthaginians.[50]

This excerpt was written by a former general in the Israeli Defense Forces, Yehoshafat Harkabi, who deemed the second-century revolt a disaster in both military and political terms. In his mind, the view of the

47

revolt in heroic terms served political ends in Israeli society. As Harkabi writes in his book, 'in contemporary Israel, one repeatedly hears the claim that great deeds are accomplished precisely because they spring from an unrealistic approach', as was the case in the revolt. He thus advocated a return to what he called a realistic approach to the past: 'to the traditional Jewish view which considered the Rebellion a catastrophe'.[51]

Harkabi's opinions led to 'a heated public debate' in Israel during the early 1980s.[52] A scholar and an ideologist of the Israeli right wing, Yisrael Eldad, argued against Harkabi's analogizing between the past events and the Israeli–Arab conflict.[53] In Eldad's mind, if Zionism had adopted Harkabi's realistic views, Israel would not have come into being. In the spirit of Theodor Herzl, the founder of Zionism, Eldad argued that the unrealistic can become part of reality.[54]

The controversy between Harkabi and Eldad received wide publicity in Israel. To rebut Harakbi's views, the Israeli government arranged a national ceremony of burial for remnants of the Bar Kokhba Revolt warriors found in the archaeological digs of the 1960s. The government committee organizing the event instructed the Ministry of Education 'to hold informational and educational activities on the period of Bar-Kokhba's revolt, stressing the tradition of heroism'.[55] As a result, the Ministry of Education Director General published a letter directing teachers to instruct students on the Bar Kokhba Revolt.[56] The political pressures failed, however, to re-establish the heroic image of the revolt in Israeli collective memory due to deep divisions in Israeli society about how to view the event.[57]

The textbook which came out in 1996 chose to side with one view in the debate, that of Harkabi. In so doing the author Bruria Ben Baruch eliminated the opposing view in the controversy which argued that the event was warranted. The text sided with one view in the present-time controversy, concealing competing viewpoints. It was creating a counter-myth in the minds of Israeli students.

Within her narrative, the author of the textbook integrated some critical elements. For example, she constantly uses the words 'possibly' or 'may have' in her narrative, as well as acknowledging the lack of historical sources in some cases. Still, she narrates the past for students and therefore does not fulfil her own commitment, as well as those of the 1995 curriculum, that students should participate in historical analysis and develop their own independent views of the past. The author avoided students' analysis of historical sources, or their narration of events. This textbook, as others before it, communicated the past in a conclusive manner. It attempted to construct a collective memory; however, this time it portrayed the event in disastrous terms.

Discussion and Conclusion

On 14 August 1999, a headline on the front page of the *New York Times* declared: 'Israel's History Textbooks Replace Myths With Facts'.[58] The article revealed that the Israeli Ministry of Education had approved a new series of revolutionary textbooks. While early generations of Israeli schoolchildren learned that Palestinians fled their homes in the 1948 war, the new generation of students would learn that 'there were localities in which the Jewish fighting forces conducted expulsion actions'.[59] The article concluded that the new school year 'marks a quiet revolution in the teaching of Israeli history to most Israeli pupils'.

A naive spectator would view these changes as commendable. Textbooks set history straight; they confront students with the questionable acts of their predecessors. Yet, a more careful look shows the problematic dimension of these alterations. Textbooks' narratives change with each generation: in one generation the Bar Kokhba Revolt appears as a victory, in the next as a defeat; from 'Jerusalem was freed' by Bar Kokhba a decade ago, to Jerusalem only 'possibly' captured today.

A key element in textbook depiction is appeasing the social and political factors. History textbooks communicate a contemporary past, one which matches the prevailing social and political needs. One textbook author cited in the *New York Times* seems to admit that his depiction of the Israeli–Arab conflict depended on changing social circumstances: 'Only 10 years ago much of this was taboo ... we were not mature enough to look at these controversial problems. *Now* we can deal with this' (emphasis added).[60] With the emerging peace in the Middle East textbooks need to update their narrative.

It is not that the scholarship included in the new series of Israeli textbooks was not known a decade ago. In fact, references to the expulsion and killing of Palestinians appeared in the memories of Israeli politicians for many years.[61] Palestinians have pointed out these events for many more years. Historians of the Second Temple era have argued about Bar Kokhba's capture of Jerusalem for decades. Only recently with the changing social and political circumstances in the Middle East did textbooks adopt these scholarly views as the *lingua franca*.[62]

The danger in altering historical accounts to appease changing social and political circumstances is obvious. With each new wind a change in depictions occurs: one textbook out, another textbook in. While today textbooks admit to wrongdoings of Israelis to Palestinians, with a new social and political environment they may replace this narrative with one which emphasizes the cruelty of Arabs towards Jews.

History textbooks narrate history for students and, in so doing, suppress alternative narratives. Textbooks present students with a supposed factual account. In some instances authors conceal, in others they select, but in all they interpret. In an essay written more than 30 years ago, Peter Schrag explained:

> History textbooks are bad, not because they are too biased, but because their biases are concealed by the tone. History texts are written as if their authors did not exist at all, as if they were simply the instruments of a heavenly intelligence transcribing official truths. The tone of the textbook is the tone of a disembodied voice speaking in passive sentences, it fosters the widespread confusion that the text is history, not simply a human construct composed of selected data, interpretations and opinions.[63]

Furthermore, authoritative accounts of history textbooks, points out Peter Seixias, do not convey the essence of knowing historically. When historical scholarship is transferred into textbooks and is presented as 'reality', it loses what signified it in the historical community of inquiry. Historical arguments among historians are 'tentative and invented, to be challenged and revised, contributions to an ongoing discussion within a community of inquiry. When taken out of that context, they dry up', as happens in textbooks.[64]

Not surprisingly, students see history as a subject which is primarily focused on accumulating information, not on argumentation.[65] History appears to students as reporting 'just the real facts', a chronology of dates and events in progression.[66] This notion of history as a simple factual chronology is reflected, among other things, in the history students read. In fact, students asked to evaluate primary historical documents' trustworthiness against that of textbooks held the latter as more credible.[67] In communicating a fixed and final account, textbooks deprive students from developing their capacity to know historically.

To alter this situation, some scholars have argued for a change in the authoritative tone of textbooks. 'If we want students to read historical texts differently from their driver's education manuals, if we want them to comprehend both text *and* subtext', points out Wineburg, 'we will have to change our lesson plans – not to mention our textbooks.'[68]

Crismore who found that 'metadiscourse' – the author's presentation of his or her ideas, beliefs, hesitations and judgement – appeared in historical books, but was lacking in textbooks, asks:

> What happens to critical reading ... when bias is not overt (as it is not in textbooks) are young readers being deceived? What happens to critical reading when attitudinal metadiscourse is delayed until adulthood and readers are not encouraged to become active participants in the reading process? ... Young readers need to learn about the domain of scholarship at an early age – where ideas come from, sources, citations, and bibliographies. Textbooks should model this.[69]

Yet, is a reform in textbooks such as Wineburg, Crismore and others call for feasible? Calls for reform in textbooks have echoed for decades, but textbooks persist with their authoritative accounts.[70] Why do textbooks avoid conceding their control and shifting the historical agency to students?

Let us first consider the change in historical understanding in modern times. The French philosopher of history Pierre Nora points out that the rise of modernity has resulted in the transformation of society's historical memory. While in pre-modern societies memory was passed down from one member of a generation to another, in modern societies, such as our own, 'there are *lieux de mémoire*, sites of memory, because there are no longer *milieux de mémoire*, real environments of memory'.[71] The role of family, community and ritual in the communication of history has declined and instead *lieux de mémoire* have risen. We now learn about the past events through national memorial sites, historical museums, television and film – not in the traditional means which informed our ancestors.

While one may argue with Nora's assessment that memory in modern societies is restricted, his notion that modern societies have transformed the means by which we come to know the past applies to textbooks. Textbooks manifest the mass historical transmission of a historical knowledge from one generation to another. Furthermore, textbooks have become a means for social groups to meet and contemplate on the essence of their *lieux de mémoire*. Textbooks represent a point of social negotiation between different groups whose prime concern is passing down to students a common past for a mutual future. The watchdog groups for textbooks in the USA as well as in Israel will testify to this.

History textbooks preserve and communicate cultural truths intergenerationally. David Olson points out the similarity between textbooks and ritualized speech. In the case of ritualized speech, the speaker appears to the spectator not as speaking the speaker's own words but those of a transcendental power. The differentiation between speaker and speech gives the words a high status. Similarly, 'the separation of speech from speaker [in textbooks] helps to put the words "above criticism"'.[72] The truthfulness of the textbook creates the basis for a common credo acceptable to the future citizenry.

The social role of textbooks dictates their tone. The authoritative tone and the narration of the past serve to pass down a memory from one generation to another. The goal is for students to have pride in their tradition, for them to cherish their origins, for them to join, identify and benefit their social group. Textbooks represent the socially valid and truthful knowledge. Competing viewpoints do not serve to communicate a heritage to the young generation; they do not enhance the group's cohesion. We should not expect the complexity of historical knowing to come from textbooks which are social tools.

Students have the capacity to think historically. Numerous studies have found that middle school students are able to take part in historical reasoning.[73] Furthermore, students employ these historical abilities in regards to their personal lives.[74] When authors are visible in the text, that is, when they express their attitudes or opinions, teenagers engage in a mental discourse with them.[75] However, since textbooks serve society to preserve its values, textbooks are structured to avoid presenting students with the challenge of thinking historically and instead communicate a narrated past to them.

The narrative of textbooks is an important means for communicating society's account of events to students. As we have seen, with all the changes textbooks have gone through in the past decades, they still remain primarily tools for the enhancement of national identification among students. History education must, however, go further and educate students to know in a critical sense, as well as to understand the limits of their ability to know. For students to know in historical terms, we need to focus our efforts on the instruction of history, on transferring the conceptual tools for thinking historically.

Acknowledgements

I am indebted to Mark Brilliant, Jon Marvin, Susan Mosborg and Sam Wineburg who reviewed drafts of this chapter. This study was possible thanks to the generous support of the Memorial Foundation for Jewish Culture.

NOTES

1. George Orwell, *1984* (New York: Signet Classics, 1949), pp. 64 and 68.
2. Maurice Halbwachs, *The Collective Memory* (1950; reprint New York: Harper & Row, 1980), p. 86.
3. Yosef Haim Yerushalmi, *Zakhor: Jewish History and Jewish Memory* (Seattle, WA: University of Washington Press, 1982), pp. 94–5.
4. Richard White, *Remembering Ahanagran* (New York: Hill & Wang, 1998), p. 4; Natalie Z. Davis and Randolph Starn, 'Introduction: memory and counter memory', *Representations*, 26, 2 (1989), pp. 1–6; Yael Zerubavel, *Recovered Roots: Collective Memory and the Making of Israeli National Tradition* (Chicago, IL: University of Chicago Press, 1995).
5. David Lowenthal, *The Past is a Foreign Country* (1985; reprint Cambridge: Cambridge University Press, 1993), p. 213; Amos Funkenstein, 'Collective memory and historical consciousness', *History and Memory*, 1, 1 (1989), pp. 5–26.
6. Jane J. White, 'Searching for substantial knowledge in social studies texts', *Theory and Research in Social Education*, 16, 2 (Spring 1988), pp. 115–40.
7. Only a few studies have demonstrated the way history textbooks have served to advance ideologies through selection and stereotyping. Jean Anyon, for one, conducted a study on economic and labour history from the Civil War to the First World War in American textbooks, and found that the textbook authors selected, omitted and presented only one-sided accounts of the events: Jean Anyon, 'Ideology and United States history textbooks', *Harvard Educational Review*, 49, 3 (1979); Frances FitzGerald, *America Revised: History Schoolbooks in the Twentieth Century* (Boston, MA: Little Brown, 1979).
8. My study included all textbooks approved by the Ministry of Education for use in classrooms. Over a period of 45 years, 11 books for sixth or seventh grade referred to the Bar Kokhba Revolt. In the references and citations I cite in this chapter, I refer mostly to the more popular textbooks used in the Israeli Jewish public schools.
9. In this context I translate the Hebrew word *nasi* as leader rather than president.
10. Menachem Mor, *Mered Bar Kokhba Otsmato ve Hekefo* (*The Bar Kokhba Revolt, its Extent and Effect*) (Jerusalem: Yad Yitshak ben Tsevi, 1991); Mary E. Smallwood, *The Jews under Roman Rule* (Leiden: E.J. Brill, 1976).
11. David Ben-Gurion, *Netsah Yisrael* (Tel Aviv: Ayanot, 1964), p. 158. Also see Uri Ram, 'Zionist historiography and the invention of modern Jewish nationhood: The case of Ben-Zion Dinur', *History and Memory*, 7, 1 (1995), pp. 91–124. Abba Eban, who was the Israeli Minister of Education during the early 1960s, writes in his autobiography that 'I found the Israeli school a very conservative place … The strong Hebrew and Biblical emphasis could, of course, be understood in terms of our need to create a national consciousness.' Abba Eban, *An Autobiography* (New York: Random House, 1977), p. 284.
12. Ministry of Education, Israel, *Tochnit ha-Limudiem le-Veit ha-Sefer ha-Yesodi ha-Mamlachti ve-ha-Mamlachti ha-Dati* (*Curriculum for National and National-Religious Elementary Schools*) (Jerusalem: 1956), pp. 17–18.
13. Ministry of Education, Israel, *Horat ha-Shoah be-Veit ha-Sefer* (*Proceedings on Teaching the Holocaust in Schools*) (Jerusalem: Ministry of Education, 1961), p. 75.
14. Zerubavel, *Recovered Roots*; Shmuel Almog, *Zionism and History: The Rise of a New Jewish Consciousness* (New York: St Martin's Press, 1987).
15. D. Issac and A. Oppenheimer, 'The revolt of Bar Kokhba: Ideology and modern scholarship', *Journal of Jewish Studies*, 36 (1987); p. 41. See also Menahem Stern, *Greek and Latin Authors on Jews and Judaism*, 2 (Jerusalem: Israel Academy of Sciences and Humanities, 1980), p. 393.
16. Moshe Shmueli, *Korot Amenu* (Jerusalem: Tarbut ve-Chinuch, 1958), p. 282.
17. *The Talmud of the Land of Israel*, vol. 18 of *Besah and Taanit*, trans. Jacob Neusner

(Chicago, IL: University of Chicago Press, 1987), p. 276.

18. Issac and Oppenheimer, 'Revolt', p. 37.
19. Baruch Avivi and Nathan Perski, *Toldot Yisrael* (*History of Israel*) (Tel Aviv: Yavenh, 1955), p. 292.
20. For example, one rabbinic sage argued with Rabbi Akiva and said to him in reference to Bar Kokhba that 'grass will rise from your cheeks [Rabbi Akiva] and the son of David will not yet have come'. Ekha Rabba, 2:5.
21. Avivi and Perski, *Toldot*, pp. 294–5.
22. Baruch Ahiyah and Moshe Harpaz, *Toldot am Yisrael* (*History of Israel*) (Tel Aviv: Sherchbek, 3rd edn. 1965), p. 211.
23. Jacob Katz, 'Ha-Historia ha-Yisraeliet ke-Gorem Hinukhi' ('Israeli history as an educational factor'), *Molad Jerusalem* (1954), pp. 73–4.
24. Jacob Katz, *With My Own Eyes* (Hanover: Brandies University Press, 1995), p. 130.
25. Jacob Katz, *Yisrael ve-ha-Amim, Kerech 2* (*Israel and the Nations, Vol. 2*) (Jerusalem: Tarshis, 1957), p. 20.
26. Ibid., pp. 20 and 24.
27. Jacob Katz, 'Le-Darco shel Sefer ha-Limud be-*Yisrael ve-ha-Amim*' ('The Method of the Textbook in *Israel and the Nations*'), in A. Morgenstein (ed.), *Three Articles on History Teaching* (1963; reprint Jerusalem: Ministry of Education, 1977), p. 16; Katz, interview by author, 23 July 1997.
28. Katz, *Yisrael*, p. 19.
29. Issac and Oppenheimer, 'Revolt', p. 45.
30. Zohn Collection, 22 December 1957, p. 18, The Archives of Jewish Education in Israel and the Diaspora in Memory of Aviezer Yellin, Tel Aviv University.
31. B.S. Bloom (ed.), *The Taxonomy of Educational Objectives* (New York: Longman, 1956).
32. Jerome Bruner, *The Process of Education* (Cambridge, MA: Harvard University Press, 1960), p. 33.
33. Ministry of Education, Israel, *Tochnit ha-Limudim be-Historiah le-Kitot Vav-Tet be-Veit ha-Sefer ha-Mamlachti ve-ha-Mamlachti-Dati* (*History Curriculum: Grades 6–9 in National and National-Religious Schools*) (Jerusalem: 1970), p. 11, objective 5.
34. Ibid., p. 11, objective 5.32, 5.22, 5.21.
35. Ibid., p. 10, objective 8.
36. Shlomo Shavit, ed., *Shiuriem be-Historia, Kerech 2* (*History Lessons, Vol. 2*) (Jerusalem: Ministry of Education, 1987), p. 113.
37. Ibid., p. 114.
38. Shlomo Shavit (ed.), *Toldot Yisrael ve-ha-Amim, Kerech 2* (*History of Israel and the Nations, Vol. 2*) (Jerusalem: Ministry of Education, 1987), p. 119.
39. L. Adar and S. Fox, *Nituch Tochnit Limudiem be-Historyah u-Bitzuah be-Veit ha-Sefer* (*An Analysis of the Content and Use of a History Curriculum*) (Jerusalem: Hebrew University School of Education, 1978), pp. 29–30.
40. Shavit, *Toldot*, p. 112.
41. Issac and Oppenheimer, 'Revolt', p. 54.
42. Shavit, *Toldot*, p. 112.
43. In fact only a minority of scholars believe Jerusalem was captured by Bar Kokhba and even a smaller number contend that he rebuilt the temple. For a review of the literature see Issac and Oppenheimer, 'Revolt', pp. 54–5.
44. The status of Jerusalem has been contested over the past decades. After the establishment of Israel in 1948, the country's borders included only the western part of the city, while the eastern side – including the site of the Temple mount – remained under Jordanian control. After the Six Day War of 1967, Israelis gained control of the entire city. Many Israelis believe that they themselves also have a historical and moral right to control the Holy City at present due to their ancestors' control over the city in the First and Second Temple.

45. Zimmerman, interview with author, 14 August 1998.
46. Ministry of Education, Israel, *Tochnit Limudiem*, p. 12.
47. Ibid., pp. 25–6.
48. Bruria Ben Baruch, *Greeks, Romans, Jews* (Tel Aviv: Tel Aviv Books, 1996), p.6.
49. The English name of the book *Greeks, Romans, Jews* includes the word 'Jews' in its title.
50. Ben Baruch, *Greeks*, p. 162.
51. Ibid., p.xiii.
52. Yehoshafat Harkabi, *The Bar Kokhba Syndrome* (Chappaqua, NY: Rossel Books, 1983), p.vii.
53. Yisrael Eldad, *Pulmus Ha-Hurban U-Lekahav: Ketsad Nityahes Le-Hurban Ha-Bayit U-Le-Mered Bar-Kokhva (Controversy: Our Perception of the Destruction of the Second Temple and Bar Kochba's Revolt)* (Jerusalem: Van Leer Foundation, 1982), pp. 65–7.
54. Ibid.
55. Mayron J. Aronoff, *The Frailty of Authority*, Political Anthropology Series, No. 5 (New Brunswick, NJ: Transaction, 1986), p. 118.
56. Ministry of Education, Israel, *Chozer ha-Manchal (Director-General Newsletter)* (Jerusalem: 1 June 1982).
57. Zerubavel, *Recovered Roots*, p. 190.
58. *New York Times*, A1, A5.
59. Ibid., A1.
60. Ibid.
61. See Benny Morris, *The Birth of the Palestinian Refugee Problem, 1947–1949* (New York, Cambridge University Press: 1987), p. 345.
62. Peter Lee, 'Historical knowledge and the national curriculum', in Hilary Bourdillon (ed.), *Teaching History* (New York: Routledge/The Open University, 1994), p. 43.
63. Peter Schrag, 'The emasculated voice of the textbook', *Saturday Review* (21 January 1967), p. 74.
64. P. Seixas, 'Parallel crises: History and social studies curriculum in the USA', *Journal of Curriculum Studies*, 25, 3 (1993), p. 313.
65. S. Wineburg, 'On the reading of historical texts: Notes on the breach between school and academy', *American Educational Research Journal*, 28, 3 (1991).
66. Tom Holt, *Thinking Historically: Narrative, Imagination, and Understanding*, (New York: College Entrance Examination Board, 1995), p. 3.
67. S. Wineburg, 'Historical problem solving: A study of the cognitive processes in the evaluation of documentary and pictorial evidence', *Educational Psychology*, 83, 1 (1991), pp. 73–87.
68. Wineburg, 'On the reading of historical texts', p. 519.
69. Avon Crismore, 'The Rhetoric of Textbooks: Metadiscourse', *Journal of Curriculum Studies*, 16 (July–September 1984), pp. 295–6.
70. FitzGerald, *America Revised*; Michael W. Apple, *Official Knowledge: Democratic Education in a Conservative Age* (New York: Routledge, 1993).
71. Pierre Nora, 'Between Memory and History: Les lieux de mémoire', *Representations*, 26 (1989), p. 8.
72. David R. Olson, 'Writing: The divorce of the author from the text', in Barry M. Kroll and Roberta J. Vann (eds), *Exploring Speaking–Writing Relations* (Urbana, IL: National Council of Teachers of English, 1981), p. 109.
73. For a list of studies which demonstrate these abilities, see Stuart J. Foster and Charles S. Padgett, 'Authentic historical inquiry in the social studies classroom', *The Clearing House*, 72, 6 (1999).
74. Holt, *Thinking Historically*, p. 6.
75. Richard J. Paxton, '"Someone with like a life wrote it": The effects of a visible author on high school history students', *Journal of Educational Psychology*, 89, 2 (1997), p. 246.

4

Historical and International Dimensions of History Education: The Work of the Committee of Seven

CHARA HAEUSSLER BOHAN

Historical and international dimensions of history education, particularly with respect to the work of the Committee of Seven, merit renewed attention in the present. Lessons from the past illuminate paths for future work in the field of history education. American historians at the turn of the twentieth century, who served on the Committee of Seven, remained committed to the principle that education was critical in a democratic society. The Committee of Seven, a subcommittee of the American Historical Association, worked to improve the teaching of history in American secondary schools. Not parochial in their perspective, the historians who served on the Committee of Seven in the late 1890s examined and evaluated history education in the United States, Germany, France, England and Canada. They believed that understanding history instruction and curricula in other countries could inform and advance the practice of history education in American schools.

Members of the Committee of Seven hoped to bring increased uniformity to the secondary history curriculum and believed that the educational systems of foreign countries could serve as an example. Although committee members conducted their research by surveying historical studies in American schools, they also sought an international comparison of educational practices with regard to the teaching of history. Therefore, at the first meeting of the Committee of Seven, held in Cambridge, Massachusetts on 16–17 April 1897, members agreed to 'study the conditions of foreign schools during the next summer' as 'such investigations would give a fresh and valuable basis for discussion'.[1] They believed their endeavour to study the history curricula and teaching practices in several industrialized nations would inform their recommendations for teaching history in American schools.

Certainly, the report that the committee ultimately published affected the US secondary history curriculum at a national level. Yet, transformation of the historical studies was not radical, and the committee's impact must be qualified. Curriculum considerations in the United States have been and remain under state and local control, despite attempts to establish national standards. Furthermore, achieving consensus on history curricula has often led to heated debate over the content and methods to be implemented. Recently, co-directors Gary B. Nash and Charlotte Crabtree of the government-funded National Standards for History project stated that: 'there have been many who have wondered if a national consensus could be forged concerning what all students should have the opportunity to learn about the history of the world and of the peoples of all racial, religious, ethnic, and national backgrounds who have been part of that story'.[2] Indeed, polarized debate over national history standards is not new. The Committee of Seven faced similar challenges in the 1890s as did those who served on the National Standards for History in the 1990s. Understanding the relationship between the past and the present can help frame future deliberations regarding history curricula.

Origin, Membership and Aims of the Committee of Seven

The American Historical Association (AHA) established the Committee of Seven. Founded in 1884 at Johns Hopkins University, the AHA was the first national association in the United States dedicated to the promotion of the study of history.[3] In 1895 several AHA members pressed for changes within the organizational structure of the association. Believing that methods of electing AHA officers were autocratic, they pressed for democratic changes within the AHA's administration. These members led a revolt against AHA founder Herbert Baxter Adams and his 'virtual one-man rule and limited view of the AHA's structure and function'.[4]

Concerned about the status of historical studies in secondary education, August F. Nightingale, chairman of the National Education Association's Committee on College Entrance Requirements, asked historians at the 1896 AHA meeting to study the practice of teaching history in American schools.[5] Against Herbert B. Adams' wishes, the association agreed to the National Education Association's request and formed a committee to recommend the history curriculum for the nation's secondary schools. Not wanting to be excluded from the deliberations,

Adams made certain he was appointed a member of the committee. Subsequently, in 1897 the AHA established the Committee of Seven.

The AHA charged the committee to make recommendations about the teaching of history and to foster increased uniformity in secondary school history offerings. The Committee of Seven considered the scope and sequence of history offerings in secondary schools and proposed college entrance requirements in the field.[6] Members of the Committee of Seven included Andrew McLauglin (chairman), Herbert B. Adams, George L. Fox, Albert Bushnell Hart, Charles H. Haskins, H. Morse Stephens and Lucy M. Salmon.[7] Six of these members were prominent historians; one was the headmaster of an elite private school.

Clearly, all committee members were highly accomplished individuals. Herbert B. Adams, who had organized the American Historical Association at its founding in 1884 and served as its first secretary, was Professor of American and Institutional History at Johns Hopkins University.[8] Charles Homer Haskins was Professor of European History at the University of Wisconsin at the time the Committee of Seven was formed. He later became Dean of Harvard Graduate School and served on the American delegation to negotiate peace at the end of the First World War.[9] Andrew McLaughlin, Managing Editor of the *American Historical Review*,[10] was Professor of American History at the University of Michigan and later at the University of Chicago; H. Morse Stephens was Professor of Modern European History at Cornell University and later at the University of California.[11]

Other committee members also possessed noteworthy credentials. Harvard historian Albert Bushnell Hart, a prolific author, had written a popular guide to the study of American history.[12] Hart was was elected president of the AHA (1909) and the American Political Science Association (1912).[13] McLaughlin (1914), Stephens (1915) and Haskins (1922) also later became AHA presidents. George L. Fox, rector of the Hopkins Grammar School in New Haven, Connecticut, was the only individual practising in a secondary school.[14] The only woman on the committee, Lucy Maynard Salmon, chaired the history department at Vassar College.[15] Subsequently, Salmon became the first woman elected to the Executive Council of the AHA, at a time (1915) when women in most states remained disenfranchised.

When Salmon suggested the addition of another woman to membership on the Committee of Seven, the association rebuffed her request. In a letter to George Burton Adams dismissing Salmon's request, fellow committee member Herbert Baxter Adams wrote: 'I am inclined to think that one woman is enough!'[16] Despite Salmon's inability to increase the female membership on the committee, her work on the report contributed to her prominence as a nationally recognized authority in history and education.

Initially, Salmon and the other members of the conference conducted a nationwide survey of secondary history curricula in the United States. After expanding their examination of history instruction to an international level, these historians made recommendations to improve history education in the USA.

The Committee of Seven certainly took into consideration the earlier work of the Committee of Ten. In 1892 the National Education Association (NEA) had authorized the Committee of Ten, under the leadership of Harvard president Charles W. Eliot, to recommend standards for the various subjects in the secondary school curriculum.[17] A special subcommittee on history, civil government and political economy, meeting in Madison, Wisconsin, developed recommendations to the larger committee for the teaching of history in the schools. Albert Bushnell Hart had served on the subcommittee as well, along with prominent historians Charles Kendall Adams, Edward G. Bourne, Ray Greene Huling, Jesse Macy, James Harvey Robinson and future president Woodrow Wilson.[18] Members of the Madison conference called for a more complete programme in history, similar to what had been common in Europe for more than 50 years.[19] Although the report of the Committee of Ten recommended a comprehensive programme of history education, it endorsed only two years of required history and one year of elective history in American high schools. For the small percentage of students who earned high school degrees in the 1890s, the subcommittee of the Committee of Ten suggested that the ninth and tenth grade be devoted to French and English history, and that American history be examined in eleventh grade. A final year could be devoted to selected historical topics and the study of civil government.[20] The Committee of Ten suggested course titles, but provided little guidance in terms of specific historical curriculum topics and content.

The Committee of Seven report went further. Indeed, its recommendations had a far greater impact on the development of history education in secondary schools than did the earlier more comprehensive report of the Committee of Ten. The Committee of Seven noted:

> In spite of all that had been done, and in spite of this awakened interest, there was no recognized consensus of opinion in the country

at large, not one generally accepted judgment, not even one well-known point of agreement, which would serve as a beginning for a consideration of the place of history in the high-school curriculum ... The task of the committee was, therefore, to discover the actual situation, to see what was doing and what was the prevailing sentiment ... and having apprehended what was best and most helpful in spirit and tendency among teachers of the country, to seek to give that spirit expression in a report that would be helpful and suggestive, and that would be of service to widening the field of agreement and in laying the foundations for a common understanding.[21]

In other words, the Committee of Seven understood its task to be an evaluation of existing history curricula and to make suggestions for reform. The Committee of Seven hoped to develop the foundations of a common history curriculum in US schools, similar to the educational practices in Germany and, to a lesser extent, France.

The Committee's Views on Concepts and Purposes of History Education

The Committee of Seven researched the condition of historical study in the USA by circulating several hundred questionnaires to schools. Approximately 250 schools responded. The committee analysed these data to determine the status of history curricula and instruction.[22] Survey questions addressed the nature of history courses taught, the time allotted for history instruction, the selection of textbooks, collateral reading and source materials, written work required of students, teacher preparation and college requirements.[23] Educational historian David Warren Saxe depicted the members of the Committee of Seven as traditional historians in contrast with the 'insurgent' members of the later 1916 Committee on Social Studies of the Commission on the Reorganization of Secondary Education. Notwithstanding Saxe's polarized portrayal, the Committee of Seven members boldly employed newly developed social science methods to investigate the status of history instruction. Methods such as the distribution of surveys and the analysis of statistical data were uncommon research techniques to historians at the turn of the twentieth century. However, they were typical of the work of the new professional social scientists such as Lester Frank Ward, Florence Kelly, Jane Addams and Carroll Wright.[24] Clearly, the 'traditionalists' who served on the Committee of Seven were 'progressive' in their approach to their research of the status of history in schools.

Committee members also embraced progressive and global perspectives with regard to educational issues. They believed that lessons could be learned by studying educational systems abroad. Three committee members spent considerable time studying foreign methods of history instruction. Salmon spent a summer in Germany; Haskins studied the educational system in France; and Fox examined English schools.[25] Professor George Wrong of the University of Toronto contributed an analysis of history in Canadian secondary schools.[26] Articles on each country were included in the appendices of the committee's report. The committee stated: 'They [foreign educational practices] are not offered as furnishing us models to which we ought to conform, but as investigations in the study of comparative education; they may, however, give to teachers of this country suggestions on the subject of general pedagogical values, methods of historical instruction, and the arrangement of studies.'[27] The committee found that the German model of history instruction 'offers to America the most lessons'[28] because German teachers were best prepared in subject matter, methods, and child development.

The Committee of Seven had clearly defined aims and well-established goals for history instruction. The primary value derived from historical study, according to the committee, was for men and women to 'see the steps in the development of the human race' and to 'come to a sympathetic knowledge of their environment'.[29] The aim of history education and teaching was not to train scholars, nor for students to learn to be historians. The end result of a secondary education, it held, should be 'acquaintance with the political and social environment, some appreciation of the nature of the state and society, some sense of the duties and responsibilities of citizenship' and 'something of the broad and tolerant spirit which is bred by the study of past times and conditions'.[30] Saxe claimed that the committee primarily fostered intellectual development.[31] However, strong practical and general citizenship elements existed in the committee's stated goals, in addition to the desire to contribute to students' mental development and learning of content knowledge.

Indeed, the committee asserted that the supreme aim of teaching should not be the accumulation of information, but rather to foster thinking and mental preparation for problems that citizens will confront in everyday life.[32] The committee's goals conveyed the Deweyian ideal that the aim of education is to enable human beings to live life to the fullest by supplying conditions which ensure growth.[33] Certainly, committee members were familiar with Dewey's thoughts; chair McLaughlin and Dewey were faculty colleagues at the University of Chicago; Lucy Salmon had stayed in Dewey's home in 1893 when he taught at the University of Michigan (where Salmon and Dewey's wife Alice had both earned degrees),[34] and Herbert Baxter Adams taught at Johns Hopkins, the institution from which Dewey had earned his PhD.

In addition, the committee stated that value can be derived from studying history because history cultivates judgement, increases ability to gather and use knowledge, develops the 'scientific habit of mind and thought', fosters library work and reading of books, and cultivates the imagination.[35] Certainly, these skills were intellectual in nature. However, the committee argued that history deserved a place in the secondary curriculum equal to that of literature, mathematics and science, rather than treatment 'as an intruder entitled only to a berth in a cold corner, after language, mathematics, science, music, drawing, and gymnastics have been comfortably provided for'.[36] A crucial component of the committee's task was to legitimate history's deserved prominence in the secondary curriculum.

History Instruction in Foreign Countries

The appendices of the Committee of Seven's report included detailed evaluations of history education in Germany, France, England and Canada. Lucy Salmon was able to study the German school system by visiting many German *gymnasia* during the summer of 1897.[37] She noted some similarities to US methods of history instruction, but also some significant differences. For example, German instructors relied more heavily on narrative when providing history instruction than did US teachers.[38] In addition, German teachers devoted a greater amount of time – an average of three hours a week – to historical study.[39] Salmon thought that more time could be devoted to studying history in US schools; however, she thought increased reliance on narrative methods of instruction was imprudent. American teachers of history were not as well prepared as German teachers, nor did such methods cultivate creativity and independence of judgement – qualities important in American culture.

Nevertheless, Salmon and her fellow committee members believed that the German model offered important lessons for US schools. First, the German method of teaching history was remarkably uniform throughout the nation. Although Salmon visited 32 *gymnasia* in 18 different locations and observed 70 different history classes, she noted: 'A visit to one school and the study of one programme would have sufficed. There are indeed variations in detail, but the fundamental principles in the arrangement of work in history are the same – a uniformity that is especially noteworthy in view of the contrast it presents to our own system, or lack of system.'[40] The curriculum in Germany included ancient, medieval and modern history with an emphasis on the study of German history particularly in the medieval period. Ancient history was primarily devoted to Greek and Roman history, and modern history focused on Europe.[41] The German history curriculum had been developed with attention to the students' psychological and mental development as well. For example, encouraging historical imagination was a critical component of early work in history. Another advantage of the German practice was that history was correlated with other subjects in the curriculum, such as literature and language. Making connections between subjects helped to reinforce student learning. A final benefit of the German model was important to the Committee of Seven's considerations. Although secondary coursework in history was ideal preparation for subsequent university studies, the course sequence was complete in itself and, therefore, adequate for the provision of a wide outlook to students who did not seek education beyond the German *gymnasium*.

Charles H. Haskins wrote the study of history in French lycées.[42] He found that historical studies in French secondary institutions had been added to the academic curriculum only in recent years. Previously, history had been taught in France as part of school courses in ancient languages. The movement to treat history as a separate subject arose largely to encourage patriotism; however, Haskins observed that 'a broader conception of aims of historical study has spread in recent years and found expression in the official instructions issued in connection with the course of study'.[43]

Similar to the German practice, the French curriculum was remarkably uniform throughout the country. The French curriculum differed from the German model in which historical topics studied in the elementary school years were repeated and discussed in greater depth in the *gymnasium*. (Salmon identified this method as two concentric circles; later in the century, Hilda Taba labelled this organization as a 'spiral curriculum'.) In France, by contrast, historical studies followed one long chronological progression begun in the elementary grades that continued through the secondary level (a linear model). The first three years of historical studies at the lycée were devoted to oriental, Greek and Roman history, and students studied medieval and modern European history with particular emphasis on France in the last four years.[44] An average of two and a half hours a week was devoted to the study of history and geography. Because Haskins found the semi-militaristic French teaching methods encouraged only passive learning, he thought they had little to offer to American schools. French teachers, however, were substantially prepared and endured rigorous examinations before earning a teaching licence from a university or *école normale supérieure*.[45] Haskins thought that a similar foundation could benefit American teachers.

George Fox conducted the Committee of Seven's study of history education in English schools. He found that the lack of uniformity in the 'scope and methods of teaching history' made analysis and generalization difficult.[46] In fact, the Committee noted in the introduction to the report:

> The situation in England does not offer many valuable lessons to American teachers. The most noticeable features are a lack of historical instruction, a common failure to recognize the value of history, and a certain incoherence and general confusion ... It is enough to say that the laissez faire idea has been carried farther and is more marked in England than in America ... one who examines the condition of historical instruction in this country, and compares it with that of France and Germany, feels that Englishmen and Americans are of one blood.[47]

Considerable variation existed among English secondary schools because most were under private control, supervised by a board of governors and a headmaster who determined the course of study and teaching methods. In general, Greek, Roman and English history were offered, but no orderly sequence or arrangement of courses dominated.[48] In addition, less time was devoted to historical study in England than in both France or Germany. Indeed, only a few schools devoted more than two hours a week to historical studies. English teaching methods featured the use of a textbook, written examinations, lectures and notetaking; the use of original sources was extremely rare. To conclude his description, Fox quoted three English authorities, one of whom was James Bryce, an eminent teacher and editor of the *London Journal of Education*, who found historical studies exceedingly poor in English schools; nevertheless, Fox expressed hope that the situation would improve.

Professor George M. Wrong of the University of Toronto discussed historical studies in Canadian schools.[49] Wrong noted that history was typically neglected in the Canadian curriculum at both the secondary and university levels. Similar to the situation in the USA, Canadian schools lacked curriculum uniformity because educational decision making occurred in localities rather than through national influence or direction. Time devoted to the study of classics and mathematics illustrated the neglect of history. The Canadian college entrance examination provided evidence of the lack of import attributed to historical studies because history was 'worth only one-third of the value of Greek or Latin, and one-sixth of that of mathematics'.[50] Although the history curriculum varied among provinces, in general course offerings included Greek, Roman, English and Canadian history. Wrong believed the Canadian history curriculum 'defective' because it did not 'form a well-balanced course of historical study'.[51] Despite Wrong's sharp criticism, he believed that the status of historical studies in Canada was gradually improving, primarily because the universities increased history offerings and established fairly rigorous guidelines for earning a specialist licence in the teaching of history.

In general, the Committee of Seven tended to favour the methods of teaching history in Germany and France over patterns in England and Canada. Clearly, the committee preferred a uniformity of the history curriculum to a system in which history offerings and teaching methods varied widely. Perhaps, the committee preferred national history curricula because this pattern would facilitate the establishment of standards and the control of educational policies. In addition, the Committee of Seven preferred chronological sequencing of history courses, similar to the German model. Nevertheless, the United States remained a country in which local and state control of curricula continued to dominate educational practices, despite the committee's efforts.

Recommendations of the Committee

After conducting and analyzing a comprehensive, nationwide survey of the teaching of history in the nation's schools and studying foreign history curricula, the Committee recommended a four-year course sequence consisting of four blocks or periods in the following sequence: (1) ancient history, which would include Greek and Roman history and the early Middle Ages, and would close approximately at AD 800;

(2) medieval and modern European history, which would pick up from the close of the ancient history course and continue to the present; (3) English history; and (4) American history and civil government.[52] The Committee of Seven believed that secondary schools should provide four years of history instruction and consider the importance of chronological sequencing in planning the order of course offerings. Hence, the committee's history course recommendations began with ancient history, progressed forward in time with medieval, modern European and English history, and concluded with American history.

The Committee of Seven did not recommend a course in general history, which a considerable number of secondary schools at the time offered.[53] A draft of the committee's report indicated that there was a wide divergence of practice and opinion about what constituted general history in the first place.[54] In some cases the course took the form of medieval history, but in a majority of schools the course was a general survey based upon one textbook, with no collateral reading. Despite the seeming consensus of opinion in the committee's published report which advised that the modes of teaching general history were neither sound nor reasonable, minutes from several meetings reveal striking disagreement among committee members about a course in general history. Indeed, secretary Hart recorded: 'The committee found itself unable at this time to come to any agreement upon the subject.'[55] Probably the lack of consensus contributed to the decision to advise against teaching general history altogether.

With regard to methods of instruction and implementation of the suggested programme, the committee advised that teachers first consider the goals or aims of history instruction. Committee members reiterated their belief that the purpose of studying history was not to fill students' heads with 'a mass of material' and lamented that history is 'stigmatized as an information study'.[56] In fact, the committee observed that attempts to store facts in students' heads were often self-defeating because many college professors marvelled over the amount of misinformation recorded on college entrance examinations. Without prescribing pedagogical practices, the committee suggested that teachers utilize a textbook, collateral reading material and maps, and require students to prepare written work, notebooks and examinations.[57]

The Committee of Seven's final report also recommended that teachers employ original sources in order to enhance students' historical study. In fact, the committee affirmed: 'The use of sources in secondary work is now a matter of so much importance, that it seems to demand special and distinct treatment.'[58] The committee noted that continued stress on memorization as an instructional method would jeopardize the retention of history in the curriculum. The committee asserted, instead, that students should be taught how to read history books, how to think about historical facts and how to analyze the relationships between evidence and historical statement. The committee's stance on the use of sources later led to some modest, but pointed, criticism from both college professors and secondary school teachers.

Despite the recommendations of the Committee of Seven, the history curriculum in American secondary schools has lacked rigid national uniformity. While common threads prevail – such as a secondary course in American history – debate has ensued throughout the twentieth century over the nature, content and methods of history courses. For example, how much attention should be devoted to political history compared to social history? How much factual content should be addressed compared to methodological processes of historical investigation? Such questions were considered by the Committee of Seven and continue to be part of the ongoing deliberations about history education in the United States.

Significance and Criticism of the Committee's Work

Despite local variations in American history curricula, the Committee of Seven's recommendations significantly affected the development of the history teaching and course offerings in the nation's schools. Many schools adopted the four-year course sequence recommended by the committee. The committee recognized that it courted criticism for its suggestion of such a comprehensive programme, but believed, nevertheless, that history warranted a prominent place in the curriculum. Furthermore, some schools already offered such a plan. The committee decided that it should promulgate an ideal programme even if some schools decided not to embrace it fully.

Evidence of the committee's long-term significance was apparent more than a decade later when articles in the *History Teacher's Magazine* – later to become *Historical Outlook* and subsequently *Social Studies* – contained myriad references to the work of the Committee of Seven. The success of the committee's work in influencing approximate uniformity to the school history curriculum was widely acknowledged.[59] In fact, Teachers College professor and historian, Henry Johnson, noted 40 years later that the report prepared by the Committee of Seven 'was the ablest document relating to history for schools ever produced in America'.[60] Indeed, the resultant standardization also facilitated constancy in college entrance requirements.

Nevertheless, moderate criticism of the Committee of Seven report arose in its aftermath. Debate about the nature and purpose of history in the secondary school curriculum ensued. For example, a 1902 report of deans and principals of secondary schools endorsed the Committee of Seven report, but differed with the committee's preference for the individual history of countries over a course in general history.[61] The Committee of Seven had earnestly debated the teaching of general history and recommended that it not be part of the secondary history curriculum. By 1909 the New England Association recommended several changes to the report of the Committee of Seven which included the provision of detailed guidelines for ancient history, the separation of American history and American government and the structuring of courses in medieval and modern history with English history as a primary content base.[62] Fred Morrow Fling, editor of 'The source methods of teaching' for *History Teacher's Magazine* in 1909, criticized the committee for what he perceived to be a restrictive utilization of source documents and he also held that the section on teaching methods was too conservative.[63]

Conclusions

When interest in the teaching of modern history became prominent in the early 1900s, the AHA appointed another committee to investigate the desirability of a revision of the course of study.[64] In this 1907 committee – labelled the Committee of Five – were two members from the Committee of Seven, Andrew McLaughlin who headed the new group and Charles H. Haskins. The other three members included James H. Robinson, Charles W. Mann and James Sullivan. Members conducted a new national survey of schools and determined that, although the Committee of Seven had been criticized for its recommendation of four years of history offerings, more than half of the high schools which replied to the survey reported that they offered four years of history.[65] Indeed, the Committee of Five reaffirmed most of the recommendations of the Committee of Seven. The Committee of Seven's work established a lasting legacy.

Clearly, the Committee of Seven's report had a considerable impact upon the American secondary school history curriculum. In fact, the dominance of history in the contemporary secondary social studies curriculum may be reasonably attributed to the monumental work of the committee members early in the twentieth century. Advocates of a social studies curriculum claimed the later work of the Commission on the Reorganization of Secondary Education had greater influence on the current secondary curriculum. Although these debates appear semantic, at the heart of such discussions are fundamental disagreements about the nature of what and how historical and social science knowledge should be taught. The continued dominance of historical studies in the secondary social studies curriculum, the increased standardization and chronological sequencing of the curriculum, the examination of foreign countries' history education, the request for improving history teachers' training as required in European schools,[66] the proposal that history occupy a prominent place in the curriculum alongside subjects such as Latin and mathematics and the recommendation that historical studies prepare 'boys and girls for the duties of daily life and intelligent citizenship'[67] indicate the Committee of Seven's significant legacy. Undoubtedly, the social studies recommendations of the Commission on the Reorganization of Secondary Education grew out of the strong foundation established by the Committee of Seven.

While national curriculum laws regarding history education do not exist in the United States, clearly increased uniformity developed during the twentieth century. Certainly, the work of the Committee of Seven can be credited as one important factor in this phenomenon. Notably, committee members examined history curricula issues not only in the United States but in other countries as well, as it carefully considered recommendations for school history programmes. German methods of history education were favoured by the Committee of Seven as providing the most useful example to American schools. The committee preferred German pedagogy and curricula because of Germany's nationwide uniformity, chronological sequencing of courses, and exceptional teacher preparation. Curriculum developments in history education during the ensuing 100 years in the United States suggest that the committee was successful in bringing a limited degree of uniformity to secondary history education. Of course, other factors – such as the development of standardized college entrance examinations in history, the establishment of the federal department of Health, Education and Welfare which provides funding for education, the growth of large textbook publishers and the expansion of legal regulations affecting education – have also contributed to the more recent standardization of history curricula.[68]

Despite the increased uniformity in history curricula, the committee recognized the importance of 'elasticity' in the curriculum so that schools could 'adapt themselves to some extent to local environment and local needs'.[69] Such recommendations recognized that most secondary history teachers happily retained a degree of autonomy when they closed the classroom door. Fortunately, teacher sovereignty in history remains a hallmark of secondary education in the United States.

NOTES

1. Albert Bushnell Hart, secretary, Minutes of the Committee of Seven on History in Schools Conference in Cambridge, MA, 16–17 April 1897, container 459, Committee of Seven on History Study in High Schools, American Historical Association Records, Library of Congress.
2. National Center for History in the Schools, *National Standards for History* (Los Angeles, CA: 1996), p.ix.
3. Charles H. Haskins to Lucy Salmon, 31 October 1902, Lucy Maynard Salmon Papers, Special Collections, Vassar College Libraries, Poughkeepsie, NY, box 47, folder 12. Hereafter cited as Salmon Papers. Haskins, corresponding secretary of the AHA, was trying to increase membership and included in his letter to Salmon a pamphlet detailing the founding history of the AHA.
4. D. Van Tassel, 'From learned society to professional organization: The American Historical Association, 1884–1900', *American Historical Review*, 89 (October 1984), p. 951.
5. Herbert Baxter Adams to H. Morse Stephens, 8 April 1897, container 459, AHA Records, Library of Congress; David Warren Saxe, *Social Studies in Schools: A History of the Early Years* (Albany, NY: State University of New York Press, 1991), pp. 53–4; Howard Boozer, 'The American Historical Association and the schools, 1884–1956' PhD dissertation (Washington University, 1960), pp. 51 and 55.
6. American Historical Association, *The Study of History in Schools: Report to the American Historical Association by the Committee of Seven* (New York: Macmillan, 1899), p.v. Hereafter cited as *The Committee of Seven*.
7. *The Committee of Seven*, p.iii.
8. Charles H. Haskins to Lucy Salmon, 31 October 1902, Salmon Papers; Laurence R. Veysey, *The Emergence of the American University* (Chicago, IL: University of Chicago Press, 1965), p. 102.
9. 'Charles Homer Haskins', *Webster's New Biographical Dictionary* (Springfield, MA: Merriam-Webster 1983), p. 452.
10. A.C. McLaughlin to Lucy Salmon, 3 January 1916, Salmon Papers, box 47, folder 13.
11. Carol Gruber, *Mars and Minerva: World War One and the Uses of Higher Learning in America* (Baton Rouge, LA: Louisiana State University Press, 1975), p. 240; H. Morse Stephens to Lucy Salmon, 19 January 1901, Salmon Papers, box 47, folder 13; Boozer, 'American Historical Association', p. 53.
12. Michael Whelan, 'Albert Bushnell Hart and the origins of social studies education', *Theory and Research in Social Education*, 22 (Fall 1994), pp. 423–40.
13. Michael Whelan, 'A particularly lucid lens: The Committee of Ten and the Social Studies Committee in historical context', *Curriculum and Supervision*, 12 (Spring 1997), p. 260.
14. Boozer, 'American Historical Association', p. 53; *The Committee of Seven*, p. v.
15. Chara Haeussler Bohan, 'Go to the sources: Lucy Maynard Salmon and the teaching of

history', PhD dissertation (University of Texas at Austin, December 1999); Chara Haeussler Bohan, 'Lucy Maynard Salmon: Progressive historian, teacher, and Democrat', in Margaret Smith Crocco and O.L. Davis Jr (eds), *'Bending the Future to their Will': Civic Women, Social Education, and Democracy* (New York: Rowman & Littlefield, 1999), pp. 47–92.

16. Herbert B. Adams to George B. Adams, 7 January 1897, George Burton Adams Papers, Manuscripts and Archives, Yale University Library.

17. See Lawrence Cremin, *American Education: The Metropolitan Experience, 1876–1980* (New York: Harper & Row, 1988); Henry Johnson, *Teaching of History in Elementary and Secondary Schools* (New York: Macmillan, 1917); Herbert M. Kliebard, *The Struggle for the American Curriculum: 1893–1958* (New York: Routledge & Kegan Paul, 1987); Edward Krug, *The Shaping of the American High School* (New York: Harper & Row, 1964); Whelan, 'A particularly lucid lens', pp. 256–68; Saxe, *Social Studies in Schools*; Diane Ravitch, *The Schools We Deserve* (New York: Basic Books, 1985).

18. Saxe, *Social Studies in Schools*, pp. 42–5.

19. Johnson, *Teaching of History*, p. 134.

20. Saxe, *Social Studies in Schools*, p. 48.

21. *The Committee of Seven*, pp. 3–4.

22. Ibid., p. 5.

23. Ibid., pp. 152–3.

24. Dorothy Ross, *The Origins of American Social Science* (Cambridge: Cambridge University Press, 1991), p. 158.

25. *The Committee of Seven*, p. 9.

26. Ibid., pp. 231–8.

27. Ibid., pp. 9–10.

28. Ibid., p. 10.

29. Ibid., p. 17.

30. Ibid., p. 17.

31. Saxe, *Social Studies in Schools*, p. 61.

32. *The Committee of Seven*, p. 18.

33. John Dewey, *Democracy and Education* (1916; reprint New York: Free Press, 1944), pp. 49–51; Lawrence Cremin, *The Transformation of the School* (New York: Vintage Books, 1961), p. 123.

34. Linda Robinson Walker, 'John Dewey at Michigan', *Michigan Today* (Fall 1997), p. 18.

35. *The Committee of Seven*, pp. 21–6.

36. Ibid., p. 20.

37. Lucy Salmon, 'History in the German gymnasia', in *The Committee of Seven*, p. 173.

38. Ibid., p. 191.

39. Ibid., pp. 188–9.

40. Ibid., pp. 173–4.

41. Ibid., p. 182.

42. Charles H. Haskins, 'History in French lycées', in *The Committee of Seven*, pp. 199–209.

43. Ibid., p. 200.

44. Ibid., p. 203.

45. Ibid., p. 207.

46. George Fox, 'History in English secondary schools', in *The Committee of Seven*, p. 210.

47. *The Committee of Seven*, pp. 12–13.

48. George Fox, 'History in English secondary schools', p. 220.

49. George M. Wrong, 'History in Canadian schools', in *The Committee of Seven*, pp. 231–8.

50. Ibid., p. 234.

51. Ibid., p. 236.

52. *The Committee of Seven*, pp. 34–5; Boozer, 'American Historical Association', pp. 56–7.

53. *The Committee of Seven*, pp. 44–52.

54. 'The present condition of history teaching in secondary schools', draft of the Committee of Seven, n.d., container 459, American Historical Association Records, Library of Congress.
55. Minutes of the Committee of Seven proceedings at Cleveland, Ohio, 27–30 December 1897, container 459, American Historical Association Records, Library of Congress.
56. *The Committee of Seven*, pp. 87–8.
57. Saxe, *Social Studies in Schools*, pp. 68–71; *The Committee of Seven*, pp. 90–7.
58. *The Committee of Seven*, p. 101.
59. James Sullivan, 'Suggested changes in course of study in history', *History Teacher's Magazine*, 2 (January 1911), p. 103.
60. Henry Johnson, *Teaching of History in Elementary and Secondary Schools with Applications to Allied Studies* (New York: Macmillan, 1940), p. 59.
61. 'The fifteenth educational conference of the academies and high schools affiliating or cooperating with the University of Chicago', *School Review* (January 1902), p. 3.
62. Professor Kingsbury, 'Modifications in the report of the Committee of Seven Recommended by the N.E. Association', *History Teacher's Magazine*, 1 (December 1909), pp. 89–90.
63. Robert E. Keohane, 'The great debate over the source method', *Social Education* (May 1949), p. 216.
64. *The Study of History in Secondary Schools: Report to the American Historical Association by the Committee of Five* (New York: AHA, 1911).
65. 'Is revision of the course of study in history desirable? Summary of the report of the Committee of Five to the American Historical Association', *History Teacher's Magazine*, 2 (April 1911), p. 181.
66. *The Committee of Seven*, p. 117.
67. Ibid., p. 122.
68. See Michael W. Kirst, 'Who's in charge? Federal, state, and local control', in Diane Ravitch and Maris A. Vinovskis (eds), *Learning from the Past: What History Teaches Us about School Reform* (Baltimore, MD: Johns Hopkins University Press, 1995), pp. 25–56.
69. *The Committee of Seven*, p. 121.

5

Children's Historical Thinking within a Museum Environment: An Overall Picture of a Longitudinal Study

IRENE NAKOU

The exploration of children's historical thinking, as expressed and developed within a museum environment, is generally of considerable theoretical interest. It is at the heart of the current debate on history and on history teaching and learning in relation to working with sources. It is also related to the current discussion on the changing character of museums and their broad educational and social role.

Focusing on children's historical thinking within a museum environment, a longitudinal field study was conducted, based on observations made on 1,079 responses provided by 141 pupils to a series of specially devised tasks relating to work with museum objects over a period of three years. Primary research questions were:

- What sort of historical thinking do children develop within a museum environment?
- Can children in the age range from 12 to 15 use museum objects as sources in historical terms?
- To which educational variables is children's historical thinking related?
- To which museological variables is children's historical thinking related?
- How far is children's historical thinking related to age?
- How could we define historical thinking and its elements in order to produce an analytical schema by which we could explore children's historical thinking, especially as it evolves within a museum environment, in terms of different (traditional, modern, postmodern) approaches to history and history education?

This longitudinal field study aimed to explore pupils' historical thinking in the first three years of secondary school, which corresponds to the last years of compulsory education in many countries. It was conducted among pupils who were educated by a traditional approach to history education, in order to observe historical thinking as it evolved in pupils who did not have any education and/or experience in matters regarding scientific historical thinking and method. Indeed, the traditional Greek system by which these pupils were educated is based on the reproduction of historical knowledge provided by compulsory history textbooks, and, thus, does not offer pupils any opportunity to work with any sort of historical source, or to activate 'scientific' historical thinking.

Our understanding of pupils' underlying historical thinking was considered of great significance to history education, because their own ideas and thoughts could provide an invaluable basis for further work and discussion to develop their historical thinking, as Thompson has suggested.[1] This consideration was mainly based on Vygotsky's argument that education and assistance can lead children to do more than they could do by themselves though only within the limits set by their state of development and according to the 'zone of proximal development'.[2] So the study was expected to be significant to history education and to museum educational programmes, which aim to advance pupils' historical thinking and knowledge. It was therefore predictable that a field study in which pupils' experience of working with sources was minimal – as a consequence of the nature of the traditional educational system – would show some of the underlying thinking as well as pupils' potential and undeveloped abilities in historical thinking. It was also expected to enable the researcher to discuss the benefits of museum practice for history learning, in relation to history teaching and learning at school.

In addition, observations on some basic factors which might influence pupils' historical thinking within a museum environment were expected to lead to a discussion of educational programmes and practices by which the educational role of museums could be enriched and better related to school history education. On this basis, the longitudinal field study answers questions about what pupils make of museum objects, and it gives a longitudinal picture of change in pupils' historical thinking on the basis of pupils' handling of relics.

The Educational Environment of Museums

The longitudinal field study of pupils' historical thinking was conducted in museums, because museums were assumed to offer an enabling educational environment in relation to many fields of human knowledge and experience, among them history. The historical ambiance of archaeological and historical museums in particular was expected to attract pupils' historical thinking from the time they entered the museum, since they were surrounded by material evidence for human life in the past.[3]

Museums were not conceived as static and neutral institutions, but as relating to their social, economic and ideological context, and, therefore, as changing according to the changing character of the different museological philosophies and theories and their associated museological approaches. Museums today were therefore theoretically investigated in relation to their type, by being schematically distinguished as 'traditional', 'modern' and 'postmodern'.

Each type of museum and its underlying philosophy was assumed to form a distinct educational environment which encourages a relevant type of historical thinking. Yet, it was assumed that all types of museum could serve as a stimulating educational environment, as long as museum practice led pupils to enter into a personal dialogue with the museum world through personal and alternative readings of the objects displayed.

In addition, the historical significance of museum objects as sources was investigated on the basis of their conception as *opera aperta*: that is, as objects that can be given several meanings, open to several and alternative interpretations, both historical and not.[4] In this sense, pupils' historical interpretations of museum objects as sources of historical information or evidence were 'read' as being closely interrelated with a series of aesthetic, psychological, museological and archaeological interpretations. Accordingly, the study of historical thinking took into consideration subjects' cultural, social and educational background, and their identity as active intellectual personalities distinguished on the basis of individual differences: general intellectual and aesthetic abilities, sensitivity and interests in historical investigation, and ways of knowing and thinking.

On this basis, the primary focus of the research was on the evolution and development of pupils' historical thinking in relation to their work with museum objects, while the museum environment was conceived as the general surrounding educational environment in which this longitudinal field study was conducted. The fact that all museums visited

75

were of the 'traditional' type did not allow the study of pupils' historical thinking in relation to different museum environments. It enabled, however, discussion of the general educational significance of museums and of museum practices relating to school history education, and pointed up some issues for further research.

Historical Thinking

Historical thinking was investigated as a complex intellectual activity being realized within the social character of historical process, and being thus conceived differently by each theory of history and its associated approach to history education. In this sense the study of pupils' historical thinking in this research relates to changing approaches to history education in Britain.[5]

On the other hand, historical thinking was conceived as involving the selection and interpretation of evidence, on the basis of which historical inferences and questions about the past are generated. Thus historical thinking was conceived as directly relating to historians' conceptions of evidence, its interpretation and its use; that is, as relating to historians' treatment of the evidence according to their theoretical view of the historical process and their effort to make sense of it. On this basis, all different types and modes of history – including traditional, modern and postmodern – were conceived as being realized on the basis of this system of conceptions, albeit seen from different perspectives.

Accordingly, an analytical schema was devised on the basis of a parallel conceptual analysis and empirical analytical work, by which the complex intellectual activity that is historical thinking could be explored in different museum environments. It distinguished between different approaches to history and history education in terms of its constitutive elements, namely, its 'methodology', 'content' and 'specific characteristics' (see further details in the Analysis section below).

The study of historical thinking on the basis of the analysis of 1,079 responses provided by 141 Greek pupils within the age range 12 to 15 years, in a museum environment, over a period of three years, was not an easy task, mainly because historical values were not transparent within the complexity, wealth and constraints of the children's thoughts. Therefore, the analytical schema must be 'read' as a mental model, produced by the research for helping us to understand pupils' historical thinking.

Moreover, the conception of historical thinking *per se* on the basis of which pupils' historical thinking was explored was, to a large extent, formed in the light of the first 'readings' of pupils' responses through which a primary attempt was made to decode its historical nature. On this basis, these children not only made the study of historical thinking within a museum environment possible, but they also enabled investigation of what historical thinking might be.

Research Methods

The method for data collection was designed with respect to the variables which were expected to influence pupils' historical thinking within a museum environment. These were individual differences and age; the different tasks set; the different museum objects with which pupils were presented and the difficulty they posed for pupils' work; historical information that was 'dependently' acquired in the museum in relation to the historical context of the objects studied; and general background historical information or knowledge that was 'independently' acquired.

A series of questions guided the method employed. How far was pupils' historical thinking related to age? How far was it related to the different tasks pupils had to respond to? How far was it related to the different types of museum objects they were presented with, and the level of 'difficulty' they posed for pupils' work?

The longitudinal field study was conducted in the natural environment of different museums, where pupils had to concentrate on pre-selected museum objects and collections, and to respond on their own and in their own words to different tasks in writing. The questions set in each task were both historical and not (history free). 'Choose an interesting museum object. Why have you chosen it?' – history free question. 'What information does this object give you about itself and its period?' – historical question.

There were three different tasks. Task 1 let pupils concentrate on one museum object; task 2 let pupils concentrate on a collection of museum objects; and task 3 interrelated museum practice with work in class. All tasks included similar historical and history free questions, so that responses to different tasks could be compared. The questions set in task 1, common for all groups, were as follows:

a. Please choose one object that you are interested in. Why have you chosen it?
b. What information does this object give you about itself and about its period?

c. What can you say about this object? [The aim of this question was to lead pupils to give a presentation of the object on the basis of their overall perception of it, not just to describe it.]
d. What are your questions about this object? (Suppose you were a historian who wished to find out about the past by studying this object.)

Data collection lasted three years, during which data on four groups of pupils were collected, mainly in connection with their work in museums, in four different museum environments. Two of the groups, namely groups 1 and 2, served as main groups, and data were collected several times, when the pupils of these groups were in secondary school grades A, B and C respectively (ages 12/13, 13/14, 14/15 years). So main group 1 served as main group A1, B1 and C1 respectively, while main group 2 served as main group A2, B2 and C2 respectively. Data from the two other 'additional' groups were collected during this same period, but only once, when the pupils of group 3 were in secondary school grade A (additional group A3), and when the pupils of group 4 were in secondary school grade C (additional group C4).

For each task the two main groups were presented with different museum objects, some of which were related to dependently and/or independently acquired historical information or knowledge. In addition, the museum objects with which pupils were presented in the first school grade did not pose great difficulty for pupils' work, while museum objects selected for the second and the third school grades posed increasing difficulty. This basic decision was based on the fact that all groups responded to common task 1, so this variable was kept constant. It will also be clear that, generally, pupils of main groups 1 and 2 would logically perform on a standard or even on a higher level as they grew older from the first secondary school grade through the second to the third. The estimation of the difficulty that different museum objects posed for pupils' work was mainly based on their general appearance, on the familiarity pupils had with their type, and on their relation to pupils' independent background historical knowledge.

In the longitudinal study, in common task 1, pupils of main groups A1 and A2 (age 12/13) were presented with museum object a, 'The calf-carrier', which is an archaic statue of a man carrying a calf. This object did not pose great difficulty for pupils' work, because of its represented theme and its relation to pupils' background historical knowledge. Pupils of main groups B1 and B2 (age 13/14) were presented with museum object b, a Hellenistic grave stele of two females – a dead woman and her female servant in an everyday scene. Museum object *b* posed some difficulty for pupils' work, because it did not relate directly to pupils' background historical knowledge and its represented theme was more complex than museum object *a*. Pupils of main groups C1 and C2 were presented with museum objects *c* (a damaged clay mould for a bronze statue of Apollo) and *d* (replicas of the Parthenon reliefs) respectively. Museum object *c* posed great difficulty for pupils' work, because of its appearance and the fact that it did not relate to pupils' background knowledge. Museum object *d* was quite difficult, mainly because the reliefs were not authentic objects, and they represented mythological scenes.

On the other hand, it was expected that pupils' historical thinking might be influenced by the different museum objects with which pupils were presented. Therefore, additional groups A3 (age 12/13) and C4 (age 14/15) were presented with museum object *b*, with which main groups B1 and B2 (age 13/14) were presented.

In addition, main group B2 responded to task 2 (concentration on a collection) as well as task 1 (concentration on a museum object), which was common for all groups, while main group B1 responded to task 3 (interrelation of museum practice with work in class) as well as task 1. This was decided in order to study how pupils' historical thinking was influenced by the different tasks. Pupils of both main groups were selected to respond to tasks 2 and 3 respectively when they were in the second grade, because, at age 13/14, they were in the centre of the age range investigated (12 to 15 years).

The methodological design

Task 1: concentration on one museum object

Grade A (age 12/13)
Grade B (age 13/14)
Grade C (age 14/15)

Main group A1	museum object *a*	low difficulty object
Main group B1	museum object *b*	medium difficulty object
Main group C1	museum object *c*	high difficulty object
Main group A2	museum object *a*	low difficulty object
Main group B2	museum object *b*	medium difficulty object
Main group C2	museum object *d*	high difficulty object
Additional group A3	museum object *b*	medium difficulty object
Additional group C4	museum object *b*	medium difficulty object

Task 2: concentration on a collection of museum objects

    Main group B2   collection *a*   medium difficulty objects

Task 3: interrelation of museum practice and work in class

    Main group B1   museum object *e*   medium difficulty object

Analysis

The category systems for the analysis of children's responses, in terms of the 'methodology', the 'content' and the 'specific characteristics' of historical thinking, were constructed on the basis of a parallel conceptual analysis and empirical analytical work, which related to modern approaches to historical thinking.

The 'methodology' of historical thinking corresponds to the different stages through which historians interpret the evidence available and generate historical inferences. The 'content' of historical thinking was conceived as a very broad theme, mainly corresponding to the conception of the 'real' and the 'historical' past, on the basis of the use of sources and their interpretation as evidence in context. The 'specific characteristics' of historical thinking correspond to specific concepts and skills, in terms of which thinking can be characterized as historical and scientific: validity, rhetoric, observing skills, use of dependent historical information, use of independent background historical knowledge, historical questioning, use of the notions of historical uncertainty, relativity and empathy and appreciation of the limitations of evidence and historical interpretation.

The full analysis of pupils' historical thinking in terms of all issues concerning its 'methodology', 'content' and 'specific characteristics' cannot be presented in a short chapter.[6] Because of its significance for the categorization of pupils' responses, only the 'methodology' analysis is presented.

In order to study pupils' historical thinking in terms of its methodology one main question was asked. What are the categories of pupils' historical thinking in terms of the 'historical methodology' pupils have used in their responses?

The 'methodology' system consisted of seven distinctive categories of 'historical methodology', and was largely dependent on Shemilt's work on 'Adolescent ideas about evidence and methodology in history'.[7]

The 'methodology' category system

Category 1. A-historical thinking: Description of the relic as an object of the present.
('It is a statue', boy, 13/14.)

Category 2. Unhistorical thinking: Description of the relic as an object of an imprecise past.
('It is damaged', girl, 13/14.)

Category 3. Pseudo-historical thinking (absence of any need for demonstration in historical terms): Reproducing historical information or knowledge.
('It is a Mycenian vase of the 14th century', girl, 13/14.)

Category 4. Pseudo-historical thinking (absence of any need for demonstration in historical terms): Unsupported inferences directly from the object.
('It must be a Mycenian vase', girl, 13/14.)

Category 5. Rational thinking: Inferences by rational processes.
('The owner of this vase must have been rich, because it is gold', boy, 13/14.)

Category 6. Historical thinking: Historical inferences by historical processes.
('This object gives us information relative to the art and artistic style of the period in which it was produced. The [artistic] figures of the period must be huge. This is shown by the size of the finding itself, which gives us an idea about the enormous size of the rest of the statue. People must have known the use of bronze so they had the necessary means for its extraction and working', boy, 13/14.)

Category 7. Advanced historical thinking – Advanced historical inferences by historical processes.
('These scales were found in royal Mycenian tombs, that means they were *kterismata*. They are gold, which means that Mycenians used gold and that the civilization was developed. The fact that they are so thin, engraved and elaborate shows us that people then did not only care about the practical aspect of an object but about aesthetics as well. This poses to us some questions, whether they were used in everyday life or whether they had a symbolic or decorative use. It is very much possible that Zeus used them to weigh the souls of people (that's why they were in a tomb). (In the *Iliad*, we read: 'Then the father of gods got

his golden scales ...') That probably means that these small instruments were especially made for burial use and that they had a symbolic religious meaning. If this is true, they give us a lot of facts about their religious ideas. Mycenians believed that, when the body of a man died, his soul went on existing and went to "Hades". In these tombs we have found many objects which lead to the same conclusion. A fact that supports the above statement is that these instruments are so thin, fine and small, that if we weighed anything real, they would break (they were found broken). So they were probably not used for weighing. The butterflies and flowers which were engraved on the thin surface are probably some symbols of that age. So we see the mentality of Mycenians, their great religious belief and their artistic sensitivity', girl, 13/14.)

Findings

The research results were very rich, concerning many aspects of children's historical thinking, in terms of many educational and museological variables. In this chapter, only some primary results on historical thinking and age are discussed analytically, in relation to museum objects of increasing difficulty, while other results and observations are only very briefly presented, together with the conclusions.

Historical thinking and age
The main research hypothesis that pupils' historical thinking might be related to age was supported by the following general qualitative observations that were made throughout various analyses and 'readings' of the data.

General characteristics observed in pupils' historical thinking at the age of 12/13
In general, pupils' responses were largely based on the use of a narrow sort of relevant independent knowledge, in the form of stereotypes, not really critically used to support their inferences. Groups A1 and A2 generated most of their historical inferences on the basis of the fact that museum object *a*, 'The calf-carrier', resembled a *kouros* – the typical Ancient Greek statue representing a naked young man. Many responses in which more complex independent historical knowledge was used

showed that pupils had formed a rather confusing frame of knowledge including both valid and invalid elements:

> I would suppose that this object is Philip the king of Macedonia. I understand this by its legs, one of which is shorter than the other. Also it would be in the 5th century because its body expresses a greater freedom. (One leg in front and the other behind) its look is smiling and its arms are not attached [to the body] ... Because he doesn't wear anything under and he has a chiton over it means that it was made in Sparta.

Thoughts were sometimes unrelated to each other, some thoughts of different content intervened between two similar thoughts related to the same aspect. In addition, one or two known elements were considered adequate to support inferences, in which the notion of historical uncertainty was usually absent: 'It shows to us a *kouros* and we understand it by its legs one of which is in front of the other. We could also say that it is a work of 580 BC.'

In many responses historical thinking was not clearly expressed, but was implied by the sequence of sentences or thoughts: 'It looks as if the object is a grave stele and the [illustrated] box shows that people believed in life after death.'

Attempts to demonstrate inferences in explanatory terms were usually deficient or incomplete. Historical inferences were often deficiently supported: '[It is] of about the 5th century because its legs are not joined.'

In a number of responses pupils' historical thinking could be characterized as simple or even naive; 'everyday', 'common-sense' ideas and weak expression probably indicates that they did not have the procedural concepts to express their thoughts in historical terms: 'It gives me the impression that in that period every person had to kill animals in order to cover his physical needs (for example, food). By this we understand how much exercise every person must have had'; 'That they had clothes, that they had boxes and seats even for their feet namely they had a developed culture.' In addition, in a few cases a logical gap appeared in pupils' thinking: 'We also see that they [the illustrated women] are seated on an engraved seat so we understand that they knew writing [how to write].'

However, a few pupils at the age of 12/13 provided responses of 'valid historical thinking' and of distinctive quality in terms of many historical issues: 'By the calf he is carrying he seems to be a *moschoforos* [a calf-carrier] and to come from Ancient Greece, after the period of *kouroi* because it seems like a *kouros*, but it is more detailed than a *kouros*.' Another pupil wrote:

> It doesn't have any colour (it would have had long ago). It has a clear expression on its face. The man is smiling. The meaning of the statue is that an X is formed by the man's arms and the calf's legs which shows their tender relation (people used to offer their best [animals] as a sacrifice to the gods). Also by having the two heads (of the man and the animal) the one next to the other we realize the difference in mental power between the animal and the man.

The fact that some pupils provided 'valid historical thinking' of relatively high quality at the age of 12/13 points up the differences that appeared among individuals of each age and among their responses, in terms of many issues concerning historical thinking. But, despite this fact, we may say that pupils' historical thinking at the age of 12/13 was characterized by the above mentioned elements, which were not present (at least not to the same extent) at the ages of 13/14 and 14/15.

General characteristics observed in pupils' historical thinking at the age of 13/14

At the age of 13/14 pupils in general supported or even tested their historical inferences relatively more analytically and efficiently, the notion of uncertainty and possibility appeared, independent historical knowledge was more critically used and in a broader sense, while the use of language was more sophisticated than at 12/13.

> First of all we can see the materials that they used for the manufacture of everyday life representations or that they used for the manufacture of representations of a certain specific significance that the makers wished to touch upon. We also see their clothes, their dressing style and some of the facts concerning their goods. In my opinion it is probably of the Classical period. It must have been sculptured to touch on certain religious elements of the period or for a mythological purpose. Surely it might be the case that it was sculptured to show elements of everyday life that relatively quite impressed them.

In this response, independent historical knowledge was critically used to express historical inferences, in a 'sophisticated' sort of language, and in relation to the notions of uncertainty and possibility.

On the other hand, there was a clear urge, at least by some pupils, to use 'scientific' concepts, although not always satisfactorily. Therefore, sometimes pupils' responses were characterized by the use of 'big words' or portentous statements. 'I could say about this object that it is not included 100% in the world of statues but of bas-reliefs.' This urge appeared at the age of 14/15 too, but only in a few responses was this use unsatisfactory: 'Since we observe that the colour is white it would be worthwhile to see it from the point of art.' Thoughts within each response were usually interrelated, and, since many historical inferences were efficiently supported, it was generally noted that longer responses were usually of higher level. This contrasts with the situation at 12/13, where long responses usually included many separate low-level thoughts, because most of the time historical inferences, while inadequately supported, were expressed in two or three sentences. We may say, that fluency in the use of language may be a necessary but not a sufficient condition for the expression of thinking in historical terms, since longer work does not just mean that children who are better equipped to express themselves do better.

Besides the four pupils who provided five responses of 'advanced' historical thinking at the age of 13/14, some other pupils too at this age expressed thoughts revealing a mature intellectual and aesthetic sensitivity.

> It is sorrowful, maybe it comes from a grave stele. It shows a woman who is giving a box to another woman who has her hand missing. It is well made, worked out in detail. We could say that the woman who is seated on the stool knows that the content of the box is a bad announcement, maybe of death.

General characteristics observed in pupils' historical thinking at the age of 14/15

At the age of 14/15 pupils' historical thinking generally appeared more developed in terms of all the elements discussed above, despite individual differences and the influence of other variables. Typical examples of the general higher level of historical thinking that was expressed in pupils' responses at the age of 14/15 are the three responses, provided by pupils of the three relevant groups, that are quoted here.

> When I first saw the object I didn't immediately understand what it is and this because it has sustained damage and losses by the centuries passed. But when I was informed [by the label] what it is

I realized how important it is for history because it indicates the technology with which the Ancients made their statues. (Group C1 – in relation to museum object *c*, the broken clay mould, that posed considerable difficulties for most pupils)

Even just the theme of this bas-relief tells a lot to me. I look at it with awe and I see how different those people's ideas were and what strange beings they believed in. Surely their belief in gods must have been great and strong. I consider that this centaur is a piece of our history. (Group C2 – in relation to a relief illustrating a scene of the mythological battle of centaurs)

Among the objects that are displayed in this hall I liked most the golden masks and especially the one of Agamemnon. I chose this object because generally the masks represent the Mycenian period. They show how much bound the Mycenians were with the idea of death. They used to adorn the face of the dead with gold. This fact makes clear that they believed in life after death. This object is a sample of a culture which was very developed in such mystic matters as death. (Group C4 – about a Mycenian golden death-mask, known as *The mask of Agamemnon*)

These three responses, provided by pupils of groups C1, C2 and C4 respectively at the age of 14/15, despite their differences and weaknesses related to a series of historical issues, indirectly indicate that they are very unlikely to have been written by pupils at the age of 12/13. This is mainly because of the concepts used ('mystic matters'), the critical use of background historical knowledge and the need to demonstrate inferences in explanatory terms. On the other hand, these responses could be characteristic of what many pupils wrote at the age of 13/14.

Historical thinking and age in relation to museum objects of increasing difficulty
These general qualitative observations were further supported by quantitative results. According to cross-sectional results, which were based on groups A3, B1, B2 and C4, presented with the same museum object at different ages, pupils' potential in expressing 'valid historical thinking' (of historical methodology and valid outcome) was increasing by age. Moreover, greater differences appeared between ages 12/13 and 13/14 than between 13/14 and 14/15. Characteristic of this is the fact that

in the cross-sectional study the same percentage of pupils (22 per cent) expressed 'valid historical thinking' at both ages 13/14 and 14/15.

On the other hand, according to longitudinal results, which were based on the two main groups presented with museum objects of increasing difficulty by age, the percentage of pupils that expressed 'valid historical thinking' at age 14/15 was dramatically decreased, compared with the two previous years, in accordance with the high difficulty museum object pupils (age 14/15) were presented with.

Characteristic of the relation of pupils' historical thinking to the level of difficulty museum objects posed for their work are the following two responses, provided by the same girl at ages 13/14 and 14/15, in relation to museum objects of medium and high difficulty, respectively.

> This Ancient grave stele is of marble and is quite big. It illustrates two Ancient women, one seated and one standing. It is quite detailed and nicely elaborated. One of the two women, the one standing, is offering to the other woman a box which most possibly includes jewels. I hypothesize from her simple dress that she is a slave-servant. On the contrary, the seated woman is dressed better and she is adorned. Her head is missing. She would rather be a noble-woman or a rich woman who died. I hypothesize that she is dead, I say this, because this presentation may symbolize that the seated woman is receiving one of her beloved objects by her servant e.g. jewels from life or a certain gift to accompany her in the underworld, in Hades.

This response is not one of the best responses provided at the age of 13/14, but, despite several weaknesses in historical issues, it shows that this pupil at the age of 13/14 was able to give a valid historical interpretation of this grave stele. This interpretation was historical because the represented theme was interpreted in historical terms; for example, human/social relations were seen in their historical context (slave-servant/noble-woman). In addition, the inferences were based on the evidence available, as clearly demonstrated in explanatory terms. This response corresponds to mature reasoning, highly developed concepts, sensitivity and active historical thinking related to background historical knowledge, and generating historical inferences on the basis of the use of the museum object in historical terms.

The following response was provided by the same girl (now in the 14/15 age group), in relation to a museum object of high difficulty: a broken clay mould for a bronze statue of Apollo.

87

It is a bronze mould of a statue of Apollo. It is in bad condition since its upper part is missing and some pieces of the whole body are missing. We see that it has been put together since it was found broken. It is of the 6th century BC. Its size is big, it is of the colour of clay and some pieces of clay are added in order to be united with the rest. Probably it was found in excavations which took place in the Ancient Agora.

We see that, despite her potential in expressing historical thinking, as shown in her response at age 13/14, and her obvious efforts to interpret this 'difficult' object, this same girl did not manage to express 'valid historical thinking', because she either reproduced the offered information a-critically ('bronze mould') or generated 'problematic' rational inferences on the basis of the evidence. It is likely that most pupils at the age of 14/15 could not treat this 'difficult' museum object historically as compared with the previous years, because the clay mould was a damaged, unfamiliar object, which did not relate to pupils' background historical knowledge. In addition, the written information offered in the museum in the form of a label did not help much, mainly because of the term 'mould', which proved to be an unknown word for most pupils aged 14/15.

General Discussion of Results

Generally, both qualitative and quantitative results seem to support three basic claims about children's historical thinking within a museum environment.

Claim 1 Historical thinking was related to age. A great number of children expressed valid historical thinking at the age of 12/13, but their historical thinking continued to develop with age, in terms of many issues concerning the level and the quality of historical thinking, such as its methodology, the validity of its outcome and the accurate use of 'scientific' concepts. Greater differences, however, distinguished children's historical thinking between the ages 12/13 and 13/14 than between the ages 13/14 and 14/15.

Claim 2 By 13/14 historical thinking seemed to be stabilized, but there were, nevertheless, crucial differences in historical behaviour between individuals.

Claim 3 Children's historical thinking was associated with a series of educational and museological conditions, besides age. In addition, as a complex intellectual activity, it was related to individual differences in terms of intellectual potential, aesthetic development, sensitivity and interest in historical investigation, ways of knowing, questioning and thinking.

Children's personal involvement in their work with museum objects is clearly shown in the following response, provided by a girl at the age 14/15:

> The object that attracted my interest is the grave of a girl. It attracts my interest because it is very rare to see a grave in a museum especially if it is so old (1000 BC). If I were in this girl's position I would not like it at all to be seen by thousands of people who would come to the museum every day. Another important thing is the relics which are in the grave, because they show the habits of the Ancient people then.

The effect of children's personal interest in the museum objects themselves on their historical thinking is an important issue for further study.

The relation of children's historical thinking to individual differences, such as aesthetic development, was indicated by the historical quality of some responses which seems to relate to a few children's ability to make comments on the aesthetic significance of the museum objects, and/or to explain the illustrated themes on the basis of the symbolism of art. One girl (age 13/14) interpreted a human figure as being a goddess on the basis of the fact that this woman, although illustrated seated, was sculpted having the same height as the standing woman. This girl not only made a type of observation that most people do not often make, but she interpreted the represented theme on the basis of the symbolic meaning of this artistic deviation from reality. 'This statue rather presents a goddess because although [the illustrated figure is] seated she is bigger than the other woman who is offering her a present.' Another girl (same age) pointed out the fact that the background was not illustrated, and interpreted this characteristic as implying the wish of the artist to highlight only the central theme.

Some pupils, but only a few, straightforwardly put some problems that arise in terms of the reliability of works of art as historical sources, on the grounds that artistic representations do not often correspond to the reality they suppose to represent.

> Using these objects as historians we begin with the fact that these objects illustrate two musicians, an element that shows to us that in

that period there was a development of music. The first question refers to whether this development relates to the Cyclades or more generally to the Greek region. But the historian must question himself whether the activity of music presents a picture of the reality of the period or if it has been inspired by another place or by a myth of an older period. Another question might be: Does the representation of the instruments correspond to reality or has it been changed in relation to the technical constraints of sculpture? Are the instruments that we see really a harp and a flute? (Boy, 13/14)

We could say that the quality of this response, in terms of historical interpretation, was related to the aesthetic development of this boy (age 13/14), his interest in historical investigation, and his potential in posing substantial (historical) questions, that could lead him to substantial (historical) answers. It must be mentioned here, that pupils' questioning showed that, although most pupils posed questions of a relatively high-quality content in tasks asking them to pose their questions, they did not use historical questioning to generate historical inferences in their responses to all other tasks. Questioning was not conceived as inherent in the nature of history, as a basic part of historical investigation.

Generally, we could claim that differences appearing in historical thinking between the different ages were associated with differences relating to several interrelated issues, such as differences in expression, in the relation of thoughts and the organization of questions within each response, and in the use of 'scientific' concepts. The general quality of pupils' historical thinking was to some extent differentiated, in terms of the interrelation of these issues, among individuals and their responses, but mainly among groups at different ages These differences were related to relevant differences concerning a series of other abilities and skills that this museum practice demanded of pupils: aesthetic development and ability to treat museum objects as objects of art, use of 'independent' historical knowledge as knowledge critically built and not as offered information, questioning, empathy and so on.

On this basis, we could say that carefully organized educational programmes that relate history education and museum education, aiming to enable children from early ages to use and interpret museum objects and collections as works open to several alternative interpretations, could have very important educational results: they could enable children to develop both their historical knowledge, thinking and skills and their potential to interpret and approach creatively material culture in general.

Conclusions

Although the full analysis of children's historical thinking within a museum environment, in terms of its 'methodology', 'content' and 'specific characteristics', has not been discussed in this chapter, some basic conclusions are presented here, in the light of this six-year dialogue with children's thinking.

Historical thinking and museological variables

Conclusion 1 Pupils' historical thinking was activated by the educational environment of the archaeological museums visited. The majority of subjects had a historical approach towards the museum world from the time they entered museums. In addition, the museum environment helped them to recall background historical knowledge and to activate their historical thinking, more than their school environment, in which children showed a tendency to reproduce historical knowledge and information a-critically. In this sense (archaeological) museums proved to offer an enabling educational environment for the evolution and development of historical thinking.

Conclusion 2 Pupils' historical thinking was closely related to the museum objects studied, in terms of whether museum objects were single 'isolated' objects or collections, 'everyday' objects or objects of art, and in terms of the level of difficulty they posed for pupils' work. Single objects were more easily treated as sources than collections of objects. Pupils' historical inferences on the basis of collections of objects were more general than their inferences generated on the basis of single objects. Everyday objects seemed to facilitate the evolution of pupils' historical thinking more than objects of art did. Despite the several difficulties that objects of art pose as historical sources, however, a great number of pupils proved to be able to treat them in both aesthetic and historical terms, and to express valid historical thinking of distinctive quality. Moreover, pupils' historical thinking was closely related to the level of difficulty museum objects posed for their work, in terms of their appearance, the presence and type of relevant information and their relation to pupils' background historical knowledge.

Conclusion 3 Pupils' reliance on 'dependent historical information' was associated with its form; extensive information offered in museums was ignored. Moreover the wording of labels (generally offering academic information that only specialists could understand) and their museological 'philosophy' (object-oriented, ignoring museum visitors' needs) greatly affected the expression of 'valid historical thinking'. More generally, any direct or indirect information seemed to affect children's thinking.

Historical thinking and educational variables
Pupils' historical thinking related to several educational variables: to the tasks and the questions set, and to the educational environment in which it was realized.

Conclusion 1 Pupils' historical thinking was associated with the questions set in terms of whether they were historical or history free (not implying a historical response). Historical questions enabled pupils to express higher levels of historical thinking than history free questions, in terms of most issues studied.

Conclusion 2 Differences in pupils' historical thinking were associated with the tasks set and the educational 'philosophy' they implied. Indeed, the tasks, not relating to a traditional approach to history education, in association with open-ended questions, enabled pupils to express historical thinking beyond the level of reproducing 'dependent' or 'independent' historical information or knowledge (acquired in the museum or previously, mainly at school). In this sense, pupils' historical thinking appeared as going beyond the limits set by their traditional history education.

Conclusion 3 Differences appeared in the level and quality of pupils' historical thinking, in terms of whether it was expressed within a museum environment or, afterwards, in class, where most pupils mainly reproduced the historical information available from relevant books.

These findings underline the relation of children's historical thinking to several educational variables and, especially, to the type of educational opportunities we offer children to activate and express their historical thinking.

Historical thinking, age and individual differences
Differences shown among individuals and responses in the expression of historical thinking in terms of several issues, indicated that, besides age and educational and museological conditions, pupils' historical thinking

within this age range was related to their personal intellectual powers, abilities and interest in historical investigation.

Significance for history education and museum education
Taking into consideration that results related to pupils who, being educated by a traditional approach, had no instruction, education or practice in matters concerning 'scientific' historical thinking and work with sources, the research conclusions might be of significance for history education because they offer a picture of pupils' historical thinking that is, more or less, articulated by their own potential in 'scientific' historical thinking.

Conclusions suggest that pupils' work with museum objects in a museum environment might be of great significance to the development of their historical thinking for the following reasons. An archaeological museum environment seems to appeal to children's historical thinking from the time they enter the museum; children are likely to 'see' objects in historical terms even in tasks that are 'history free', that is not implying a historical answer.

The museum offers an environment that appeals to children's interest because it displays objects. Objects address both children's intellectual powers in historical investigation and a series of different abilities and skills involving aesthetic, empathetic, psychological and social development and sensitivity, because objects stimulate our general interest in them even by their very existence.[8] Therefore, a museum seems to be a very good educational environment for setting open-ended questions and tasks that ask children to pose their own questions.

The fact that museum work with objects according to tasks relating to open-ended questions let some children express historical thinking at a high historical level is a very optimistic element. It underlines the significance of children's work with museum objects for the development of their historical thinking, especially if their work is related to carefully devised tasks that advance children's own potential in historical interpretation. In this sense results are in agreement with the argument of Dickinson *et al.* that it is not enough to let children work with concrete objects; it is important to let children 'understand them as saying something about the past'.[9]

The advantages of pupils' work with objects are associated with the fact that, although most written texts are written to record a meaning, objects are made for their meaning; they are the meaning. This fact underlines objects' unique value, and the necessity to interpret them not only on the basis of their represented theme, but on the basis of their physical existence as well. Each child, according to his or her age, abilities, knowledge and interests, can develop his or her own potentialities because objects do not pose language problems that written texts are likely to pose to children's work (even at the age of 15).

Museum objects do not narrate a closed story; they are open to children's interpretation. In contrast, the story that a written text tells is a closed story; 'supporting an amphisemy between the sense of time and of causality, it implies an unfolding, i.e. an understanding of the Narration'.[10] In other words, it is very hard for children to go beyond the 'understanding of the Narration' and to interpret it in terms of historical uncertainty and questioning.[11] Therefore, the use of both objects and texts in history education might advance children's historical thinking more globally, in relation to many historical notions, abilities and skills.

Written primary texts usually refer to men and their story. Museum objects relate to everyday life in the past and 'hence make historical knowledge [and thinking] more populistic, pluralistic, and public'.[12] They may reveal children's and slaves' past, or 'her-story', which is usually hidden by history.

The fact that objects do not tell a certain story lets children investigate ways by which they can decode their meaning: what they are and what they imply. This situation is very interesting for education. Children are likely to recall background historical knowledge and experience and to use both of them to go beyond their particular education because museum practice appeals to children's imagination. Therefore, if the museum objects generally relate to children's background historical knowledge, their historical thinking can be advanced in a museum environment by recalling and using this knowledge creatively.[13] On the other hand, if they do not relate to background historical knowledge other abilities and skills can be advanced, like children's imagination and hypothesizing in terms of historical uncertainty.

Indeed, children tend to use a series of abilities, skills and understandings that would potentially enable them to understand and 'translate' visual images into conceptual and verbal representation, and to articulate historical speech.[14] On this basis, children's work with museum objects may have broad implications for their general development. In this sense, it is very important for education to let children 'read' objects – 'material culture'. The broad educational significance of such practices relates to the culture of our times, according to which a plethora of visual images and signs replace long and detailed written information. The school has to cultivate a new type of literacy to enable children to meet current purposes and needs.

The advantages of pupils' intellectual, historical and aesthetic development by their exposure to authentic objects as well, even if they are sometimes as humble as a broken clay tool, have to be carefully studied as a counterbalance to their exposure to the bright electronic 'reality'. In addition, the fact that a museum environment offers the challenge of a personal dialogue with the displayed relics at a moment of time, in which the past and the present meet, in contradiction to the speed electronic media have introduced to life, and its implications for thinking, are matters which deserve careful study.

This dialogue enabled these children as a whole, despite the effect of their particular traditional history education, to express historical thinking beyond the limits set by their history education, in terms of historical methodology, content and specific characteristics. Although pupils' historical thinking was confined by their traditional history education within the borders of a ready-made, unquestionable historical 'knowledge' – an educational condition which implies that the past is known – many pupils expressed historical thinking of 'scientific' methodology and of rich historical content. In addition, a number of pupils' implied the idea that the past cannot really directly be known. This fact was considered very positive. It shows that pupils' potential went beyond these limits in terms of issues concerning primary philosophical assumptions on the basis of which different theories of history and their associated approaches to history education are differentiated.

NOTES

1. D. Thompson, 'Understanding the past: Procedures and content', in A.K. Dickinson, P.J. Lee and P.J. Rogers (eds), *Learning History* (London: Heinemann Educational, 1984), p. 180.
2. L. Vygotsky, *Thought and Language* (1934; revised edn by Alex Kozulin, Cambridge, MA: Massachusetts Institute of Technology, 1989), pp. 184–9.
3. The theoretical investigation of museums, their educational character and the significance of museum objects was primarily related to the work of T. Ambrose (ed.), *Education in Museums – Museums in Education* (Edinburgh: HMSO, 1987); R. Arnheim, *Visual Thinking* (Berkeley, CA: University of California Press, 1969), and *Art and Visual Perception: A Psychology of the Creative Eye* (Berkeley, CA: University of California Press, 1974; J.P. Boylan (ed.), *Museums 2000: Politics, People, Professionals and Profit* (London: Museums Association, Routledge, 1992); I. Hodder, *The Archaeology of Contextual Meanings* (Cambridge: Cambridge University Press, 1987), and *The Meaning of Things* (London: Routledge, 1991); E. Hooper-Greenhill, 'Museums in education: Towards the end of the century', in T. Ambrose (ed.), *Education in Museums: Museums*

in Education (Edinburgh: Scottish Museums Council, HMSO, 1987); E. Hooper-Greenhill, 'The Museum: The socio-historical articulations of knowledge and things', PhD dissertation (University of London Institute of Education, 1988), *Learning and Teaching with Objects: A Practical Skills Based Approach* (Leicester: Department of Museum Studies, University of Leicester, 1988), *Museums and the Shaping of Knowledge* (London and New York: Routledge, 1992), *The Educational Role of Museums* (London and New York: Routledge, 1994), and *Museums and their Visitors* (London and New York: Routledge, 1994); D. Lowenthal, *The Past is a Foreign Country* (Cambridge: Cambridge University Press, 1985); and S. M. Pearce, 'Objects as meaning, or narrating the past', in Pearce (ed.), *Interpreting Objects and Collections* (London and New York: Routledge, 1994).
4. See Pearce, 'Objects as meaning.'
5. The theoretical investigation of history and historical thinking was primarily related with the work of R. Ashby and P.J. Lee, 'Children's concepts of empathy and understanding in history', in C. Portal (ed.), *The History Curriculum for Teachers* (Lewes: Falmer Press, 1987), and 'Children's ideas about testing historical claims and about the status of historical accounts', unpublished paper presented at the AERA annual meeting, New York, 1996; T. Bennett, 'Texts in history: The determinations of readings and their texts', in D. Attridge, G. Bennington and R. Young (eds), *Post-structuralism and the Question of History* (Cambridge: Cambridge University Press, 1987), and *Outside Literature* (London and New York: Routledge, 1990); M. Booth, 'Inductive thinking in history: the 14–16 age group', in G. Jones and L. Ward (eds), *New History Old Problems: Studies in History Teaching* (Swansea: University College of Swansea Faculty of Education, 1978), and 'Ages and concepts: A critique of the Piagetian approach to history teaching', in C. Portal (ed.), *The History Curriculum*; E.H. Carr, *What is History?* (London: Penguin Books, 1991); R.G. Collingwood, *An Autobiography* (Oxford: Oxford University Press, 1939), and *The Idea of History* (Oxford: Oxford University Press, 1946); A.K. Dickinson and P.J. Lee, 'Understanding and research', in Dickinson and Lee (eds), *History Teaching and Historical Understanding* (London: Heinemann, 1978), 'Making sense of history', in Dickinson, Lee and Rogers (eds), *Learning History*; A.K. Dickinson, A. Gard, and P.J. Lee, 'Evidence in history and the classroom', in Dickinson and Lee (eds), *History Teaching*; K. Jenkins, *Re-thinking History* (London and New York: Routledge, 1991), and *On 'What is History?' From Carr and Elton to Rorty and White* (London and New York: Routledge, 1995); P.J. Lee, 'Explanation and understanding in history', in Dickinson and Lee (eds), *History Teaching*, 'Why learn history?' and 'Historical imagination', both in Dickinson, Lee and Rogers (eds), *Learning History*; P.J. Lee, R. Ashby and A.K. Dickinson, 'Progression in children's ideas about history', in M. Hughes (ed.), *Progression in Learning*, BERA Dialogues; 11 (Clevedon: Multilingual Matters, 1996); D. Shemilt, *History 13–16 Evaluation Study* (London: Holmes McDougall, 1980), 'Beauty and the philosopher: Empathy in history and the classroom', in Dickinson, Lee and Rogers (eds), *Learning History*, and 'Adolescent ideas about evidence and methodology in history', in Portal (ed.), *The History Curriculum*; and H. White, *Metahistory: The Historical Imagination of Nineteenth-Century Europe* (Baltimore, MD, and London: Johns Hopkins University Press, 1973).
6. I. Kriekouki-Nakou, 'Pupils' historical thinking within a museum environment', PhD dissertation (University of London Institute of Education 1996'.
7. See Shemilt, 'Adolescent ideas'.
8. Lowenthal, *The Past*; Pearce, 'Objects as meaning'.
9. See Dickinson, Gard and Lee, 'Evidence in history', p. 3.
10. Roland Barthes, *Le degré zéro de l'écriture* (Paris: Editions du Seuil, 1972), pp. 34–5.
11. See also Shemilt, 'Adolescent ideas'.
12. D. Lowenthal, *The Past*, p. 244.
13. See also Booth, 'Ages and concepts'.
14. See also P.J. Rogers, 'Why teach history?', in Dickinson, Lee and Rogers (eds), *Learning History*, pp. 20–38.

6

Children's Ideas about Historical Explanation

PETER LEE, ALARIC DICKINSON
AND ROSALYN ASHBY

Project CHATA (Concepts of History and Teaching Approaches), funded by the Economic and Social Research Council, has paid particular attention to the development of children's understanding of second order historical concepts of enquiry and explanation between the ages of 7 and 14 years.

This chapter concentrates on work in relation to children's ideas about historical explanation and will:

1. suggest broad models of the development of some aspects of children's ideas about historical explanation;
2. comment on the degree to which the 'seven-year gap' found in science and mathematics is also present in history (where the ideas of some 7-year-olds about explanation appear to be as sophisticated as those of most 14-year-olds);
3. offer evidence that children's ideas about causal explanation and about explaining by giving reasons may develop independently.

Background

Progression in teaching and learning is a central concern of both Project CHATA and the National Curriculum in England and Wales. The past two decades have seen increasing interest in second-order historical concepts as a means to provide a structure for progression in history; not to replace historical knowledge, but to take school history beyond the aggregation of historical facts, or the memorizing of accounts. One effect of the National Curriculum has been to consolidate this development. Against this background CHATA set out to try to map the development of children's ideas about history, working with a notion of progression in which more powerful concepts solve problems which defeat less powerful ones.

CHATA has investigated the concepts of evidence, accounts, cause and rational understanding. (The latter, somewhat clumsy label denotes understanding in which reconstruction of purposes, values and beliefs plays a central role.) For children's ideas about rational understanding, CHATA was able to build on a continuing tradition of small-scale qualitative research.[1] Although research into children's ideas about causation has been somewhat less extensive, there has been important pioneering work, most notably in Britain by Shemilt, in the USA by Voss *et al.*, and in Spain by Carretero and Limón.[2]

CHATA has worked with the assumption that children's second-order historical concepts are best treated as tacit understandings, changing over time through exposure to school and the wider culture. Among the methodological choices made by CHATA, the decision to approach children's ideas about history through substantive historical tasks from which those ideas would be inferred, rather than through direct questions, was partly dictated by the age of the younger group of children, and partly by experience of earlier small-scale work. Use of pencil-and-paper data in Phase I (enhanced for 7- and 8-year-olds by interviews) allowed the project to work with a much larger sample than previous small-scale studies, and to acquire evidence of ideas in a range of content, on several occasions.

Research Design

The project has proceeded in three main phases and an extension phase. Phase II – exploring teaching approaches – is not discussed here.

Phase I: Investigation of children's ideas about enquiry and explanation in history
In Phase I written responses were collected from 320 children between the ages of 7 and 14 (Table 6.1), across three task-sets, on three separate occasions. Each task-set employed similar questions and explored the same target concepts, but addressed different historical content within the

TABLE 6.1: MEAN AGES OF YEAR GROUPS

	Year 3	Year 6	Year 7	Year 9
Mean age	8 yrs 1 mth	11yrs 2 mths	12 yrs 1 mth	14 yrs 1 mth

National Curriculum in England. The tasks were constructed to be self-standing, providing children with the necessary material to respond. The purposive sample was drawn from three primary and six secondary schools (Table 6.2).

TABLE 6.2: PHASE I SCHOOLS

School	Phase and type	Intake	Year 3	Year 6	Year 7	Year 9
A	primary	urban	17	29		
B	primary	small town	16	18		
C	primary	rural	22	28		
D	secondary comprehensive	urban			24	24
E	secondary comprehensive	suburban			24	25
F	secondary comprehensive	urban			23	
G	secondary comprehensive	small town				10
H	secondary selective (girls)	urban +			14	16
I	secondary selective (boys)	suburban +			15	15
Total in each year group			55	75	100	90

N = 320

Follow-up interviews were conducted with 122 children, including all those from year 3, on all three task-sets. The year 3 interview responses were analyzed along with the pencil-and-paper responses; the remaining interviews were used only to check that the written responses were not seriously misleading.

The written tasks took the form of four slim booklets. The children were asked to complete these by writing, ticking boxes, ordering statements or drawing arrows. For the 11- and 14-year-olds around 90 minutes, including a break, was available for a complete task-set, and for the younger children an entire day was set aside. The year 3 children were read the background information, and were then taken through the tasks by a research officer with considerable experience as a primary school teacher; their work was broken into short periods interspersed with organized games in the playground.

Phase III: Progression of children's ideas in different teaching and curriculum contexts
In order to acquire a better understanding of the progression of pupils' ideas in the context of different teaching and curriculum approaches (not

discussed here), interview data from 92 pupils between the ages of 7 and 14 years (a sample of 96 reduced to 92 by attrition) were collected on two occasions. New, modified tasks were designed specifically for use in these Phase III interviews with children, together with appropriate interview schedules. The sample was drawn from three primary and four secondary schools (Table 6.3).

TABLE 6.3: PHASE III SCHOOLS

School	Phase and type	Intake	Year 3	Year 6	Year 7	Year 9
J	primary	rural	7	8		
K	primary	urban	8	7		
L	primary	suburban	8	8		
M	secondary comprehensive	suburban			8	6
N	secondary comprehensive	urban			8	8
O	secondary selective (girls)	urban			8	
P	secondary selective (boys)	urban				8
Total in each year group			23	23	24	22

N = 92

Phase IV: Small-scale longitudinal study
The 23 year 3 children from Phase III formed the sample for the longitudinal extension. They were interviewed in July of years 4 and 5, using tasks isomorphic with those of Phase III (same questions and interview schedule structure, different content).

Methods

Each of the three task-sets included a range of tasks designed to elicit children's ideas about historical explanation. Historical information was offered to the children in the form of simple narrative and specially drawn pictures. Some tasks asked children to use the information to explain why something happened by reference to antecedent conditions – crudely, causal explanations. Others asked for explanation of an action or social practice – explanations in terms of rational understanding, sometimes rather misleadingly called 'empathy'. (In our work 'empathy' is construed as an achievement and a disposition, not as a special power or process.)[3] The decision to operate with the divisions outlined here was prompted by indications in the trials phase that children's ideas about causal explanation and about explaining by giving reasons may develop separately.

Rational understanding
The tasks exploring children's ideas about understanding past action and social practices were designed to investigate different aspects of these ideas in each of the three task-sets. The first task-set, in asking why Claudius invaded Britain ('when it cost the Romans more than they got out of it'), focused on individual action, and both the purposes and the circumstances in which the action was taken were relevant to an explanation. In the second task-set two issues were addressed: why the Romans had a law that all slaves in a household should be killed if a master was murdered by a slave, and why the law was enforced in the particular case in question. This also suggested explanation by reference to purposes and situation, but in a wider social and institutional context. In task-set 3 the issue was why the Anglo-Saxons used the ordeal – by fire and by water – to decide whether someone was guilty of a crime. Here purposes were, on the face of it, already given: the problem was to explain why particular means were adopted.

In all this our assumption was that explanation of individual action and of social practices is an important part of historical explanation and understanding, and that in understanding past actions and social practices, as in making sense of everyday life, it is often important to know what individuals or groups of people believed, valued and sought to attain. Such understanding involves establishing how people in the past saw the situation (their particular circumstances and wider sets of beliefs and values) and what they were trying to do (their intentions) in order to reconstruct their reasons for doing what they did.

The notion of 'rational understanding' links, through 'empathy', to a long tradition of research on perspective taking.[4] There is space here only for two brief comments. First, Piaget's work dealt with adolescents' ability to relate different perspectives of model mountains, and more recent investigations have looked at everyday, child-friendly situations in which the perspective taking is part of a social activity, such as hiding from police-officers. The more 'embedded' nature of the child-friendly tasks devised by Hughes and others,[5] and the fact that they were social, gave new insight into perspective taking, but this does not alter the fact that physical relationships were still central. In history, perspective taking may involve physical viewpoints, but the primary task is understanding people's ideas, beliefs and values, and relating them to action or practice.

Second, although in some sense children must know how to make sense of other people's actions in order to survive in the everyday world, it cannot be assumed that they therefore have an intuitive grasp of historical understanding. People in the past did weird things, and it does not seem part of everyday intuitive understanding to assume that these made sense.

Causal explanations

Several different approaches were used to elicit ideas about cause, illustrated here by reference to items from the first task-set. The children were given text and specially drawn pictures covering background information on Rome and Britain and the events of the Roman Conquest. The question which followed took the form of a paradox (Figure 6.1).

FIGURE 6.1: CAUSE QUESTION PARADOX, TASK-SET 1

> There were lots of Britons in Britain.
> The Roman army that went to Britain wasn't very big.
> The Britons were fighting for their homes.
>
> **SO WHY WERE THE ROMANS ABLE TO TAKE OVER MOST OF BRITAIN?**

This was asked first in the form of an open question, for which children had to write a few lines in answer. The immediately following question was designed to ascertain whether children could distinguish reasons for action – why the Romans invaded Britain – from causal factors contributing to Roman success (Figure 6.2).

The children were then asked to draw arrows linking boxes to give the best explanation they could of why the Romans were able to take over most of Britain. The boxes contained statements about the Roman Empire or about the Britons (Figure 6.3). Children were told that an arrow from one box to another meant that the first box helped explain the second, and that they could have as many or as few arrows as they needed. They were also told that more than one arrow could go into or out of a box.

Finally, in the third approach, two different – very brief – explanations were offered to the children. One set out two simple background conditions for Roman success, and the other offered an event which was both a key step in the Roman Conquest, and an immediate cause of the Romans' success (Figure 6.4). Subjects were asked 'How can there be two different explanations of the *same* thing?' Subsequent questions asked whether one explanation was better than the other, how they could check to see if one was better than the other, and how they could check to find out if either was a good or bad explanation. One part of the rationale behind these questions was an attempt to discover whether there is any kind of depth-structure in children's handling of causal explanation.

FIGURE 6.2: CAUSE, REASON AND INFORMATION TASK

BOX 1
The Roman army trained a lot and the Roman soldiers were used to fighting as a team.

BOX 2
The Roman Emperor Claudius ordered the invasion of Britain in AD 43.

BOX A
THE ROMANS WERE ABLE TO TAKE OVER MOST OF BRITAIN

BECAUSE:

BOX 3
The Romans wanted to make sure they could get tin and pearls from the Britons.

BOX 4
Claudius wanted to show that he was a great Emperor.

BOX 5
The Britons lived in different groups which sometimes fought each other.

BOX 6
The Emperor Claudius had a limp.

FIGURE 6.3: CAUSAL STRUCTURE TASK WITH YEAR 7 ANALYTICAL RESPONSE

Question 12. Why were the Romans able to take over?

[The boxes on this Chart are not in any special order]
Choose any boxes which help explain why the Romans were able to take over.
<u>Join them up with arrows to show best why the Romans were able to take over.</u>
Make the best explanation you can.
An arrow from one box to another means: <u>the first box helps explain the second box.</u>
Use as many joins as you need. You can have more than one arrow to or from a box.
BUT don't make joins that don't help explain why the Romans were able to take over.

Make the middle box happen!

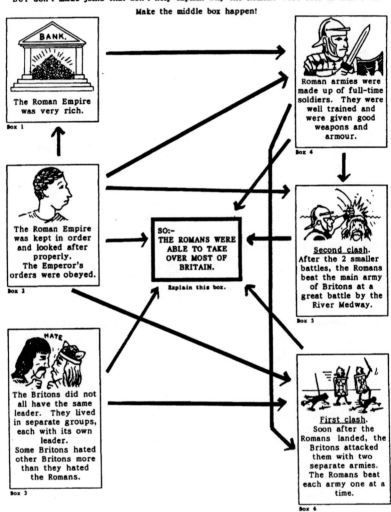

104

FIGURE 6.4: ALTERNATIVE EXPLANATIONS

The Romans were *really* able to take over most of Britain because the Roman Empire was rich and properly looked after.	The Romans were *really* able to take over most of Britain because they beat the Britons at the battle of the River Medway.

Discussion and Analysis of Phase I Results on Aspects of Historical Explanation

Rational understanding

The differences in focus (mentioned above) in the three task-sets were reflected in children's responses within the broad pattern of progression reported below.

Outright bafflement was frequent only with the Saxon ordeal, where, on the face of it, the purpose – to detect guilt – was already given. Almost all year 3 children could offer a purpose to explain Claudius' invasion of Britain. Explanation by deficit (the idea that people in the past lacked basic knowledge or simply could not do certain things) was common among younger children. Half the children in years 3 and 6, falling to one-quarter at year 9, attributed the treatment of the slaves to the inability of the Romans to find out who was guilty. More than 50 per cent of the year 3 children, and still 30 per cent at year 9, attributed the ordeal to the fact that the Saxons 'had no other way' of detecting the guilty or lacked police and courts or knew nothing about physics and medicine.

Younger children were more likely than older ones to give explanations in terms of personal wants or intentions, and were much less likely to look beyond intentions to the situational context of actions or institutions. Very few year 3 children appealed to the situation to explain either Roman treatment of slaves or the Saxon ordeal, and Table 6.4 shows that even in explaining individual action, where some year 3 children did think in terms of the situation in which Claudius found himself, there was a marked tendency for younger children to concentrate on intentions.

TABLE 6.4: CLAUDIUS, TASK-SET 1:
CHOICE OF INTENTIONS AND PURPOSES, SITUATION, OR BOTH, AS
EXPLANATORY (PERCENTAGES OF YEAR GROUPS)

	Intentions	Situations	Both
Year 3	78.8	1.9	19.2
Year 6	68.0	9.3	22.7
Year 7	40.8	5.1	54.1
Year 9	23.6	6.7	69.7

For both individual action and social institutions there was evidence of a shift with age from personal to role explanations (often stereotyped), that is, explanation by role and stereotype. The Romans made the law about slaves because that is what Romans were like. Claudius acted as he did because he was Emperor (see Table 6.5). As Tanya, year 6 and aged 11, put it: 'No [I'm not puzzled] because he was just another emperor.'

The 'Situational analysis reasons' column in Table 6.5 provides substantial evidence of a shift with age to explanation in terms of the logic of the situation. A few children in year 6 explained action as taking place in a situation which offered opportunities or set constraints, and more than half in year 9 did this.

TABLE 6.5: CLAUDIUS, TASK-SET 1:
REASON TYPE BY YEAR GROUP (PERCENTAGE OF YEAR GROUPS)

	Personal wants	Personal reasons	Emperor role wants	Emperor role reasons	Situational analysis wants	Situational analysis reasons
Year 3	56.9	11.8	5.9	25.5	0.0	0.0
Year 6	21.3	14.7	6.7	50.7	0.0	6.6
Year 7	3.1	4.1	3.1	51.1	1.0	37.7
Year 9	1.1	4.5	1.1	40.5	0.0	52.8

In explaining Roman slavery the situation was sometimes taken into account, but in modern terms: it would be difficult to sell slaves from a household where a master had been murdered, or the law was to be explained as a means of deterring other slaves from doing the same thing. Many children explaining the ordeal recognized that a mechanism of some kind was required to make sense of Saxon behaviour, and suggested that God would be seen as 'helping' (Table 6.6). Thus there is evidence in some responses to all three task-sets of explanation in terms of the logic of the situation, but in modern terms.

TABLE 6.6: SAXON ORDEAL, TASK-SET 3:
MECHANISMS FOR THE ORDEAL (PERCENTAGES OF YEAR GROUPS)

	Year 3	Year 6	Year 7	Year 9
God was helping	9.1	17.3	33.0	40.0
God was giving a sign	0.0	5.3	8.0	15.6
God was seen as directly intervening in life	1.8	1.3	8.0	12.2

Table 6.6 (third row) also shows a small number of children tying the ordeal to beliefs more specific to the time, a move belonging to the next category, explanation by reference to the way in which people saw the action or institution in question. In the Claudius task some older children made it clear that there were certain things Claudius could not have known, and that he had no guarantee that Rome would gain financially or economically from the invasion. Some (5 per cent in year 7 and 7 per cent in year 9) also took account of the temporal context in which Claudius was operating, and fitted his actions into wider policies (for example, past emperors' attitudes to Britain, and British aid to the Gauls).

In the Roman slave task a few children referred to beliefs about the status of slaves (as property for example), and others emphasized the symbolic importance of the law. Children in this category saw the ordeal as fitting into beliefs about hierarchy. Explanations of this kind were beginning to take into account the wider framework of social and material life, a category suggested by earlier small-scale work.[6] A few responses in Phase I showed signs of such ideas.

Two general considerations also seem to merit reporting. For most children, even at year 9, explanation and justification were closely linked: explanation in terms of reasons was judgemental. But this did not necessarily lead to a deficit view: older children recognized that judgements made from a past standpoint will not be the same as those made from their own position. For example, the idea that the Saxons, at any rate, would have thought the ordeal fair or right, increased in frequency with age (Table 6.7).

TABLE 6.7: SAXON ORDEAL, TASK-SET 3:
PEOPLE THOUGHT DIFFERENTLY (PERCENTAGES OF YEAR GROUPS)

	Year 3	Year 6	Year 7	Year 9
They had different beliefs from us	1.8	17.3	20.0	16.7
The Saxons thought it right	9.1	20.0	27.0	34.4
Recognition of problems in understanding	1.8	2.7	1.0	7.8

Cause

Explaining the outcomes of actions From six boxes (containing two factual statements, two reasons for action and two causal conditions for the outcome of the action – see Figure 6.2) children were asked to choose two to give the best explanation of the success of Claudius' invasion of Britain. Year 3 children were more likely to choose a combination of reasons and causes than to choose two causes. Many younger children gave reasons for Claudius' decision to invade as if they explained the successful outcome. Interestingly, this was predicted by some year 9 children. Beki, year 9, responded to the invitation to suggest why others might choose the wrong boxes by writing: 'Some people may have chosen Box 3 because it gives a reason why they wanted to, not how the Romans managed to take over.' But other children converted 'reason' or 'fact' items into causes (Table 6.8), most frequently by treating reasons as strengthening desires, and hence as making a successful outcome more likely (for example, suggesting that Claudius might threaten to kill his troops if they did not win).

Table 6.9 shows the pattern of choices of 'best' items adjusted to take account of conversions. In responding to this question, a few year 3 children distinguished clearly between reasons for action and causes of outcomes, indicating ideas more sophisticated than those of most year 9 children. (These results are discussed more fully in an earlier publication by the authors.)[7]

TABLE 6.8: CONVERSIONS:
'CONVERSIONS': PERCENTAGES OF YEAR GROUPS CONVERTING FACTS TO
REASONS OR CAUSES, OR REASONS TO CAUSES

	F to R	F to C	R to C
Year 3	0.0	3.6	3.6
Year 6	1.3	1.3	12.0
Year 7	8.0	5.0	37.0
Year 9	2.2	8.9	58.4

Note: F = fact, R = reason, C = cause

TABLE 6.9: COMBINATIONS OF TWO 'BEST' CHOICES:
ADJUSTED FOR 'CONVERSIONS' (PERCENTAGES OF YEAR GROUPS)

	FF, FR, FC, RR	RC	CC
Year 3	11	61	28
Year 6	17	32	51
Year 7	1	20	79
Year 9	5	13	82

Note: F = fact, R = reason, C = cause

Causal structure Asked to make links between boxes showing causes of Roman success, only a very few children in year 3 and year 6 found it hard to go beyond selecting one or two boxes. Most year 3 children could produce linear chains which made sense, some grouping clusters of items within a chain on the basis of content links (what items were 'about') rather than causal links. There was an increase with age in the number of children making valid temporal chains. Some children omitted boxes which could not be made to fit a genuinely causal chain, indicating awareness of the need to construct more than one chain, but still apparently unwilling to depart from a linear structure.

By year 9 approximately 40 per cent of children were producing analytical structures, with multiple start points, and multiple entries or exits to and from boxes, including the explanandum box. (See Figure 6.3 for an example of such a response, and Conclusions below for a model of progression of ideas.)

Figure 6.5 shows the large step between year 6 and year 7 in the incidence of modal or consistent analytical responses across task-sets. If strict causal validity in an analytical structure is the criterion, however, the step is between year 7 and year 9.

FIGURE 6.5: ANALYTICAL STRUCTURE AND VALIDITY ACROSS
THREE TASK-SETS (PERCENTAGES OF YEAR GROUPS)

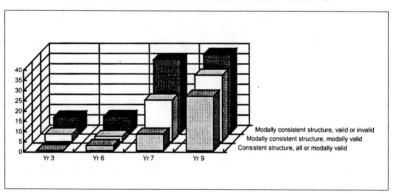

'Because' Ideas about the *status* of explanations changed. Children were asked if there was any important difference between two boxes, one of which contained two statements, and the other an explanation created by joining the statements with 'because' (Figure 6.6). There was a significant move between years 3 and 9 from denying to asserting

FIGURE 6.6: 'BECAUSE' BOXES

The Romans took over Britain. The Roman army had good weapons.

The Romans were able to take over Britain because their army had good weapons.

---

differences between the boxes. Reasons given included: the boxes differed in content; the first box gave two facts and the second an explanation; it was possible in the second box for the first statement to be true and the second false. Younger children were more likely to say that the boxes were the same (Figure 6.7).

FIGURE 6.7: PERCENTAGES OF YEAR GROUPS SAYING THE BOXES WERE THE SAME OR WERE DIFFERENT

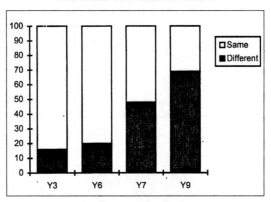

Brief Report on Phases III and IV

The data for these phases of the project were extensive and rich, covering the same concepts as Phase I. Initial analysis of the Phase III data shows clear but uneven signs of progression in causal structure and rational understanding. There is space here to mention just a few findings relevant to this paper.

Phase III

1. Children's starting points at the first visit differed greatly. One year 3 girl was already giving explanations of action in terms of 'roles',

110

whereas for one-third of her cohort the request for an explanation was baffling. In year 9 one girl produced an additive causal structure, while nearly a quarter of her cohort were giving valid analytical explanations.

2. Children's ideas about understanding and cause appear to be decoupled, in terms both of sophistication and progression. In year 3, by the second visit, five children were still baffled by a past institution, but three of them were constructing valid linear explanatory schemes. Only two of the 23 year 3 children showed progression on both concepts.

3. Movement differed in the year groups. The biggest gains on causal structure were in year 6, with ten children giving clear signs of progression, and on rational understanding in year 3 (9) and year 7 (9).

4. The pattern of changing ideas differed between schools. Differences between schools were more pronounced on rational understanding than on causal structure. In school J only two children made progress on rational understanding compared with seven in school L and five in K, but on causal structure more children made progress in J than in K. In schools K and L history was taught as both a separate subject and as part of school topics. In school J history registered only as part of the topics in progress at any particular time.

5. The most marked difference in progression in the secondary schools was in year 9 at school M, where history was taught as part of an integrated humanities course: only one of the children made any progress on the concepts under investigation, and then only on causal structure.

Phase IV

The Phase IV longitudinal extension provides strong indications of progression between years 3 and 5, although small numbers dictate a degree of caution.

1. There was little indication that development proceeded in parallel within the concept pairs (cause and rational understanding, or evidence and accounts). Nine children made sufficient progress to register changes of category on either causal structure and rational understanding, but not both. Of the remaining 11, seven made progress on both, and four made no progress on either. (Results in the

area of historical enquiry were similar: 13 children made progress on one or other of evidence or accounts, but not both.)

2. There were large differences between children's ideas at year 3. Two year 3 children clearly made (logical) distinctions between 'so' and 'and then' in constructing linear explanations, while four simply joined one card to the explanandum box.

3. By year 5 the spread had increased. In general, while some children's ideas changed considerably, others remained static, sometimes at a very low level.

4. Some salient shifts in ideas about explanation in history may be picked out. For example, by year 5 additive causal structures had disappeared, and linear structures were the norm. (See Conclusions for model.) Two children were on the verge of producing analytical structures (see Figure 6.3). A considerable expansion in the range of ideas occurred in rational understanding, where 12 children in year 3 had given explanations of action in personal terms, and six found the request for explanation itself baffling. By year 5 two children remained baffled, but more than half had moved to or beyond explanations appealing to roles.

Conclusion

Models of progression
From the analysis so far carried out it is possible to outline broad changes in children's understanding of individual concepts. These might be summarized as follows.

Explaining the outcomes of action

1. Wanting makes things happen.

2. Desires only make things happen if they are strong enough.

3. Even 'strong' desires require a mechanism to account for outcomes.

4. Desires cannot on their own account for outcomes.

Causal structure

1. Single items, or items operating separately but additively, cause events.

2. Items connect linearly, but, so long as they are all part of the story, order is inconsequential.

3. Order in a chain is determined by content (clusters of items 'about the same thing').

4. Temporal order fixes relationships in a chain: temporal and causal connections are not distinguished.

5. Events are the outcome of linear structures with causal links between items.

6. Events are produced by complex structures of independent or conjoined chains, with multiple links between items.

Rational understanding

1. Bafflement: there is no way to make sense of some past actions, institutions or practices.

2. Explanation by deficit: people in the past were not as clever as us, or lacked basic knowledge, or simply could not do certain things.

3. Explanation in terms of personal wants or purposes.

4. Explanation by role and stereotype.

5. Explanation in terms of the logic of the situation (offering opportunities or setting constraints) understood in everyday terms.

6. Explanation by reference to the way in which people at the time saw the action or institution in question.

7. Explanation in terms of the wider context of ideas and material life.

The 'seven-year gap'
There seem to be grounds for suggesting that the 'seven-year gap', found by the Assessment of Performance Unit in science and mathematics, is also present in history. The ideas of some 7-year-olds – albeit a small proportion – about explanation and the nature of historical knowledge, are as sophisticated as those of most 14-year-olds. For example, some year 3 children made valid (logical) distinctions between 'so' and 'and then' in constructing linear explanations. Moreover, a few year 3 children distinguished clearly between reasons for action and causes of outcomes, indicating ideas more sophisticated than those of most year 9 children.

Thus, Tom, year 3, in explaining why he ruled out Box 3 ('The Romans wanted to make sure they could get tin and pearls from the Britons') made a clear distinction: 'Well, 'cos you see, just because they wanted them it doesn't mean that they're going to be able to take over.' It seems possible that the gap is less marked in areas where ideas are more specific to history (for example, ideas about historical accounts and rational understanding) than in areas where they may be more generic (for example, causal structure). Table 6.5 above shows that none of the year 3 children in the Phase I sample thought it appropriate to consider the logic of the situation when explaining why Claudius decided to invade Britain. Even so, one year 5 child in the extension phase tried to reconstruct the situation, ideas and values of Elizabeth I in order to explain her delay in ordering the execution of Mary, Queen of Scots, appealing to wider policy considerations in a way not found in many year 9 children in this type of task.

Decoupled conceptual strands
It seems that children's ideas about causal explanation and about the explanation of actions do not develop hand-in-hand in most instances; we need to think in terms of different strands here. Both may be seen by curriculum planners and those concerned with assessment as falling under the heading 'explanation', but this does not mean that a single attainment target (spelling out one path by which children's ideas about explanation develop) can accommodate both. It is important to differentiate at least these two broad areas of explanation if teaching is to be targeted effectively.

Prospects
Insights into the development of children's ideas about history offer the prospect of basing history education on progression rather than aggregation, and of allowing history teaching objectives to be couched in terms which are discipline determined rather than content determined. This would allow history teaching to develop powerful intellectual (but specifically historical) tools, within pluralist and open historical content. From a research perspective, a further worthwhile step would be small-scale collaborative work involving researchers in several countries in order to develop 'close-cultural' comparison of progression in second-order understandings. There is also a need to explore further the relationship between substantive knowledge and second-order progression. Such work could be of benefit to history education at all levels around the world.

NOTES

1. In particular, R. Ashby and P.J. Lee, 'Children's concepts of empathy and understanding in history', in C. Portal (ed.), *The History Curriculum for Teachers* (Lewes: Falmer Press, 1987), pp. 62–88; H. Cooper, 'Young children's understanding in history', PhD dissertation (London: University of London, 1991); A.K. Dickinson and P.J. Lee 'Understanding and research', in A.K. Dickinson and P.J. Lee, (eds), *History Teaching and Historical Understanding* (London: Heinemann Educational, 1978), pp. 94–120; Dickinson and Lee, 'Making sense of history', in A.K. Dickinson, P.J. Lee and P.J. Rogers (eds), *Learning History* (London: Heinemann Educational, 1984), pp. 117–53; P. Knight, 'A study of teaching and children's understanding of people in the past', *Research in Education*, 44 (1990), pp. 39–53; D. Shemilt, *History 13–16 Evaluation Study* (Edinburgh: Holmes McDougall, 1980), and 'Beauty and the philosopher: Empathy in history and the classroom', in Dickinson, Lee and Rogers (eds), *Learning History*, pp. 39–84.

2. For important pioneering work, in Britain see D. Shemilt, 'The devil's locomotive', *History and Theory*, 22, 4 (1983), pp. 1–18; in the USA see J.F. Voss, M. Carretero, J. Kennet and L.N. Silfies, 'The collapse of the Soviet Union: A case study in causal reasoning', in M. Carretero and J.F. Voss (eds), *Cognitive and Instructional Processes in History and the Social Sciences* (Hillsdale, NJ: Lawrence Erlbaum, 1994), pp. 403–29; and in Spain see M. Carretero, M. Asensio and J. Pozo, 'Cognitive development, historical time representation and causal explanations in adolescence', in M. Carretero, M. Pope, R. Simmons and J. Pozo (eds), *Learning and Instruction* (Oxford: Pergamon Press, 1991), pp. 27–48, M. Carretero, L. Jacott, M. Limón, A. López-Manjón and J.A. Léon, 'Historical knowledge: Cognitive and instructional implications', in Carretero and Voss (eds), *Cognitive and Instructional Processes*, pp. 357–76, and M. Limón and M. Carretero, 'Evidence, evaluation and reasoning abilities in the domain of history: An empirical study', in J.F. Voss and M. Carretero (eds), *International Review of History Education: Vol. 2, Learning and Reasoning in History* (London: Woburn Press, 1998).

3. See P.J. Lee 'Historical imagination', in Dickinson, Lee and Rogers (eds), *Learning History*, pp. 85–116.

4. H. Borke, 'Piaget's view of social interaction and the theoretical construct of empathy', in L.S. Siegal and C.J. Brainerd (eds), *Alternatives to Piaget* (London: Academic Press, 1978), pp. 29–42; Margaret Donaldson, *Children's Minds* (Glasgow: Fontana Press, 1978); J.H. Flavell, 'The development of inferences about others', in T. Mischel (ed.), *Understanding Other Persons* (Oxford: Blackwell), pp. 66–116; and J. Piaget, *The Child's Conception of Space* (London: Routledge & Kegan Paul, 1956).

5. See M. Hughes, 'Egocentricism in pre-school children', PhD dissertation (Edinburgh: Edinburgh University, 1975).

6. See Ashby and Lee, 'Children's concepts of empathy'.

7. P.J. Lee, A.K. Dickinson and R. Ashby, 'Children making sense of history', *Education 3–13*, 24, 1 (1996), pp. 13–19.

7

Significance in History: Students' Ideas in England and Spain

LIS CERCADILLO

This study focuses on a comparative analysis of progression in the understanding of a specific second-order concept, historical significance. This kind of research belongs to a tradition – originally British – of qualitative studies developed around the understanding of structural concepts in history education. The comparative approach works at two levels: first, in the relationship between two educational systems, those from England and Spain; second, in the comparison of cognitive development across three bands of age: 12–13, 14–15 and 16–17 years.

Two main sources contribute to attain a definition of the notion of significance in this project: the theoretical discussion held by philosophers and historians, and the empirical analysis of students' ideas. 'Significance' is at the heart of the subject matter of both academic and school history. It is fundamental to understand a distinctive feature of the discipline: discrete events are not understandable without their link to a frame of reference and a sense of authorship behind them. Academic and school history are not the same thing, but reducing the gap between both 'histories' becomes necessary in order to reach a more sophisticated historical understanding.[1] Therefore, the idea of contextuality and the relativization of historical knowledge are important for students if they are to realize the implications of the (re)construction of the past by historians. Teachers need to confront the question of how historical interpretations differ and why, because this has turned into a core issue in history curricula in Europe and North America. However, in contrast to other structural concepts such as empathy or causality, the notion of significance has been neglected until very recently in the domain of history education research.

116

'Significance' is a key concept in any exploration of students' ideas about the general question of interpretations and progress in the construction of historical knowledge. This concept is defined through questions such as: What makes things significant in history? Is significance in history seen only as fixed, as an intrinsic value of historical occurrences or is significance viewed as tied to context, as a referential value? Students' ideas about significance can be ordered across these extreme (and additional middle) stages, in a process which sums up, at least, two variables: cognitive development and teaching/learning experiences (along with influences from outside school). The extent to which these ideas may be similar or may diverge when arising in two different European countries was one of the goals of this work.

Specific aims of the present study were:

1. exploring English and Spanish pupils' understanding of a particular historical second-order concept – significance – in its different attributions, and in its relationship to historical accounts;

2. categorizing and mapping the understanding of these concepts to delineate patterns of progression in history learning in two countries, England and Spain;

3. investigating the possible similarities and differences in the categorized ideas of progression in both countries.

Grounded on empirical data, the delineation of patterns of progression may provide a coherent framework to the history curriculum and assessment at secondary school. It can also contribute to elaborate a more homogeneous design of history curricula across European countries, not just in content but, most importantly, in historical understanding.

Academic Context of the Research

This kind of research is rooted in various traditions that have developed innovative educational theory and teaching practices related to history, both by psychologists and subject matter specialists. These traditions include the new history movement in England (in the 1970s and 1980s), studies linked to the recent educational reform in Spain (in the 1980s and 1990s), research from a cognitive approach to learning in the last decade in North America and current research in England.

Early British research in history was mainly grounded on Piaget's theories. The application of the Piagetian developmental model of thought to history led to a series of studies in the 1960s and 1970s by Hallam.[2] They concluded that history demanded levels of formal operational thinking which pupils could not achieve below 16 years of age. Alarmed by these negative conclusions and interested in the unique nature of historical thinking, some authors argued for a new framework for research: an open-ended analysis not based on the formal operational thinking modelled by Piaget, but on history's particular structure.[3] The first work on pupils' second-order ideas from an epistemological, history-specific, non-Piagetian standpoint was carried out by Dickinson and Lee.[4]

New approaches to history education developed in the 1970s and 1980s had come to be referred to as the 'new history'. The most comprehensive model of an empirical approach to teaching on the basis of the new history was the Schools Council History 13–16 Project (SCHP), in which an important number of British secondary schools participated from the mid-1970s onwards. SCHP questioned the Piagetian models of age. The project's founders argued that traditional history education could lead students to possess copious amounts of historical information, while having no idea where this information came from. Nonetheless, they could reach higher levels of understanding if history was conceived as a distinctive form of knowledge, and its curriculum structured around the nature of historical enquiry and historical explanation, not merely on factual knowledge. SCHP had a strong impact upon pupils' historical understanding.[5] Educational researchers started to turn to the conceptual analysis of philosophers about the epistemology of history, and to the ideas teachers and students hold about particular historical concepts, especially those which conferred on history its distinctiveness – second-order or organizing concepts. These concepts are the object of understanding; skills are the mechanisms of that understanding, whereas substantive concepts are the medium within which pupils' historical understanding can be developed.

A question was pending. Can history offer a 'pure' form of conceptual complexity, described in terms of levels that are content-free? The need to answer that question and to overcome some of the obstacles that the study of substantive concepts presented are some of the reasons why a shift to an emphasis on structural or second-order concepts was made.[6] Cause, reason, empathy, time, continuity and change, relevance and significance, are 'organizing' concepts of the discipline; they act as the medium to apprehend history's internal logic. To reach a sophisticated historical understanding, substantive content should be shaped by second-order concepts and historical procedures. Students tend to hold certain tacit ideas which facilitate or hinder their historical understanding; the knowledge of the ideas pupils have about organizing concepts, and the subsequent construction by researchers of an underlying hierarchy, are means to approach students' reasoning development in history. In this way, it is possible to delineate patterns of progression, or hierarchies of conceptual complexity in history learning, which are applicable to all kinds of content.[7]

Notwithstanding the pioneer character of British research in the field, during the last decade an increased interest in history teaching and learning has been developed among some academic groups in other countries (including the USA, Canada, Germany and Spain), especially among educational psychologists. Investigations are addressing a multiplicity of historical topics, from children's historical misconceptions to the analysis of textbooks, from teachers' elaboration of instructional explanations to the comparative study of causal reasoning in experts and novices.[8]

Recent studies have tended to confront second-order ideas as overarching concepts, such as evidence and enquiry, rational and causal explanation, or narrative discourse and accounts in history. They are establishing solid bases for the development of further research. An overarching structural element in history is significance. The study of this notion is a way to approach the question of interpretation, an alternative way to face the distinction between structural or causal explanations (analytical discourse) and intentional explanations of history (narrative discourse).[9] Here narrative is considered as inherent to history writing. Concentration on significance allows us to by-pass the duality intentional/causal explanation.

Enquiry into students' ideas about historical significance can lead us to important implications for teaching and learning. First, one of motivation: if there is no meaning in history, if they do not grasp what they are asked to know and understand, what is the use of studying it? Second and no less important, that of thought development: how students' reasoning in this particular strand contributes to their general historical knowledge and understanding.

Some researchers started from analysis of substantive content, not from focusing on second-order ideas.[10] However, in the 1990s most research on historical significance and education has followed the approach of students' motivation. This work is concerned with what is considered important for children and adolescents themselves, as students; what is significant at each age group and for different cultural groups.[11] In order to define the notion of significance, two approaches are addressed here. The 'multicultural approach' mentioned above and a second focus that understands significance in the context of historical accounts.

Historical significance can be attributed at two levels: as basic meaning, which corresponds to the historical fact (and includes the condition of intrinsic significance), and as secondary meaning, which relates to the broader notion of historical interpretation.[12] In this last case, significance is almost always a relative matter, because it implies relating one event to another, and because the relationships between events depend on the point of view or perspective that historians take to construct their accounts.

The nature of significance is also defined by reference to its sources, or types, which establish the relationship between events and processes in an account. The significance of any occurrence may change because historians select different points of view which spring from different sources. We consider here the following possible attributions of significance: contemporary (linked to rational understanding), causal (in connection with relative importance and causal explanation), pattern, symbolic and significance for the present and the future.

Ultimately, the question is knowing more about students' ideas to help them make sense not only of events and episodes of history, but also to make sense of the 'story' in which those events and episodes are located. A key point may rest in Shemilt's advice to learners, teachers and researchers:

> Students should not be taught that 'p' is important whereas 'q' is not as though these were facts. Rather *they should be taught to debate the significance of events according to specified criteria.* They may, for example, learn to differentiate between the immediate and the historical, or long-term, significance of events; to use and to apply the concepts of 'change' and 'development', 'trend' and 'turning point'; and to understand that the significance attributed to events varies according to the questions posed by the historian, and to the spatial and temporal contexts of the narrative within which those events are to be located.[13]

A preliminary picture of students' awareness of elements that determine significance has been presented by the Project CHATA work on global differences in accounts,[14] based on stories offering different tone, time-scale and theme, and asking also for reasons why particular events may be described differently. That work provides a starting-point for this more specific investigation and also suggests methodologies for approaching students' ideas about alternative accounts. The present investigation goes beyond the CHATA research in closely targeting the notion of significance, and in comparing, for the first time, students' understandings in two countries.

Institutional Context: England and Spain

Educational systems

The interest of a comparison between students from England and Spain is explained because the reformist movements that led to the implementation of new curricula in these two countries developed in part as a consequence of a common deeper reflection on the importance of educational research. The changes in teaching and learning have followed parallel pathways in both countries, though much research in history education in the last three decades was pioneered in Britain, as explained above.

TABLE 7.1: ENGLISH AND SPANISH EDUCATIONAL SYSTEMS

	Grade English	Age	Grade (Spanish)	
Key stage 1	Year 1	5–6		
	Year 2	6–7	1°	Educación
Key stage 2	Year 3	7–8	2°	primaria
	Year 4	8–9	3°	
	Year 5	9–10	4°	
	Year 6	10–11	5°	
Key stage 3	Year 7	11–12	6°	
	Year 8	12–13	1°	Educación
	Year 9	13–14	2°	secundaria
Key stage 4	Year 10	14–15	3°	obligatoria
	Year 11	15–16	4°	(ESO)
A-levels	Year 12	16–17	1°	Bachillerato
	Year 13	17–18	2°	

Some of that research has inspired and substantiated the basic lines of development of reformed curricula in the two countries: the National Curriculum (NC), set up in England since 1988, and the Law for the General Organization of the Educational System (LOGSE), established in Spain since 1990[15] (see Table 7.1).

Since the implementation of that legislation, the study of significance as a structural concept has gained a direct relevance for teaching and learning history in both countries. Although understanding of the concept of significance is not explicitly statutory for all year groups, there is an implicit requirement for key stage 4 and A-levels (and their Spanish equivalents). However, there is no clue for progression in the indications of both general laws, a key question if any criteria for assessment in this particular concept need to be established.

Educational traditions

Comparative educational research may contribute to deepening our understanding of the difficulties of learning from others. Students in England and Spain have been exposed, because of their relation to different educational traditions, to different teaching practices. Or this is, at least, a common assumption.[16] Conventionally, the teaching of history in England focuses on the use of sources and in-depth studies, on discussion and a sense of uncertainty in the epistemological study of the discipline. In Spain history teaching tends to be centred on content, coverage and chronology, and didactic methods are preferred to enquiry. These could work as starting hypotheses, but when two educational systems need to be compared, the danger lies in identifying too simplistically, educational traditions in teaching practices. For this study, more complex similarities and differences emerged than common assumptions might foresee, through the analysis of the data generated in pilot studies and the main sample.

In the design of this research, the question of the relationship between substantive content and second-order ideas, of knowledge and understanding, was always present, though such a clear-cut dichotomy continues to be a matter of controversy. The choice of second-order concepts – particularly historical significance – was viewed as more suitable for a comparative approach. If research were grounded on substantive concepts, it would be more difficult to link the investigation done in different countries. However, once patterns of progression in both countries were constructed, it became clear that concepts such as historical significance in history are apprehended relatively independently of the events narrated, making practicable a more qualified comparison.

Methods and Research Tools

Methods

Methods followed in this study are mainly qualitative: the exploration of pupils' ideas works through 'non test-like' kinds of activities. Written tasks, both in open and closed questions, were designed not to get a 'right' answer, but to delve into student's thinking about history. Interviews were intended to clarify, complement or deepen students' written answers, in order to obtain further in-depth data. However, the size of our main sample – 144 students in the main study – also allowed a quantitative analysis in some specific aspects, such as comparison of levels of progression by grade and country, once patterns of progression had been delineated in the qualitative analysis. The goal was not so much to provide a foundation for making claims about general populations as to identify the range of responses that occur in a particular setting in two different countries.

The enquiry starts with listening to students and looking at their responses, to decide how those responses can be categorized in order to construct patterns of progression which can be comparable across three groups of age and across two cultures. The criteria employed to categorize students' responses stem from the theoretical debate carried out by philosophers and historians, which establishes a conceptual apparatus, always subject to further discussion, in terms of what to think about students' responses.

Sample features and administration procedures

Early work for pilot studies and for the final study was centred on the design and trial of appropriate targeted material. The goal was that data generated by students' responses could be deployed to construct models of how progression may take place through different levels of historical understanding. For the main study, small groups of students were chosen from different kinds of schools. The number of schools involved in the main study was six in each country. In order to attain a representative sample of schools, they were also matched by geographical location: urban, suburban and rural. In England, the selection of schools was made in inner-city London, Cambridge, Cambridgeshire and Essex. In Spain, it took place in inner-city Madrid and Community of Madrid.

Empirical data for the main study were obtained from three age bands: 12/13, 14/15 and 16/17 years, which correspond respectively to year 8, year 10 and year 12. The number of participants was 72 students in each country, making a total of 144 students. In Spain and England, mixed-ability groups of four members each were selected for each age-band. Each group aimed to include one high-ability student, two middle-ability and one of low-ability, preferably two girls and two boys. They were matched by ability, gender and social background across countries as groups, not individually. Selection was made by the researcher (at random) from lists elaborated by the teachers. Groups were matched by social background through schools because, although all participants for the final study were selected from state and comprehensive schools both in England and Spain, performance results and social background varied from one school to another.

Data gathering for the main study was accomplished during the second and third terms of the academic year 1997–98. It was carried out in two separate periods in each country, one for each of the two task-sets that were presented.

Research tasks
Tasks were designed to be self-contained. Two topics were chosen. The first one was the defeat of the Spanish Armada in 1588. It aimed at comparing the perceptions of English and Spanish students of a familiar topic, which is commonly taught at school in both countries, but which has different significance for each one. The second topic was the campaigns of Alexander the Great. Picked as 'neutral' content, the choice of this topic implied two main things: no direct involvement of any of the students – Spanish or English – was presumed; and it was expected to be a topic not generally taught in school, either at compulsory level or at A-level or Bachillerato. Both themes were organized in the form of two competing accounts, or different interpretations of the same matter in connection with the question of significance. (See the stories in the Appendix.)

Types of Significance: Model of Progression

Data analysis
The main focus of this chapter is on the categorization of students' epistemologies when confronted with issues of historical significance in its various types. After successive stages of analysis of the main empirical data, categories were developed and redefined. The analysis of

124

responses was based on the following stages: (a) successive readings and rereadings; (b) the inductive construction of categories; and (c) the coding of each appearance of indication for the categories in students' responses. For category systems, particularly in this broad strand ('Types of significance'), counter-coding was carried out by an independent coder and agreement of 90 per cent was achieved.

Categories of progression in this strand were devised on the grounds of the distinction and variety of types of attributions and their association with two other concepts – contextuality and importance.[17] Specifying the different attributions or possible senses in which we speak of an occurrence as significant will operate as an indicator to classify students' ideas. Our typology of significance is shown in Table 7.2.

TABLE 7.2: TYPES OF SIGNIFICANCE

| Contemporary |
| Causal |
| Pattern |
| Symbolic |
| Present/Future |

The nature of significance was defined here by reference to its attributions or sources, which establish the relationship between events and processes in a historical account. Historians start from different viewpoints that emerge from different sources, among which we have determined our classification to satisfy the following research questions:

- Do students see significance in history as fixed or variable?
- In the case that they see significance as variable, to what extent are they aware of the possible different attributions that may work within a historical account?
- Do they consider that the 'logic of the narrative' obeys different theories of causal weighting and different emphasis on a particular type of significance?

These questions were answered inferentially through several items from our research tasks. For the present chapter, question 1 from the Spanish Armada task (SA Q1) and question 1 from the Alexander the Great task

125

(AG Q1) were selected. Having read the stories from each task-set, pupils were asked: 'Some historians think that the Spanish Armada's defeat / what Alexander did was really important; others think it wasn't. What do you think? Was it important or not? Explain why it mattered *or* why it did not matter.'

The main characteristics and pointers for the categorization of each type in students' responses are presented below.

Contemporary significance The event is seen as important by people at the time in the context of their perceptions, beliefs and view of the world. In students' responses everything is treated as inclusive (anything is considered as such that applies, in general terms, the perspective of people at the time). We study students' justifications about possible different perceptions of an event as significant, depending on what agents are considered. For instance, in the case of the Spanish Armada, we observe whether they are attentive to the different viewpoints of contemporaries, such as the English and the Spanish, or whether their own nationality prevents them from perceiving the others' side: 'I think the Spanish defeat was very important as Philip lost some of his subjects' confidence ... Philip lost his reputation of being an invincible warrior'. (Sarah, year 8, Sp 4, SA Q1, written response)[18]

Causal significance This situates an event or process in relation to its causal power; hence its significance is in part dependent on later events or consequences. An awareness of this type always indicates a degree of contextuality in our empirical data. Particular features and uses of language may act as rules to systematize data coding. Hints for causal significance are verbs such as 'help', 'make', 'benefit', 'enable', 'change', 'achieve', 'instigate', 'result', 'allow'; expressions such as 'have an influence', 'due to', 'contribute to'; consequential links such as 'therefore', 'so', 'that is why', 'in that way'; or the use of counterfactuals and such like. The nature of causal significance may be defined in pupils' answers by aspect (economic, social, political, religious, cultural), geographical space (England, Spain; Greece, Persia) and time-scale (immediate, short-term, long-term): 'I think the Spanish Armada was important because otherwise the Spanish Empire would have grown and people and countries would lose their individuality; they would be forced to become Catholics despite their beliefs'. (Charlotte, year 10, En 4, SA Q1, written response)

Pattern significance This indicates a higher level of sophistication in students' answers. It is always allied to contextuality, and usually refers to concrete models of emplotment, such as the concepts of progress and decline. Markers for data coding within this category are those terms which allude to the event or process as a turning-point or a trend in a developmental account, such as words like 'milestone'; or expressions such as 'the world might not be the same way it is now', 'he broadened the horizons', 'he achieved new things', 'he opened up the world', 'it was a first step', 'he was ahead of his time' (in AG tasks); or 'it marked the beginning', 'from then on', 'it was the start of', 'since then', 'that way it started' (in SA tasks).

> I think it was an important defeat, for England as much as for Spain. In the case of Spain, it meant the beginning of the Empire's decline, above all economically, which went on until the XVIII century. For England, it was the beginning of one of its best periods. Not only it [England] improved after the defeat, but also it remained to be a Protestant country and increased its territories. (Elena, year 12, Sp 1, SA Q1, written response)

Symbolic significance This may operate from the perspective of people of the past and from the perspectives of subsequent presents; we need then to disentangle this category from other types, like significance for contemporaries or significance for the present and the future. Unlike the latter type, symbolic significance is attached specifically to notions of moral example (lessons from history) and mythical past. It implies a particular 'use of history', related to issues of national identity and partisanship, but it can also be connected to more general or a-historical concepts, such as piety or transcendental moral ideas. In all cases, this type of significance is recognized in both English and Spanish educational systems as one of the distinctive features that make history an essential part of the curriculum. Through the analysis of students' wording, we can establish markers for data coding. General expressions such as 'it showed', 'it gives an indication', 'it proved', 'it highlighted' usually indicate this type of attribution; it can also be expressed by more definitive terms, such as 'teaches us', 'set a good example for others', 'he was an inspiration for', 'was a role model', and so on. 'Yes, because once he built new towns, he could spread the Greek culture from those towns, and *that is good*. Besides, afterwards Napoleon read about him *to follow his example*' (Ana, year 10, Sp 3, AG Q1, written response, emphasis added).

127

Significance for the present and the future Closely related to importance and causal weighting, it only operates in the long term, when the bond with the future is emphasized. In our data, links will be shown to the category of intrinsicality and to the notion of subjective significance. With respect to the concrete context of research tasks, empirical data may work at different levels of progression, from a Calvinistic causal logic in the sense of linear endless transmission[19] to a contextualized comparison of different presents, that at the same time establishes the effects in psychological terms: 'I think it was important and that it did matter. What Alexander achieved was an amazing feat over such a large area ... The idea of such a large empire at that time is amazing, before that of Rome, and also of such a military success ... We still think he's quite a big figure today' (Liz, year 12, En 6, AG Q1, written response).

TABLE 7.3: NUMBER OF RESPONSES BY YEAR GROUP AND COUNTRY FOR EACH TYPE OF SIGNIFICANCE

Question 1		Year 8			Year 10			Year 12		
		En	Sp	Total	En	Sp	Total	En	Sp	Total
	SA	15	17	32	12	12	24	17	16	33
CS	AG	20	24	44	18	22	40	20	24	44
	Total	35	41	76	30	34	64	37	40	77
	SA	16	14	30	22	21	43	22	20	42
CA	AG	10	7	17	18	16	34	21	20	41
	Total	26	21	47	40	37	77	43	40	83
	SA	3	3	6	8	7	15	12	14	26
PA	AG	6	4	10	8	2	10	13	8	21
	Total	9	7	16	16	9	25	25	22	47
	SA	5	0	5	6	3	9	14	5	19
SY	AG	7	1	8	15	1	16	14	4	18
	Total	12	1	13	21	4	25	28	9	37
	SA	3	1	4	5	1	6	6	4	10
PF	AG	4	0	4	6	2	8	12	4	16
	Total	7	1	8	11	3	14	18	8	26

Note: EN = English students; n = 24 / year   CS = contemporary
Sp = Spanish students; n = 24 / year   CA = causal
SA = Spanish Armada task-set   PA = pattern
AG = Alexander the Great task-set   SY = symbolic
Total = 24 × 2 countries × 2 tasks = 96 / year   PF = present/future

FIGURE 7.1: TYPES OF SIGNIFICANCE, QUESTION 1

Total

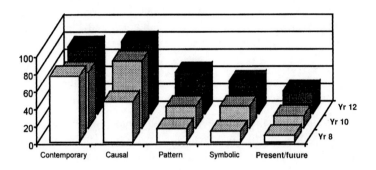

English

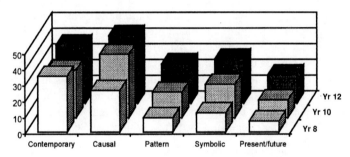

Spanish

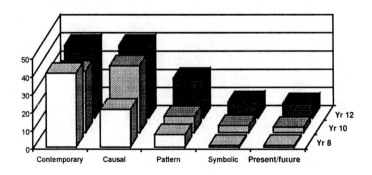

Quantitative Study by Types of Significance

The first objective in our quantitative analysis is knowing the number of responses that include each type or attribution, by year group, country, task and question. Data are shown in Table 7.3 and Figure 7.1. From these data several patterns emerge:

(a) The most frequent types of significance mentioned in students' responses are contemporary and causal, this being the case in both countries and across different content in all year groups.

(b) Contemporary significance is the type most frequently indicated among younger students (year 8), by a considerable margin over other types, including causal significance. It is even more frequent in the Alexander tasks than in the Spanish Armada set, and slightly more frequent among Spanish students of all grades in the Alexander set.

(c) Pattern significance ranks third in all three year groups, but the proportion of responses is much higher in year 12 than in year 10 or year 8. Across countries, the pattern type is better represented among English participants of all grades in the Alexander tasks, whereas it is represented by almost the same number of responses in the Spanish Armada tasks. Yet it is interesting to note that while there is exactly the same number of answers in year 8 and year 10 in both countries, in year 12 the proportion is higher within the Spanish group in the Armada set.

(d) Symbolic significance is the fourth type in frequency of answers both in England and Spain, but it shows a very much higher number of responses among English students. In this particular feature, differences across countries are striking in both task-sets.

(e) Significance for the present and the future is the least frequently represented among all students, particularly the younger, including those of year 10. Nonetheless, there are variations across countries. As in the case of symbolic significance, the relation with the present is almost absolutely ignored among Spanish students in years 8 and 10, and only one-sixth of year 12 students allude to it, whereas a small proportion of English students in the lower grades and half of students in year 12 do mention this kind of significance. Those general trends were corroborated by data from other items in the research tasks.

Analysis suggests, then, that pattern and symbolic notions of significance and significance for the present and future may be considered as possible indicators of progression in historical understanding. Usually, pupils who mention some of those three types do mention contemporary and/or causal types as well. Contemporary and causal notions may be seen as a prerequisite for a more complete perception of significance in history.

The idea of progression in types of significance described above is empirically grounded. It is the older students who tend to mention a greater variability of types. One-third of students from year 8, almost half of students from year 10 and the majority of those from year 12 who mentioned pattern, symbolic or 'connection with the present' notions of significance did also suggest contemporary or causal notions in their responses. This could be interpreted as indicating that these students reached particular levels of understanding, but went beyond those to achieve more sophisticated modes.[20]

In the consideration of variety of types of significance, then, contemporary and causal alone were located at a lower level than other types, even if internal variations in the former occurred. This led us to disregard internal variations in contemporary and causal attributions, that is, variations within types (such as differentiation of short- and long-term consequences in causal significance) in pursuit of variations across attributions. A second indicator of progression was the consideration of significance as variable within or between attributions or types of significance. Therefore, variable significance between accounts is always regarded at a higher level than fixed significance, even if only the contemporary and the causal types are indicated.

Bearing those reasons in mind, the model of progression in types of significance was defined as follows:

Level 1: No allusion to any type of significance

Level 2: Intrinsic and single significance

Level 3: Fixed contextual significance: significance is fixed within/ across attributions (contemporary and causal only)

Level 4: Fixed contextual significance: significance is fixed within/ across attributions (besides or other than contemporary and causal)

Level 5: Variable contextual significance: significance varies within/ across attributions

5.1: contemporary and causal

5.2: besides or other than contemporary and causal.

In the following section we consider concrete examples across age groups and countries which reveal internal variations and degree of sophistication within each level. Then we will chart students' responses by levels of progression from a quantitative perspective.

Discussion of Examples

Level 1: No allusion to any type of significance
At this level, significance is viewed as fixed, attached to the occurrence in itself; a-historical moral views may appear. It may involve problems of general comprehension. In the following examples, sometimes the explanation is constructed by means of disconnected events, with no clear relation to the occurrence that is being treated (see Eva's example, below). There is no mention of any type of significance, and explanations are usually established in everyday terms, with no reference to the concrete stories or to the historical context in general (see Carl, below).

> England and Spain were confronted. Great Britain became independent... Spanish was spoken more than Chinese and English. (Eva, year 10, Sp 3, SA Q1, interview)

> I don't think it was important for Armada's defeat because the Spanish should keep what they have and leave England alone. The Spanish should never come over to England in the first place. (Carl, year 8, En 5, SA Q1, written response)

These kinds of responses do not code for contemporary significance, because students here speak in a-historical terms, with neither implicit nor obvious approach to the perspectives of the contemporaries.

Level 2: Intrinsic and single significance
This level entails a consideration of significance as fixed, in intrinsic terms, measured always by the contemporary type. A wide range of elaboration in ideas, nevertheless, underlies the rigid limitation of levels. But what is definitive here is the capacity of students for seeing the notion of significance exclusively in the contemporaries' terms.

> What Alexander did was important, because he invaded Asia Minor and he kept winning victory time after time. (Yetti, year 8, En 2, AG Q1 written response)

Yes, he is important, because nobody else could equal the Empire he had. The Persian Empire had a reputation of being very well disciplined warriors; the Macedonians were also like that. (Manuel, year 12, Sp 1, AG Q1, written response)

Here significance is assessed by the fact of the conquests and victories, not by the implications of those (at least, explicitly); it is considered intrinsically, attached to the importance of the conquest in itself, not with reference to one or various context(s).

Level 3: Fixed contextual significance: significance is fixed within/across attributions (contemporary and causal only)
The bulk of answers within this level are categorized as 'causal only' or 'contemporary and causal in association'. For a majority of pupils significance may be reduced to the attribution of 'importance', that is, issues of significance of an occurrence in history are mainly explained by its consequences, in general terms. Variation in the degree of sophistication within this level is considerable, ranging from ideas that are very close to intrinsicality, where contemporary significance and immediate causal types of significance can be difficult to define and disentangle (Pupinder, below), to ideas about causation that include different time scales and aspects (Clare, below).

> I think it was important what Alexander had done, because it was what his father was going to do, but he died, or it could be that Alexander wanted more power and wanted a bigger empire.
>
> Yes, he made Greece a popular and powerful country. (Pupinder, year 10, En 3, AG Q1, written response and interview)
>
> It was important that Alexander spread his armies over a large area as it spread the knowledge of the Macedonians to many people and places.
>
> ... spread of Greek culture ... They had a lot of knowledge, didn't they? (Clare, year 12, En 5, AG Q1, written response and interview)

In the first example, the evaluation of importance starts from a previous state of affairs: he makes a connection with consequences, but significance is the same across attributions. In the second example, significance is seen across different time-scales: immediate (spread of armies) and long-term (spread of knowledge), but within a single type – causal.

133

Level 4: Fixed contextual significance: significance is fixed within/across attributions (besides or other than contemporary and causal)
This level classifies those responses which distinguish different types of significance, but make no reference to the possible conflict between accounts in the consideration of types, or to the internal variation of types. A typical example from the Spanish Armada task-set could be:

> I think the Spanish Armada's defeat mattered. It was the beginning of lots of other things, like loss of respect for Philip II and his army. It started Spain's loss of land and colonies because the defeat showed that Spain could be beaten. It led to hope, respect and a feeling of power for the British who then continued to attack Spain, weakening it. (Emma, year 10, En 2, SA Q1, written response)

Emma makes an analysis of the significance of the Armada's defeat based on immediate consequences for England and Spain ('loss of respect for Philip II and his army'; 'led to hope ... for the British'), on the view of the Armada as a turning-point ('It was the beginning of lots of other things ... It started Spain's loss of land') and on the symbolic repercussions of the event ('the defeat showed that Spain could be beaten'). She gives indication of an awareness of different focuses of significance that we call causal, pattern and symbolic.

At the same level, a Spanish example, this time from year 8 and in Alexander's task-set could be this one:

> I think it was important, because Alexander the Great did not want just to conquer Persia, but he wanted to explore new lands as well, and he built more than seventy new towns. Besides, he opened new trade routes and he brought the single silver currency, which would improve trade.
>
> I think it is important, he discovered new lands, he did not only conquer, but he wanted to discover new things, he opened the way for other people who tried to do what he had done, but somewhere else ... the world became bigger, people started to think. (Víctor, year 8, Sp 1, AG Q1, written response and interview)

Víctor starts his evaluation of Alexander's importance in intrinsic terms, very accurate in detail and focused on Alexander's intentions, but then he goes a step forward when he considers repercussions of a different order. These are: causal (economic aspects, short-term consequences); pattern (Alexander's expansion as a turning-point in history, economically and, above all, culturally); symbolic (other people followed his example).

134

Level 5: Variable contextual significance: significance varies within/ across attributions

Responses falling into this level are characterized by the discrimination of various layers of significance *within* and *across* accounts, through the reference to different attributions of significance and the allusion to a conflict between accounts (in question 1), whether the conflict is perceived as factual or criterial. To illustrate the lower category within this level, in which significance is seen as variable but is limited to contemporary and causal attributions, the following example has been selected:

> I think that the defeat of the Spanish Armada was important because the English had more confidence in their queen after it. It mattered because if the English had lost confidence in their monarch, there may have been a rebellion which would have threatened Britain's ability to remain a powerful country. In some ways, the defeat was less significant as it failed to bring the war between the Spanish and the English to an end.
>
> The Spanish and the English lost quite a lot of money. (Alice, year 10, En 4, SA Q1, written response and interview)

Alice makes a distinction of different degree of importance when the context changes: the defeat was important to make the English situation clear, since the Protestants won, but it did not have the same importance in solving the Spanish–English war. This answer was categorized, therefore, under the contemporary and causal types; then she would belong to level 5.1 of our scale.

In the examples shown below, both students are aware of variations of significance across the two accounts (at a factual level), but add further attributions apart from contemporary and causal, thus giving us the criterion for their classification at a higher category than previous examples of this level.

> I think it did have a great importance, not because of the fact in itself, but rather because of the feeling of frustration that this caused, apart from the immense human and economic losses that this caused. I think that with this fact, Great Britain dominated the seas at the expense of Spain.
>
> Spain got into a crisis, she lost her naval power, since then Spain went down, little by little. (Alberto, year 12, Sp 2, SA Q1, written response and interview)

135

Here Alberto is aware of the immediate impact of the defeat on its contemporaries ('human and economic losses'), but he explicitly denies its intrinsic importance with historical distance ('not because of the fact in itself'). The key point is that all these students relativize the significance of the event in their consideration of diverse types of significance and different degrees of importance through contexts.

A similar approach is made by Stuart:

> I think that the Spanish Armada's defeat was important but not very. It helped along with other things to weaken Spain as a power. However it did not completely destroy Spain. Without other causes, Spain may still have been powerful for a long long time [*sic*]. People's opinions of Philip II changed. He didn't seem so powerful. Overall though, Spain recovered and is nowadays a well-developed country.
>
> It was quite important, but not really really important. Other things led to the downfall of the Spanish Empire, not just the Armada's defeat. Afterwards, Spain remained quite powerful. (Stuart, year 10, En 3, SA Q1, written response and interview)

To him, significance changes according to context *across* attributions: contemporary, mid-term consequences and in a very long-term process. It also changes *within* attributions in that the evaluation of importance for contemporaries (Philip and the Spanish) is relative: the defeat is seen as a quite important event, but not as the main cause of a later decline; it is clearly a contributory cause. The defeat's importance is played down when it is located in a broader pattern of development. This is a very sophisticated way of reasoning for pupils of year 10, as the number of responses for this level of progression shows (13 English against three Spanish in year 10 out of 24 in each country). More English than Spanish pupils fall into this level in years 10 and 12.

The highest degree of sophistication is reached in the combination of different types of significance and an awareness of the conflict as a criterial issue, for instance, in the account constructed by Israel:

> It was not that important from the battle's point of view; they just missed the chance to invade England, but they didn't lose lands. From the historical point of view, it is very important indeed; since this defeat, the beginning of the Spanish decline started. If we look at what happened later, to Spain … If this is taken as a starting-point. (Israel, year 12, Sp 5, SA Q1, interview)

Although the Spanish perspective is predominant here, this pupil establishes clear criteria to define importance: the point of view that one may take, either evaluating the defeat in its intrinsic terms (negative as immediate consequences for the Spanish Empire), or in its historical significance (positive as the starting-point for the Empire's decline).

Quantitative Study by Levels of Progression in Types of Significance

Students' responses were charted according to the scale shown above. Progression is charted according to: (a) the consideration of fixed versus variable significance and (b) the variety of types of significance represented in the number of responses for each group, and according to the specific types of significance touched in each year group; pattern, symbolic and significance for the present and the future indicate a higher degree of elaboration in historical thinking.

TABLE 7.4: NUMBER OF RESPONSES FOR EACH LEVEL OF PROGRESSION IN TYPES OF SIGNIFICANCE BY GRADE, COUNTRY AND TASK-SET

Question 1		Year 8			Year 10			Year 12		
		En	Sp	Total	En	Sp	Total	En	Sp	Total
	SA	2	3	5	1	1	2	0	0	0
Level 1	AG	1	0	1	0	1	1	0	0	0
	Total	3	3	6	1	2	3	0	0	0
	SA	5	9	14	0	2	2	0	0	0
Level 2	AG	7	14	21	1	5	6	0	2	2
	Total	12	23	35	1	7	8	0	2	2
	SA	9	6	15	8	8	16	3	3	6
Level 3	AG	6	4	10	3	10	13	4	7	11
	Total	15	10	25	11	18	29	7	10	17
	SA	7	4	11	10	10	20	12	10	22
Level 4	AG	7	3	10	10	3	13	9	9	18
	Total	14	7	21	20	13	33	21	19	40
	SA	1	2	3	6	3	9	8	11	19
Level 5	AG	3	3	6	9	5	14	12	6	18
	Total	4	5	9	15	8	23	20	17	37

Note: En = English students; n = 24 / year
Sp = Spanish students; n = 24 / year
SA = Spanish Armada task-set
AG = Alexander the Great task-set
Total = 24 students × 2 countries × 2 tasks = 96 / year

FIGURE 7.2: TYPES OF SIGNIFICANCE, QUESTION 1
– LEVELS OF PROGRESSION

Total

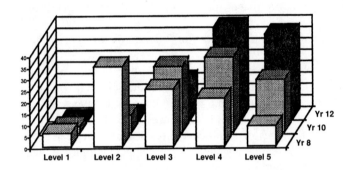

English

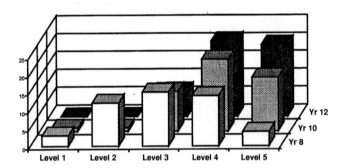

Spanish

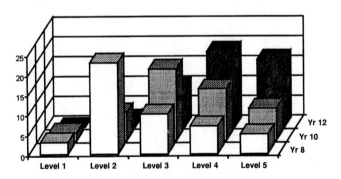

The main features of Table 7.4 and Figure 7.2 might be interpreted as follows:

Level 1 The lowest level in the scale, applies to a very small proportion of answers, and only responses from year 8 and year 10 fall into this classification ('no allusion to any type of significance'). No year 12 students in either country are categorized at this level.

Level 2 ('intrinsic and single significance'), however, includes one-third of students from year 8, the Spanish ones in a bigger proportion. No English student in year 12 reasons at this level, and there are only two cases in Spain. From these data it can be inferred that there is a much stronger tendency in younger students than in older ones to justify issues of significance exclusively in contemporary terms.

Level 3 ('fixed contextual significance: contemporary and causal only'). Almost one-third of answers in year 10 fall into this level, but Spanish year 10 pupils are better represented in it than the English ones. Most answers from English year 10 pupils fall into level 4. For year 8, less than one-quarter of Spanish responses and one-third of English ones correspond to level 3. Almost one-fifth of responses from year 12 belong to level 3, again in a bigger proportion in Spain.

Level 4 Almost half of responses from year 12 are classified under level 4 ('fixed contextual significance: besides or other than contemporary and causal'). For English students from year 10 this level is first in number of answers and for year 8 it is third (after level 2 and level 3). Twice as many year 8 English students belong to this level as Spanish year 8 students. The distribution of responses that include different types of significance apart from contemporary and causal seem to confirm the meaning given to these types as indicators of higher levels of ideas.

Level 5 ('variable contextual significance'; 5.1, 'contemporary and causal'; 5.2, 'besides or other than contemporary and causal') corresponds to one-third of responses from year 12, this time in a higher proportion for the English ones in the Alexander set; in the Armada set, the proportion is slightly higher for the Spanish. Less than one-fifth of responses from year 10 (most from English pupils) and a tiny sample from year 8 (again, most from English pupils) may be allocated to Level 5. As the distribution in number of responses shows, English students reach the last levels of progression (levels 4 and 5) in a higher proportion than Spanish students in years 10 and 12.[21]

The model of progression delineated in this research integrates a categorization that addresses students' ideas about importance and other related notions that have to do with significance and historical narratives, associated with diverse types of significance. These ideas develop from an unawareness of issues of importance and types of significance as connected to historical tasks, through notions of importance and significance understood only in intrinsic terms, with no reference to a wider context or variation by types, towards ideas about significance as contextual, but fixed within or across attributions, with different consideration of types and, beyond that, to the understanding of significance as contextual and variable within and across attributions. Progression is confirmed in the samples of both countries, but cross-cultural differences are detected; English students' ideas seem to develop towards higher levels of progression at earlier ages than Spanish students; more English students than Spanish ones operate within advanced sets of ideas in all year groups, particularly at younger and intermediate ages.

Conclusions

1. Progression in English and Spanish students' ideas runs from responses that indicate no awareness of the notion of importance or contextuality in historical matters, and make no allusion to types of significance or refer to the contemporary type only (levels 1 and 2), towards responses that establish some kind of criteria to assess significance in different contexts and mention various types (level 5.2).

2. We found a crucial boundary allocated between level 4 and level 5, when students learn that the significance of any occurrence is relative to its frame of reference and to the different perspectives particular accounts may imply. This boundary is evident after the analysis of two indicators: (a) the consideration of significance as variable between accounts and across types of significance; and (b) the mention of types of significance other than contemporary and causal.

3. English students' responses in this sample reach a higher order of ideas on types of significance (higher levels of progression) at earlier ages than Spanish ones. This difference remains consistent in both tasks. However, at age 16–17 the gap across countries is considerably reduced.

4. With regard to the variability of types, the most frequent types of significance mentioned in students' responses are contemporary and causal. The majority of students justify the significance of an occurrence in history in causal terms, by an appeal to the consequences of that occurrence. In younger students (in both countries), there is a strong tendency to assess significance exclusively in contemporary terms. Pattern and symbolic types and significance for the present and the future are employed in a much higher proportion by older students than by younger or intermediate ages. The mention of these types is more frequent among English participants in all year groups and across task-sets (except for Spanish year 12 in the Armada task-set). These differences across countries, in both task-sets, are more striking in the symbolic notion.

NOTES

1. Education is necessarily normative, but school history has to point in a certain direction; this should be academic history. See K. Jenkins, *On 'What is History?' From Carr and Elton to Rorty and White* (London and New York: Routledge, 1996).
2. R. Hallam, 'Piaget and thinking in history', in M. Ballard (ed.), *New Movements in the Study and Teaching of History* (London: Temple Smith, 1970), and 'A study of the effect of teaching method on the growth of logical thought with special reference to the teaching of history', PhD dissertation (University of Leeds, 1975).
3. M. Booth, 'A recent research project into children's historical thinking and its implications for history teaching', in J. Nichol (ed.), *Developments in History Teaching*, Perspectives 4 (School of Education, University of Exeter, 1980), and 'Ages and concepts: A critique of the Piagetian approach to history teaching', in C. Portal (ed.), *The History Curriculum for Teachers* (Lewes: Falmer Press, 1987).
4. A.K. Dickinson and P.J. Lee, 'Understanding and research', in Dickinson and Lee (eds), *History Teaching and Historical Understanding* (London: Heinemann Educational, 1978), pp. 94–120.
5. D. Shemilt, *History 13–16 Evaluation Study* (Edinburgh: Holmes McDougall, 1980).
6. This is evident in Dickinson and Lee, 'Understanding and research'; Shemilt, *History 13–16 Evaluation Study*, 'The devil's locomotive', *History and Theory*, 22, 4 (1983), pp. 1–18, 'Beauty and the philosopher: Empathy in history and the classroom', in A.K. Dickinson, P.J. Lee and P.J. Rogers (eds), *Learning History* (London: Heinemann Educational, 1984), pp. 39–84, and 'Adolescent ideas about evidence and methodology in history', in Portal (ed.), *The History Curriculum for Teachers*; R. Ashby and P. Lee, 'Children's concepts of empathy and understanding in history', in Portal (ed.) *The History Curriculum for Teachers*, and 'Information, opinion and beyond', paper given at the symposium Elementary and Secondary Students' Historical Understanding: Recent findings from the USA and Europe, AERA conference, San Diego, CA, 1998; P.J. Lee, R. Ashby and A.K. Dickinson, 'Progression in children's ideas about history', in M. Hughes (ed.), *Progression in Learning*, BERA Dialogues, 11 (Clevedon: Multilingual Matters, 1996), and '"There were no facts in those days": Children's ideas about historical explanation', in M. Hughes (ed.), *Teaching and Learning in Changing Times* (London: Blackwell, 1996); I. Barca-Oliveira, 'Adolescent students' ideas about

provisional historical explanation', PhD dissertation (Institute of Education, University of London, 1996); H. Cooper, *The Teaching of History in Primary Schools* (London: David Fulton, 1997); P. Lee, '"None of us was there": Children's ideas about why historical accounts differ', in S. Ahonen *et al.*, Historiedidaktik, Norden 6, Nordisk Konferens om Historiedidaktik, Tampere 1996 (*History Didactics: Sixth Nordic Conference on History Didactics, Tampere 1996*) (Copenhagen: Danmarks Laererhøjskle, 1997); and P. Lee, and R. Ashby, 'History in an information culture', paper given at the AERA Annual Meeting, San Diego, CA, 1998.

7. See Lee, Ashby and Dickinson, 'Progression in children's ideas'. Examples of patterns of progression already constructed are: causation (Shemilt, *History 13–16 Evaluation Study*); evidence (Lee, Ashby and Dickinson, 'Progression in children's ideas'); rational explanation (P.J. Lee, A.K. Dickinson and R. Ashby, '"Just another emperor": Understanding action in the past', *International Journal of Educational Research*, 27, 3 (1997), pp. 233–44; accounts (Lee, 'None of us was there'); and provisional explanation (Barca-Oliveira, 'Adolescent students' ideas').

8. T. Trabasso and L. Sperry, 'Causal relatedness and importance of story events', *Memory and Language*, 24 (1985), pp. 595–611; C. Perfetti *et al.* 'How students use texts to learn and reason about historical uncertainty', in M. Carretero and J. Voss (eds), *Cognitive and Instructional Processes in History and the Social Sciences* (Hillsdale, NJ: Erlbaum, 1994), pp. 257–83; S. Wineburg, 'The psychology of learning and teaching history', in D.C. Berliner and R.C. Calfee (eds), *Handbook of Educational Psychology*, (New York and London: Macmillan, 1996), pp. 423–37; B. von Borries, 'Representation and understanding of history', in J.F. Voss, and M. Carretero (eds), *International Review of History Education, Vol.2, Learning and Reasoning in History* (London: Woburn Press, 1998); M.J. Rodrigo, 'Promoting narrative literacy and historical literacy', in Carretero and Voss (eds), *Cognitive and Instructional Processes*, pp. 309–20; J. Domínguez and J.I. Pozo, 'The learning of causal explanations in history: concepts and procedures', paper presented at the Second International Seminar on History Learning and Instruction, Las Navas del Marqués, July 1994; and M. Carretero, A. López-Manjón and L. Jacott, 'Explaining historical events', *International Journal of Educational Research*, 27, 3 (1997), pp. 245–54.

9. J. Wertsch and M. Rozin, 'The Russian revolution: Official and unofficial accounts', in Voss and Carretero (eds), *Learning and Reasoning in History*.

10. M. McKeown and I. Beck, 'Making sense of accounts of history: Why young students don't and how they might', in G. Leinhardt, I. Beck and C. Stainton (eds), *Teaching and Learning in History* (Hillsdale, NJ: Erlbaum, 1994), pp. 1–26; and I. Beck and M. McKeown, 'Outcomes of history instruction: Paste-up accounts', in Carretero and Voss (eds), *Cognitive and Instructional Processes*, pp. 237–56.

11. P. Seixas, 'Historical understanding among adolescents in a multicultural setting', *Curriculum Enquiry*, 23, 3 (1993), 'Conceptualizing growth in historical understanding', in D. Olson and N. Torrance (eds), *The Handbook of Education and Human Development* (Cambridge, MA and London: Blackwell, 1996), pp. 765–83, and 'Mapping the terrain of historical significance', *Social Education*, 61, 1 (1997), pp. 22–7; L. Levstik, 'Any history is someone's history: Listening to multiple voices in the past', *Social Education*, 61, 1 (1997), pp. 48–51; T. Epstein, 'Sociocultural approaches to young people's historical understanding', *Social Education*, 61, 1 (1997), pp. 28–31; and K. Barton, "Best not forget them": Positionality and students' ideas about significance in Northern Ireland', paper presented at AERA annual meeting, Montreal, April 1999.

12. C.B. McCullagh, *The Truth of History* (London: Routledge 1998).

13. D. Shemilt, 'Review essay' on L. Kramer, D. Reid and W. Barney, *Learning History in America: Schools, Cultures and Politics* (Minneapolis, MN University of Minnesota Press, 1994), in *History and Theory*, 35, 2 (1996), p. 260. The emphasis has been added.

14. Lee and Ashby, 'History in an information culture'.

15. Department for Education and Science (DES), *History in the National Curriculum* (London: HMSO, 1991) and Department for Education (DFE), *History in the National Curriculum* (London: HMSO, 1995); MEC *LOGSE (Ley Orgánica 1/1990, de 3 de octubre, de Ordenación General del Sistema Educativo)* (BOE 4-10-90) (Madrid, 1990).
16. M. McLean, *Educational Traditions Compared* (London: David Fulton, 1995).
17. 'Contextuality' is the underlying notion in students' ideas when the significance of an occurrence is evaluated with reference to a wider context. 'Importance' here is understood in two senses: (a) a specific component of causal explanation; and (b) a wider notion as overlapping 'significance'.
18. Examples will be identified by student's first name, year group, school (either English or Spanish), number of school, task-set and question.
19. See Shemilt, 'The devil's locomotive'.
20. It is _not_ asserted here that pattern, symbolic and present/future types themselves are higher levels than contemporary and causal, but that possession of a richer armoury of concepts to handle significance certainly is.
21. Multidimensional frequency analysis was performed for Question 1. The positive correlation between level and year is clearly evident in the figures in Table 7.4; for example, year 8 was heavily weighted for levels 2 and 3, year 10 for level 4 and year 12 for levels 4 and 5. Progression was demonstrated, therefore, on the basis of the distinction of types of significance in students' responses within each year group (χ^2=81.36, df=8)., The general trend noted, that English students tended to reach more sophisticated levels of understanding at an earlier age and in a higher number than Spanish ones, was confirmed statistically (χ^2=15.96, df=4, p<0.01). These interactions are mostly ascribed to differences at year 10. Chi-squared analysis of data showed a significant association between level and country, again for year 10 (χ^2=10.6, df=4, p<0.05). For this year, English students reached higher levels of progression than Spanish ones.

APPENDIX

STORY 1

Chapter 1

The Greeks feared the Persians, who had been powerful enemies for a long time.

Alexander became king of Macedonia (in the north of Greece) when his father was killed. He took over his father's plans to rule Greece and invade Persia. Thanks to his father's reforms, Alexander had a well trained army and efficient weapons.

Alexander's military success was due to his skill as a general, and to the loyalty he inspired in his troops. He shared his soldiers' dangers and was injured many times in battle.

Chapter 2

On his advance throughout the Persian Empire, Alexander appointed Persians, not just Greeks and Macedonians, as leaders and generals.

STORY 2

Chapter 1

The Greeks feared the Persians, who had been powerful enemies for a long time.

When Alexander became king of Macedonia (in the north of Greece), he decided to invade Persia. He had a well trained army and efficient weapons.

Alexander's campaigns were not just of conquest; he also wanted to explore new lands. From the beginning of his expeditions, he took with him experts in history, science and geography.

Chapter 2

In his march towards the East, Alexander founded more than seventy towns, most of them with his name. Each town had around ten thousand people from different races. The city of Alexandria in Egypt still bears his name today.

143

He built more than seventy new towns. They were built partly to provide a base for governing and defending the area round about them.

Alexander tried to adopt the local habits of the peoples he conquered, to gain their loyalty. But Macedonian generals often resented the fact that Alexander considered all races in his empire as equals. Besides, the Greeks thought their culture was superior to that of the Macedonians or the Persians.

Chapter 3

Alexander was called 'great' because of his military genius. But his ideal of an empire based on Greek culture and racial equality was never achieved.

After his death, when he was only thirty-two years old, Alexander's generals fought between them and his empire fell apart.

Most of the towns Alexander built quickly fell into ruins after his death. The kingdoms which succeeded Alexander dominated the Greek speaking world, but not for very long. Two hundred years later they were invaded by Rome, which would become a big empire.

STORY 1

Chapter 1

Before the sending of the Spanish Armada, Elizabeth feared the power of Philip. He could help the English Catholics who did not want her as Queen. Elizabeth was determined to keep England Protestant and independent from Philip. She sent armies to help Dutch Protestants in their struggle against Spain.

Philip wanted to avoid religious divisions to keep his Empire together and tried to stop any foreign interference in his countries. In 1588, Philip decided to send an Armada to invade England, but he did not succeed.

Chapter 2

After the Armada's defeat in 1588, the Spanish said: 'We have lost our reputation as invincible warriors.' Philip lost some of his subjects' confidence.

Alexander opened up new trade routes from the West to the East. He introduced a single silver coin to enable merchants to buy and sell goods anywhere in his empire.

Chapter 3

He was only thirty-two years old when he died, but after him the world opened out; it seemed to people a much bigger place, in the way it did later on after the discovery of America.

The towns Alexander built were one of his longest-lasting achievements. These towns helped spread Greek ideas and ways of living into all the lands he ruled over.

In Roman times, Julius Caesar, Augustus and other Roman emperors visited Alexander's tomb in Alexandria (Egypt), to pay tribute to him.

For the next fifteen hundred years, many people wrote about the life of Alexander, not only in Europe, but in Persia and India as well. Even much nearer our own times, in the nineteenth century, the French emperor Napoleon used to read about Alexander's life to learn from his example.

STORY 2

Chapter 1

Before the sending of the Spanish Armada, Elizabeth feared the power of Philip. Holland belonged to the Spanish Empire, so the Spanish controlled some of the seas round English shores. Elizabeth wanted to prevent this.

Philip had to face English attacks on his merchant ships and a revolt in Holland, backed up by the English. In 1588, he sent an Armada to invade England, but he did not succeed.

Chapter 2

After the Armada's defeat in 1588, the war between Spain and England went on. English ships still attacked Spanish merchant ships.

England continued to be an independent country. Holland also benefited from the defeat of 1588; Spain accepted that Holland was no longer part of the Spanish Empire;

Holland became an independent country sixty years later.

Queen Elizabeth became more popular in England. The English thought God was on their side. They said: 'God blew and they were scattered.' Philip still sent new armadas, although they did not succeed because of storms. Elizabeth decided then to spend more money on new fleets.

Although England continued to be an independent, Protestant country, the defeat of the Armada did not prevent Philip II from being the most powerful king in the Western world.

The Dutch revolt against Spain continued. It actually went on until 1648, when Holland finally became a separate country.

Chapter 3
In the seventeenth century, the English and also the Dutch continued to attack Spanish colonies in America and Asia.

Different uprisings happened in areas of Spain itself. They were backed up by other countries, such as France or England. The size of the Spanish Empire made it hard to keep it together. Even so, Portugal was the only part of the Spanish Empire (apart from Holland) to become independent from Spain before 1700.

During this same period of one hundred years or so, the English managed to establish settlers in North America, mainly in parts that the Spanish had ignored.

In 1700, Spain still controlled more land in Western Europe than any other country, and had the biggest Empire in America and the Pacific.

The defeat of the Armada was a decisive setback to Philip II and the Spanish Empire. It was the beginning of the Empire's decline. In the hundred years that followed, the Spanish economy gradually became weaker.

The war cost a lot, and state debts increased both in England and Spain. In spite of these economic problems, Spain had one of the most powerful armies until 1800.

Chapter 3
In the seventeenth century, the English established settlers in North America and in India.

During the eighteenth century, Britain gained control of the world's sea routes by defeating Spain and France in a series of wars, such as in Trafalgar (1805). Spain lost most of its European Empire in 1713, and most of its American colonies in 1830.

From the 1800s, the invention and use of new machines allowed Britain to be the first country in selling industrial goods to the rest of the world. By the end of the nineteenth century, Britain had a big Empire. Most of its countries became independent by 1950.

Though the Spanish economy developed much later, nowadays both England and Spain are two well-off countries within the European Union, and today more people throughout the world speak Spanish than any other language except English and Chinese.

145

8

Development of Historical Explanation in Children, Adolescents and Adults

ANGELA BERMÚDEZ AND ROSARIO JARAMILLO[1]

The purpose of this research was to broaden knowledge of structural qualitative changes in students' understanding of history in order to construct a tentative model of the relationship between historical agents and their context in students' explanations of historical events. We approached the problem from a cognitive–constructivist perspective that states that the development of thought is strongly associated with experiences within domain-specific areas, not only in questions of content matter, but also considering the theoretical questions pertaining to the discipline.[2]

A mapping of the theoretical debate involved in the creation of historical knowledge and explanation was constructed,[3] mainly concerning the tension between structural and intentional explanations. This mapping was contrasted with the psychological and pedagogical research on students' understanding of historical explanation.[4]

Our analysis finally focused on the following categories and subcategories:

Category: Historical agent
1. Ability of empathetic reconstruction of historical agents' intentions, actions and social practices in their context.
2. Ability to understand historical agents' political and social identity, and to differentiate agents depending on their group affiliations.

Category: Explanation of historical events
1. Ability to understand the influence of circumstances on intentionality (freedom or determination to act of historical agents depending on their context) and of the agents' ability to influence and/or change their context depending on different causal factors.

2. Complexity and form of causal explanations both in the amount and type of factors included and in the type of theoretical web created.
3. Ability to understand and define the characteristics of times of major change. (Why deep social changes occur at the time they do.)
4. Relation between explanatory theory and historical events. Ability to build proper generalizations in order to explain an event within disciplined theories and ability to move back and forth from theories to concrete examples.

For the purpose of this chapter we selected number two of the 'historical agent' category and numbers one and two of the 'explanation of historical events' category.

Research Method

The clinical interview method was used to gather information on the theoretical models underlying students' historical understanding and explanations of the national independence of Colombia. We selected the 30 interviews that seemed to show the clearest structures of thought that could allow us to establish student's differentiation of elements and the complexity of relationships among these elements. We compared many students at elementary and secondary levels, a few at the university level, and three expert historians whose answers were used to create 'ideal types'. Based on the analysis of these interviews, we constructed the following progression model describing the development in the quality of student's explanations at five levels. Students are classified at four levels; the fifth level corresponds to expert historians.

Levels of Development in Comprehension of Historical Agents and Explanation of Historical Events

Level 1: Criteria

Criteria for constructing understanding of the historical agent	Criteria for the construction of historical explanation
• Identity. • Differentiation among agents. • Reference to individual and/or collective agents. Collective agents treated as undifferentiated aggregate of people who are either mentioned with the name of an individual (Spain is the king of Spain) or	• Influences of the circumstances on intentions and actions and of the agent over his/her circumstances. • Complexity and structure of the explanation. Relationship between intentional action and circumstances in explanation of historical events.

are kept as totally ethereal and uncharacterized.

- Individual and collective agents' identity is based on personality and appearance traits, usually stereotyped by inadequate generalizations of an individual's characteristics. The way of being, the interests and the intentions of agents are immutable and part of their nature.
- Essential criteria in order to define identity given by virtues and moral vices independently of historical context and of their social groups.
- They speak in the words of the agents themselves.
- Dualistic differentiation of agents: antagonistic and Manichean opposing groups, identified by their moral traits (greedy, self-centred conquerors vs. generous, noble subjugated Indians).
- Consideration of only one group of the agent's belonging; differentiation may be based on nationality, hierarchy of power, class or ideology; cannot articulate simultaneous belonging to more than one of those groups ('a pro-monarchy Creole').
- Can only make a first degree differentiation between groups; cannot differentiate at the interior of any group. ('Cannot see that Creoles can have both pro-independence and monarchist people simultaneously belonging to that same group'.)

- Circumstances generate agents' actions but do not affect nor modify their intentions. Intentions are immutable and proceed from agents' free will.
- Agents act on the impulses of their personalities. It is with that personality that agents respond to situations described in very general terms.
- The structure of the explanation is simple and relationships are only one way. It has the shape of a chain: an intention, an act; another intention, another act. Visually, it has the shape of a fan in which the centre is the intention from which acts or events stem out in only one direction, without any relationship between them.
- When relationships between events show up, students explain them by one event serving as an example for the agents of another event or by having a domino effect where the first event triggers all the others by simple imitation of it.
- Causal explanations only exist if there is a concrete historical agent who has the desire and will to carry it out. Events are reduced to the actions of some of the participants. There is always someone responsible for things happening. ('High prices are caused by greedy kings and they trigger a conscientious leader to revolt.')
- References to contexts are so imprecise and stereotypical that they can refer to any time in history.
- Mechanical and unidirectional relationship between the wish of an agent and the occurrence of the event.
- It is inconceivable that an agent would act independently of his/her intention or without being conscious of it. Omnipotent leaders. The only limitations are phenomena which escape human control such as earthquakes, death etc. Events that never happened, did not do so because no one ever wished them to happen.

Level 1: Interview excerpt – an 8th grade student

Interviewer: Why do you think Independence took place?

Student: Because we were not happy with the way we were treated by the Spaniards. We wanted to govern ourselves. It was awful to put up with a government that simply does not treat you right.

Interviewer: What was the way we were treated like?

Student: They dominated us and they imposed taxes on bodies and we paid without getting anything in return. We had no right to be represented (in parliament). They were the only ones who governed and because of that we became independent so that we could have a government for ourselves, in order to be able to change everything that we did not like. It seems to me that the leaders of the independence – Bolivar, Santander – what they wanted was the common good. They were generous, they wanted to help the people, they wanted to help them progress. But two people are not enough. Bolivar, during his time, was able to, but he died. Same as what happened with Jefferson. And the United States has gone through some tough times. It is not eternal.

Interviewer: Both countries had leaders who were worried about the common good. Why was it then that the United States was able to make it and the other countries were not?

Student: I imagine it was the method used by the government. Because they said, we are going to eradicate slavery, and that was it, that's what they did.

Level 2: Criteria

Criteria for constructing understanding of the historical agent

- Collective agents seen as aggregate of people but not as social groups with shared traditions, experiences, purposes etc.
- Abstract collective agents such as institutions (the crown, the state) are personalized in their leaders.
- Agent still possesses a natural identity and intentions but these can be affected and partially modified by the contexts. Contexts influence and partially modify predefined interests but do not determine them.
- Understands the behaviour of the agents as a response to the circumstances and not as an immutable trait of personality, virtues or vices.
- Individual or collective agents can belong simultaneously to more than one group, and implications of these belongings in identity can be co-ordinated in simple ways.

Criteria for the construction of historical explanation

- Social circumstances more clearly differentiated as social, economic, and such like, situations but with little historic understanding.
- The circumstances do not conform to contexts in which people become themselves; it is just an environment where people act.
- Historical agents able to mark the path of events with their own actions. Their ability to change circumstances can only be restricted by other agents with whom they cannot come to an agreement. The intention of the agents continues to have relatively omnipotent causal power.
- Leaders are created by circumstances and not only by their own conscious election.
- Historical events are usually explained by means of a mechanism in which agents react to their circumstances acting with intention and generating transformations

149

- In *ONE* of the two basic opponent groups, new opposing sub-groups can be differentiated. A group of people live in some common contexts but others are not shared, so that they may have different interests and behaviours in relation to one common situation (elite and common people or Creoles, Indians and Blacks in spite of all being Americans).
- Each one of the groups conceived in a homogeneous and monolithic fashion.
- Relationship between main opponent agents as well as second-order agents continues to be dualistic and antagonistic.

with their actions. ('The Crown prohibited trade because Spain was broke.')
- Attempt to establish relationships between some events and others or some circumstances and others. Explanation in circumstantial (non-personal) terms is viable until the abstract relation between diverse social structures needs to be established. Person loses ability to maintain argumentation in strictly political, economic domain and transfers it to the will of the agents.
- In spite of the presence of actions and events in the explanations, these bear no difference among themselves. There is a tendency to think that every event is an intentional act.
- Historical explanations of greater complexity because of types of elements included (group and individual intentions) and political, economic contexts, and number of elements simultaneously considered. Density of relationships established between different elements is scarce.
- Structure of the explanation appears as an incipient spider-web with simultaneous sets of short causal chains. There is no distinction in the temporal status.
- Explanations lack an encompassing character in which some phenomenon is inclusive of another.
- Spatial horizon is amplified and the articulation with what is going on in other places becomes clearer, although still without an idea of a world system or a totality with structural links.

Level 2: Interview excerpt – the same student, one year later, ninth grade[5]

Interviewer: Why don't you tell me about what happened during the Independence?

Student: The Independence of Colombia took place because of the lack of satisfaction there was because of the problems the Creoles had with the Spaniards, because they were dominating politically and economically and the time had come for us to have control over what we were doing … The domination was in the area of commerce, there were things that the Creoles could not trade in, there could not be any Creole political leaders; everything we had was for Spain. Nothing remained here. There was slavery.

Interviewer: Why could they not trade or participate in politics?

Student: Because we were a colony. Back then, Spain would handle all of those things.[6]

Interviewer: Why didn't Spain want there to be any trade?

Student: Because Spain was broke, we were the ones who were producing and Spain was spending away what we were producing. They were broke because they had waged a war with the Arabs. The kings had many whims; they were not handling the money properly, for the benefit of the people; instead they were spending it away.

Interviewer: Why is it that in other countries this was not happening but it was happening in Spain?

Student: The kings did not care about the good of the community, only their own good: 'Who cares if we screw up the future of a nation. We have the savings of the colonies and any time we need to, we can get money out from them and that way we keep our people happy, and we were even happier.'[7]

Interviewer: Why did the Crown not want the Creoles to participate in trade?

Student: There was the movement of the Enlightenment. Any kind of exchange could be used against Spain because people were in the mood for freedom. To trade meant to open up a space where there could be economic independence.

Interviewer: Tell me more about trade and the Enlightenment.

Student: It is two different things but in both there are personal contacts. Through trade they come in contact with other cultures. In commerce it was the economic independence from Spain. They begin to maintain themselves: 'When one is trading and producing, then where do the profits go?' When they realize that everything goes to Spain: 'No, this cannot go on like this; it must come back here, something must remain for us, otherwise, what are we doing?'

On the side of culture there was the Enlightenment. People were generally unhappy. I do not know how they were able to find out what was going on in the world, but when they realized that the French Revolution was going on and about their ideals then they said: 'No, with this we can support ourselves. We can teach people about nationalism, freedom, independence, and do away with Spain once and for all.'[8]

Interviewer: Why do you think that almost all the revolutions, the one in the United States, the one in France, then the one in Nueva Granada, the one in Mexico, took place more or less at the same time?

Student: Technology, cultural movements, the problems of the Monarchy began to be clear. The Creoles were realizing all of this ... I don't know if the kings had agreed to abuse the colonies or if it was because they thought that the colonies were becoming stronger in trade and that they could not defend themselves on their own. They started to oppress them more and the only thing they attained was a total explosion. It is that everything took place more or less at the same time.[9]

Level 3: Criteria

Criteria for constructing understanding of the historical agent	*Criteria for the construction of historical explanation*
• Collective agents seen as social groups who share common experiences, purposes and traditions. • Identity of the individual and collective agent depends upon interests derived from belonging to social, political and economic groups. • Mechanical and deterministic conception of the relationship between context and historical agents. This makes for belonging and identity to be poorly differentiated, scarcely prone to change and partially stereotyped. • The more abstract collective agents such as political and social institutions have a defined identity because of their role within the system, independently of who exercises their functions. • Beginning of a third-degree differentiation. Greater groups are differentiated within, creating subgroups which are determined by their particular social conditions. But within these subgroups, cannot identify factions or tendencies within the social subgroups because agents are all determined by one same social condition. • Identification of common characteristics and interests between groups which were previously differentiated. These integrating 'reconciliations' are more complex and precise.	• Understanding of the influence of circumstances over intentions and interests of historical agents, because of recognition of circumstances as the growth media from way back that had an influence on agents' ideas, actions, interests or the way they perceive reality. • Greater precision in the historical placement of the agent's circumstances and in the way that interests are generated, but how circumstances influence historical agents is still simplistic and mechanical and, to a certain extent, stereotyped. The insufficient degree of differentiation of the historical agent or of the events of his/her time compels the characterization of a whole social group or subgroup to be described under a very general category. Only a skeleton of historical reality is available because there is not enough knowledge of detailed facts. • No tension is perceived between conditioning agents and freedom. • Agents can act upon the system depending on its strength and the rhythm of transformation of social structures. • Agents continue to be active leaders of the trends in their society, but now explanations are complemented with involuntary events and processes and with the dynamics of the social system. But they are so entirely characterized as a result of their circumstances, that they lose.

- The dualistic character of antagonism is conquered once antagonisms between differentiated subgroups are seen, but this antagonism continues to be quite Manichean.

their individuality and become totally replaceable.
- Explanation based on interaction between actions, interests and circumstances.
- Intentions clearly related to circumstances of the agents and there is an understanding that there are events that are not intended. Often, intentions are stated in terms of political or economic projects.
- An agent is not yet conceived as having contradictory interests and thus can never be doubtful of his/her course of action. The agent is never drifting off course, nor a victim of destiny, nor trapped in contradictory conflicts of interest.
- No longer any references to moral and personal intentions as essential criteria for the explanation.
- A system of ideas transforms the existing mentality and thus people act accordingly.
- Representation of society as part of a relatively complex world system with elements of different times, space, social dimensions and individual and collective intentionalities related among each other. Political, economic and ideological spheres become articulated in a complex and dynamic totality in which particular events take place. The dynamics of the way the system works is multidirectional but relationships are not reciprocal. The essential form of the explanation is a more complex tri-dimensional spider-web.

Level 3: Interview excerpt – 9th grade student

Interviewer: Tell us about Independence.

Student: The Independence in America has three precursors: the French Revolution, the Industrial Revolution, the Revolution of the Commoners and the unhappiness of the Creoles, of the social classes.

Interviewer: Why were the Creoles unhappy at that time?

Student: Those who had the political or administrative power were the Spaniards. The economic power was in the hands of the Creoles. Then what they wanted was to have the political power so that they would be able to trade since the Spaniards were the ones who gave out the clauses for this purpose. If the Creoles had both powers, they would be able to produce and export and therefore their earnings would be greater and they would not have to send their earnings out to Spain.

The French Revolution comes with human rights. As a result of the revolution, these decrees were formed and if they had not been formed, people would continue to think about discrimination ... It helped the lower classes to have a new way of thinking. 'If we are free then why are we allowing others to rule us?' The French Revolution also helped Independence when Napoleon enters Spain and takes over. If it had not been like that then I think that the American countries would be just now becoming independent.

The Industrial Revolution was not a precursor but it helped the Independence. It took place in almost all of Europe, especially England. I think they had fights amongst the greatest powers. For England it was a good thing that Spain would lose, would fall from that power. The Creoles needed money to buy weapons, food. Then the Industrial Revolution affected them; then in exchange it was to receive natural resources (if it can be said) from America. They received wool, cotton, coal, salt, etc. Then that stuff would be sent to England in exchange for the weapons and so on.

It was not so important, the part of the weapons but that financially they lent them [*sic*]. For example, in Africa there was weapons production. Then England would buy them at a low price, would send them to America at a higher price and in exchange they would obtain a lot of profit.

Level 4: Criteria

Criteria for constructing understanding of the historical agent

- Collective intentions understood as social projects.
- Individual characteristics of the agent recovered in order to characterize his identity.
- Co-ordinated belonging to various social, economic, political and ideology groups makes it possible to generate diverse and even contradictory interests and a more flexible identity.
- Identity can also derive from ample visions regarding philosophical, social and political ideals which transcend the immediate interests determined by

Criteria for the construction of historical explanation

- Intentions of the agent are conditioned by a social context that generates interests, ways of perceiving reality and perspectives of the future. But a tension between conditioning and freedom is perceived. Agent can also act rationally and with freedom be able to transcend these determinants.
- Freedom begins to be understood as the ability to opt rationally for one action or another.
- Same circumstances can influence in diverse ways the different agents of a group or subgroup; thus they can have

belonging to a social or economic group. If ideals conflict with other interests it is not possible to solve this contradiction synthetically: one affiliation has to dominate over others or they coexist incoherently.

- Differentiation of the members of a subgroup can be made, not only in terms of their individual behaviour but also in terms of the tendencies or factions among them. Particular traits which differentiate one and another faction can be stated, among other traits which are common.
- Since elements and interests common to the various factions can be abstracted from differences, alliances between subgroups can be understood, and explained.

different intentions and act differently although they may have many things in common.

- Historical agents continue to be essentially active and leaders of the paths of their society.
- The possibility to transform circumstances is restricted because of the contradictions of interests between agents and/or because of the contradictions of interests that the same agent may have in relation to a given situation.
- Individual traits can partially influence development of events. It is possible that in the absence of certain leaders things would have taken a different turn.
- Keeps interactive character between intentional act and circumstances but without mechanical dynamics. Non-intentional acts added.
- The problem that actions produce unintentional results or ones different from those the agents wanted is resolved. Understand agents may initiate an action with a given intention and that on the way either they are swept away by the circumstances they did not control well or because their interests change as do the results of their experiences.
- Causal and hermeneutic explanation begin to be combined.
- The system has attained a higher level of concretion and detail in the characterization of the elements of the relationships that exist among them.
- Systemic explanation with greater complexity due to its multidirectional interdependent and reciprocal relationships. Transformations within the elements and relationships of the system affect the system in its totality. Causal chains now do not only occur simultaneously.
- Additionally, various outcomes given the same event are brought forth: a political event may have certain kinds of consequences in the economic sphere which may be entirely different from the ones that occur in the ideological sphere.
- They have no difficulty in establishing explicit relationships between stable structures, gradual changes of medium duration and sudden changes.

Level 4: Interview excerpt – seventh-semester university history student

Interviewer: What was the Independence all about?

Student: It was about a confrontation between Creoles and Spaniards. Some influenced by liberal ideals – all of the liberal thought of the Enlightenment – and another group of Creoles and Spaniards influenced by the ideas of absolutism, the so-called royalists. I think it was a, confrontation between liberals and absolutists. It was a result of what was going on in Europe at the time, with absolutism and the current of liberal thought.

Interviewer: Why did the patriots have those ideals?

Student: They were inspired by those ideals because they were searching for an ideological and social revolution. What they were after was a reform of the whole colonial world in which they were immersed. The same was happening in Spain.

Interviewer: Who was it that was interested in Independence?

Student: In the case of the Spaniards who were interested in independence, they come to this because there were Spaniards who were equally liberal in the peninsula and in the colonies, who agreed with a liberal project that would reform the State and society. Actually what they were looking for was a liberal order in which Spain would keep the colonies. What they were after was to modernize the Spanish imperial system, but in the end they are swept away by this whole current. With all the movements that were generated, with all the disarray of the colonial order, I believe they were sunk in there.

Level 5: Criteria

Criteria for constructing understanding of the historical agent	*Criteria for the construction of historical explanation*
• Diversity of individual and collective agents that act in a partially intentional way because of the limitations of the various systems of belonging. • Refined identities, toned down and not stereotyped by co-ordination of individual elements (experience), social elements (belonging) or historical elements, which mould identity. • Co-ordination of the contradictions of identity of the agents. Even if they have	• Understanding of the intentions of the individual or collective agent is maintained within the social context which conditions it, but it now possesses concrete examples which describe how the agents consciously or unconsciously generate the context. • Conditioning relationship between circumstances and intentions liberates from mechanical and partial representations and wins the flexibility in which agents may transcend determination and act in divergent

been incomprehensible to them, they are clear to the person thanks to their temporal perspective.

- Individual identities and collective dynamics as a synthesis of the conditioning and action transform circumstances, generating new conditionings, new possibilities and needs for decision making and action.
- Agents are placed before conflicts involving choices because they have interests and loyalties which are often countered by various affiliations.
- Since the agent acts upon varying circumstances, people can understand why some agents change their ideals or political or philosophic attitude without it necessarily meaning that there has been treason or actions lacking in logical thinking.
- Sometimes agents may transcend their personal or group interests rationally notwithstanding the determinations. These people build their identity with their freedom.
- Fourth-level differentiations with refined and detailed examples which progressively identify the new fractions within other more ample fractions and differentiate individuals within whole groups. This permits understanding and explaining antagonisms between factions of the same subgroup and alliances between factions of diverse subgroups (for example, traders of the Atlantic coast with different interests, to traders of a city in the Andean south) and can simultaneously co-ordinate these antagonisms with their respective alliances.
- Recuperation of the partially diluted individual historical agent, which can be differentiated from the totality or the group as a synthesis of the interaction of his/her individuality and his/her social being. The agent can have a proper name but he/she is the product of his/her context. The agent can also be an abstract subject though representing a social context.

or apparently contradicting directions.

- The influential circumstances are very rich and complex, full of precise and well documented data and that is why it is well understood that agents are driven towards sometimes similar and sometimes different actions. In this sense, people act rationally before the alternatives that the historian knows in detail or knows how to research.
- Freedom means the ability to understand the multiple determinations that allow the agent to transcend his/her circumstance to a certain degree and opt for alternatives in thinking, having intentions or acting within a range of options limited by the conditions of the culture and according to the ideological horizon of the times and by the psychological conditions or personal conditions, conscious or unconscious, social, economic or political of the given agent.
- Ability of transformation of the leader related with level of change in which the system is at the time.
- Political leaders have the ability to act because they have a vision of social leadership.
- A dialectical relationship is built in which the circumstances that condition the agent at the same time are transformed by the historical agent who acts on the circumstances generating new conditionings, new possibilities and needs for action and decision.
- Description of a process in terms of the system and structures in the process of transformation in which collective and individual agents may articulate with the process and even push it forward.
- Agents act with intentions that can be clear, be progressive and also question the system. But the capability for action of the agent is mediated by the conditions of possibility of the system.
- There is a simultaneous presence of the two types of explanation: intentional and structural. Now is found in the individual the personal impulse towards the opportunity within the historical circumstances.

- The relationship between circumstances and intentions is made in reference to the influence of circumstances in the intentions – teleological causal relationship – or in reference to the hermeneutic reconstruction of the sense of the actions for the agents. A hermeneutic effort must be made to understand agents within the meaning of their actions in their own contexts.
- There are actions and intentions with a high probability of existence during a period of time more than at another given period of time.
- Complexity of systemic explanations is increased over the previous level because the person additionally moves around easily at different levels of resolution of social reality from macroscopic visions to microscopic or local visions. Connects geographic phenomena (local, regional, inter-national), social structures (economic, political, ideological) and temporal structures to build historical events which may be events or processes in which both condition each other and serve an explanation.
- Temporal perspective which allows the finding of profound or underlying causes in combination with eventual situations and phenomena.
- Consequences of diverse characteristics are brought forth as in the previous level but with a greater richness of detail.
- Complex narrative with analytic explanations or analytic descriptions of social processes interrelated within a temporal flux of processes.

Level 5: Interview excerpt – historian and university professor
Historian: For the common man, in this whole period of change, his greatest worry was local interests, and if there is something in the process of change which will alter or affect its local well being, it will generate a reaction with greater intensity, it is going to enter into civil war. Some localities are affected by their interests during the uprising. For example, Cartagena has a serious problem with Bogotá. They have been trading since way back but it was resolved in a different way in the colonial system and in another way when the system disappeared. In Cartagena it is especially the Cartagenian traders and the bureaucracy that is

more likely to perceive the problem with Bogotá. The problem is double; it is the interior of the country with its head in Bogotá trying to impose some products on Cartagena to trade with them. What the provinces of the interior are after is to win over the coast for their products. Cartagena is not interested in merchandise from the interior because it can get them cheaper and better in the Antilles. Then Cartagena is going to say: 'All of what I am obtaining through customs is being taken away by Bogotá, for the interests of Bogotá and that money which I get here has to go to Bogotá which in turn gives me back only a fraction if anything at all. The customs are mine and all that I make from my customs is mine.'[10]

There is a collective behaviour between the social sectors which one can more or less identify. As agent, the Creole is going to search for his autonomy but this same autonomy leads to a division as a collective and we have to consider them as small groups. It can be a collective but having the same interest they generate diverse situations. Then, with the principle of autonomy, civil war comes around.

Then comes a period of dismantling because it is easy to think about what one wants to do but it is very hard to make it work because of the way the system is. For example, you want to tear down a monopoly. That is the ideological principle. But then the tobacco monopoly must disappear on principle and if so then what is the republican state going to live from? They need a source of finances and it cannot be the one who declares the doctrine as the best one – that it is the only tax, the direct tax – because there is no way of collecting it. Then it has to continue to maintain the tobacco monopoly otherwise the state has no resources. The state, in fact, went broke.

Conclusions

A first conclusion as a result of this investigation confirms our initial hypothesis in the sense that historical thought in students does not evolve from an explanation that is intentional and exclusively centred on the will of historical agents, reaching finally a structural kind of explanation, as is suggested in the works of authors such as Carretero, Jacott and Hallden.[11] What we have found is that the two types of factors are present in the explanations at every level, and what does change is the way in which the intentions and circumstances and their mutual relationships are understood. Both become progressively more differentiated, articulated and complex. The process by which explanations become more and more complex depends not on the substitution of an intentional type of explanation by one of the structural type but on the progressively more intricate and systemic articulation of the circumstances and the agents.

These results coincide with those found by other researchers[12] for the development of the ability of empathetic understanding of history in which they show a progressive complexity of intentional understanding as they inscribe them within more precise historical contexts.

As people manage to build the representation of society as a complex and dynamic system, with various different and related elements in multidirectional and reciprocal ways, they also manage to build a representation of the identity of agents and the intentions of their actions in much more abstract, toned down terms, free from stereotypes and unbecoming generalizations. Furthermore, these intentions are explained not only because of the particular interests and conditions of the agents but also because of their placement within a global system. This complexity also allows for an understanding of the possibilities and limitations for agents to transform their context by resolving, in a dialectic fashion, the relationship between freedom and determination.

In this sense, the construction of causal explanation does not seem to develop independently from the development of the understanding of the sense of the historical agents' actions. Sooner or later, the causal chains that connect the events that have taken place in the social, economic, political and ideological circumstances will be mediated by the agents' acts. In these cases, which are frequent in the vast majority of the explanations, the person has to be able to explain the events from the intentional perspective, in one way or another in order to be able to continue with his causal–circumstantial explanation. In the same fashion, understanding of the agents' intentions and acts cannot develop in the absence of a parallel development of the complexity of causal explanations, because this would inevitably cause them to be out of context.

In any case, this is a problem that needs to be investigated further by exploring the differences which may appear between historians of diverse theoretical stands and by pinpointing the processes through which the building of intentions and the manner in which the tension between conditioning and freedom is resolved. Likewise, it is important to resolve this problem with regard to the language used in the explanation, be it analytic or narrative, or a combination of the two.

The results of this investigation suggest that the frontier between a logical, general structure of reasoning and the specific forms of reasoning of historical thought is more difficult to establish than authors such as

Booth and Gardner suggest,[13] and than we had thought initially. We believe it is necessary to reconsider the similarities and common traits and not only the differences. This position is taken in view of the following:

- There is a similarity between empathetic understanding of history and the development of moral judgement as they both depend on the ability to have non-centred perspectives.[14]
- The reconstruction of the identity of the agent depends very closely on the operations of differentiation and coordination similar to the logical–mathematical ones described by Piaget.
- Placing of agents into context depends closely on a systemic thought which can be described in historical terms as well as in formal terms.

The ability to produce non-centred explanations depends, to a large extent, on the ability to hold a healthy scepticism and a self-critical stance which have common elements in methods of all areas, even though they are resolved in ways that are increasingly more complex as we enter the area of the social sciences.

The return to the 'old ideas' would have to be understood, obviously, from a perspective in which the differentiation in the logical structures of each discipline, which was what was obtained during the previous debates, is not lost.

We think it is of critical importance to explore the relationship between the development of historical thought and the development of social intelligence. By social intelligence we mean the ability to understand the social situations in a systemic and dynamic way and to act on them in such a manner that the individual decisions and actions integrate social and personal interests and purposes. Social intelligence is, additionally, deliberant because it confronts social reality from the standpoint of critical reflection – that is also self-critical – and the argumentative debate over the various points of ideological, social, political and economic conflict that are an integral part of a democratic society.

Many people would be willing to accept this relationship, but it requires more theoretical and empirical exploration in order to be understood. This work suggests that this occurs not only because history gives us a reference point which allows us to understand each other better as historical agents but because it develops the necessary forms of thought in order to understand contemporary social reality and its political culture,[15] in a sophisticated and complex manner.

161

This idea, interesting no matter what the social context, is even more so in the case of Colombia given the seriousness of our social crisis which reflects, among other things, the frailty of our civil society and political culture.

The development of historical thought supposes the development of reasoning skills, which are part of social intelligence. The first of these is empathic understanding of the rationale behind historical events. To overcome ethnocentricity and anachronisms and to understand the meaning of social traditions and customs in the past, students must learn to make empathic, contextual and hermeneutic analyses. We found an interesting similarity between the development of this competence and the development of moral judgement described by Lawrence Kohlberg.[16] This is probably because of the fact that, in both cases, students have to shift from a self-centred point of view to the other person's perspective (personal, social, temporal) and co-ordinate both his/hers and theirs in order to be able to build a mental representation of society that considers diversity as a main feature.

The second is the ability to articulate the actions of historical agents with the social structures and context in which these act and to build complex networks of causal and intentional relationships which explain historical social events. This competence can also be at the base of a more sophisticated and analytical understanding of current issues and conflicts, being able to handle their social, spatial and temporal complexity and avoiding explanations that are simplistic, based purely on the will of the people, or dividing the world into good and bad characters.

The third is the ability to co-ordinate the relationships of conditioning and freedom in transforming action. The way in which people develop their understanding of the conditioning or determining factors, that either hinder or promote freedom to act in order to change social relations, could be related with the development of political awareness and disposition. We believe that this disposition is influenced by the expectations and comprehension one has of the transforming dynamics of society and of the sense and possibility of political participation of civil society in these processes. Many changes take place after a medium or long period of time in ways that are not visible to people who perceive instead a hopeless state of sameness. Understanding history may aid in the comprehension of, for example, the interaction between profound structural changes with other transformations that derive from intended or unintended actions, that change is not simply a matter of free will, and that structural changes are slow and difficult. They might also realize that it is precisely only by understanding the long duration structures that one can act upon them.

Since social knowledge is not value free, values need to be made explicit and discussed. This is where its value lies and not where it is weak. Teachers need to become aware of the need to critically analyze values and to prepare students to discuss the ethical content of daily personal and social decisions as a form of educating the mind for citizen action. We think that it is in the 'praxical' relationship between a thorough understanding of the historical discipline and making decisions in our daily life that people will grow in both their personal intelligence and their moral self.

This research provides evidence, although not exhaustive, that the conventional teaching methods of history in our country are not helping in the development of thought or understanding. Our interviews showed students in the fourth grade who had the same type of reasoning of students from the tenth and eleventh grades, probably because the former had been taught by analytical and inquisitive teachers, more interested in their students' thinking than in having them memorize facts. Most of the students after eight years of history classes were still making stereotyped, anachronistic and simplistic judgements in all of their analyses. This suggests the importance of teaching around central historiographic and epistemological problems. In our present research we are exploring the hypothesis that working with the essential theoretical questions of the discipline is a powerful tool in the development of deep historical understanding and in the ability of transferring knowledge in order to solve academic and daily life problems in a new, autonomous and creative manner.

It is clear that qualification of reasoning is strongly associated with the reflexive experience that the student may have had in terms of historical questions and in constructing explanations about problems in such a way that they make sense. However, the analysis of our interviews also shows that the complexity of the arguments depends in great part on the richness and precision of the information that the student may possess and which allows him/her to move confidently and fluidly among the theoretical explanatory formulations and concrete examples. The relationship between forms of reasoning and information networks requires a much greater exploration, not only in order to grasp the role that each one plays in the complexity of explanations, but in order also to better understand their interdependence and the way in which these networks are qualified.

163

There are three inspiring references concerning this point: what has been set forth by Rogers[17] regarding the learning of history as the construction of frames of reference; the suggestions made by Lee[18] on the possibility of thinking about a qualitative development of these frameworks; and the idea expressed by Ricoeur[19] in terms of the fact that history takes form in the minds of people as a map of the past in which diverse histories interlock with one another, independently of the different interpretations of the different events. These ideas suggest that we cannot dismiss the role that good and traditional teaching may have had in the past when centring its attention on the careful learning of a wide range of contents. Today, it seems clear that we must carefully consider the relationship between 'teaching how to think' and 'teaching what to know', an equilibrium that has been lost in many innovative pedagogical approaches under the assumption that the important thing is only 'teaching how to think'.

Acknowledgements

This research was financed by COLCIENCIAS (National Institute of Research Development), Colegio San Francisco de Asís and Javeriana University, Bogota, Colombia. Special thanks for its support.

NOTES

1. The authors welcome correspondence on this research; their email addresses are bermuda@andinet.com and rosario@pz.harvard.edu respectively.
2. The work of the following authors has been of special interest and value to us: S.R. Carey, M. Evans, E. Jay Honda and C.M. Unger, '"An experiment is when you try it and see it works": A study of seven students' understanding of the construction of scientific knowledge', *International Journal of Science Education*, 11 (1989), pp. 514–29; M. Carretero, J.I. Pozo and M. Asensio (eds), *La Enseñanza de las Ciencias Sociales* (Madrid: Visor, 1989); M. Carretero, 'Perspectivas disciplinares, cognitivas y didácticas en la enseñanza de las ciencias sociales y la historia', in *Construir y Enseñar: Ciencias Sociales e Historia* (Buenos Aires: Aique, 1995); M. Carretero and J. Voss (eds), *Cognitive and Instructional Processes in History and the Social Sciences* (Hillsdale, NJ: Lawrence Erlbaum, 1994); A.K. Dickinson and P.J. Lee (eds), *History Teaching and Historical Understanding* (London: Heinemann Educational, 1978); A.K. Dickinson, P.J. Lee and P.J. Rogers (eds), *Learning History* (London: Heinemann Educational, 1984); H. Gardner, *Frames of Mind* (New York: Basic Books, 1983), *The Unschooled Mind: How Children Think and How Schools Should Teach* (New York: Basic Books, 1991), and *The Disciplined Mind: What All Students Should Understand* (New York: Simon and Schuster, 1999); David N. Perkins, *Smart Schools: From Training Memories to*

Educating Minds (New York: Free Press, 1992); J.I. Pozo and M. Carretero, 'Las explicaciones causales de expertos y novatos en historia', in Carretero, Pozo and Asensio (eds), *La Enseñanza*, and 'El adolescente como historiador', *Infancia y Aprendizaje* (1983); D. Shemilt, *History 13–16 Evaluation Study* (Edinburgh: Holmes McDougall, 1980); S. Wineburg, 'The psychology of learning and teaching history', in D.C. Berliner and R.C. Calfee (eds), *Handbook of Educational Psychology* (New York: Macmillan, 1996), pp. 423–37.

3. Of special value to us have been: M. Block, *Introducción a la Historia* (1952; reprint Mexico: Breviarios del Fondo de Cultura Económica, 1987); Ernst Breisach, *Historiography* (Chicago, IL: University of Chicago Press, 1983); R.G. Collingwood, *The Idea of History* (Oxford: Oxford University Press, 1946); G. Colmenares, 'Sobre fuentes, temporalidad y escritura de la historia', *Boletín Cultural* 10, 24 (1989); W.H. Dray, '"Explaining What" in History', in P. Gardiner (ed.), *Theories of History* (Chicago, IL: Free Press, 1959); E. Florescana, 'La historia como explicación', in C. Pereyra (ed.), *Historia ¿Para Qué?* (1980; reprint Mexico: Siglo XXI, 1995); P. Gardiner (ed.), *Theories*, and (ed.), *Philosophy of History* (Oxford: Oxford University Press, 1974); Peter Gay, *Style in History* (New York: Norton, 1974); C.G. Hempel, 'Reasons and covering laws in historical explanation', in P. Gardiner (ed.), *Philosophy*; E.J. Hobsbawm, 'The revival of narrative: Some comments', *Past and Present*, 86 (February1980); P. Novak, *That Noble Dream: The Objectivity Question* (Cambridge: Cambridge University Press, 1988); C. Pereyra, *El Sujeto de la Historia* (Madrid: Alianza, 1984); P. Ricoeur, *Time and Narrative*, vol. 2 (Chicago, IL:University of Chicago Press, 1984), and *Oneself as Another* (Chicago, IL: University of Chicago Press, 1992); A. Schaff, *Historia y Verdad* (Mexico: Grijalbo, 1974); L. Stone, 'The revival of narrative', *Past and Present* 85 (1981), pp. 3–24; J. Topolski, 'Towards an integrated model of historical explanation', *History and Theory* (1991); P. Veyne, *Cómo se Escribe la Historia: Foucault Revoluciona la Historia* (Madrid: Alianza Editorial, 1984); W.H. Walsh, *An Introduction to Philosophy of History* (1951; reprint London: Hutchinson, 1967); H. White, *The Content of the Form: Narrative Discourse and Historical Representation* (Baltimore, MD: Johns Hopkins University Press, 1987), and *Metahistory: The Historical Imagination of Nineteenth-century Europe* (Baltimore, MD: Johns Hopkins University Press, 1973).

4. The following work was of special interest to us: R. Ashby and P. Lee, 'Children's concepts of empathy and understanding in history', in C. Portal (ed.), *The History Curriculum for Teachers* (Lewes: Falmer Press, 1987); M.A. Britt, J.F. Rouet, M.C. Georgi and C.A. Perfetti, 'Learning from history texts: From causal analysis to argument models', in G. Leinhardt, I. Beck and C. Stainton (eds), *Teaching and Learning in History* (Hillsdale, NJ: Lawrence Erlbaum, 1994); M. Carretero, M. Asensio and J.I. Pozo, 'Cognitive development, historical time representation and causal explanations in adolescence', in M. Carretero, R. Pope, J. Simons and J.I. Pozo (eds), *Learning and Instruction: Vol. 3, European Research in an International Context* (Oxford: Pergamon Press, 1991); M. Carretero, L. Jacott and A. López-Manjón, 'Perspectivas actuales en la comprensión y enseñanza de la causalidad histórica: El caso del descubrimiento de América', and 'La explicación causal de distintos hechos históricos', in Carretero (ed.), *Construir*; A. Dickinson and P. Lee, 'Making Sense of History', in Dickinson, Lee and Rogers (eds), *Learning History*; O. Hallden, 'Learning history', *Oxford Review of Education*, 12, 1 (1986), pp. 53–66, and 'On the paradox of understanding history in an educational setting', in Leinhardt, Beck and Stainton (eds), *Teaching and Learning*; L. Jacott and M. Carretero, 'Historia y relato: La comprensión de los agentes históricos en el descubrimiento (encuentro) de América', in Carretero (ed.), *Construir*; P. Lee, 'Explanation and understanding in history', in Dickinson and Lee (eds), *History Teaching*; C. Portal, 'Empathy as an objective for history teaching', in Portal (ed.), *History Curriculum*; D. Shemilt, 'Beauty and the philosopher: Empathy in history and

classroom', in Dickinson, Lee and Rogers (eds), *Learning History;* C. Stainton and G. Leinhardt, 'Telling the tale: Narrative explanation in history', paper presented at the AERA annual meeting, New Orleans, April 1994; S. Wineburg and J. Fournier, 'Contextualized thinking in history', in Carretero and Voss (eds), *Cognitive and Instructional Processes*; and papers presented in 1994 at Las Navas del Marqués, to the Second International Seminar on Cognitive and Instructional Processes in History, by J. Topolski, 'The structure of the historical narratives and the teaching of history', A. Riviere *et al.*, 'History and intentionality: A developmental study', J. Dominguez and J.I. Pozo, *et al.* 'The learning of causal explanations in history: concepts and procedures', and a CHATA Project research paper by P. Lee, A. Dickinson and R. Ashby, 'Researching children's ideas about history'.

5. This interview was of special interest. The same student was interviewed one year later, after being taught by a teacher who emphasized analysis of causal relationships and constructing time lines in her classes. If we compare the two excerpts, it is clear that the student's understanding of historical subjects is simplistic – typical of the previous level – while her understanding of the situation and the temporal organization of relations is much more complex.

6. This could an incipient manifestation of a growing competence to build a complex scenario. Contrasting with a level 1 response, this student is explaining that the reason why Creoles could not trade or hold political positions was that they were living under a 'system' in which things worked in a particular manner, and not, for example, because Spaniards were greedy.

7. At this point, when having to give an answer that requires complex connections among the political, economic etc. subsystems, the student loses the ability to sustain the argumentation that demands interdependent contexts and falls back into a person-based explanation with implicit moral overtones (the kings' selfishness and the greediness with which they spend people's taxes).

8. Different from the previous level, this case shows unsettling circumstances which make people not only unable to stand it any longer but to conceive their reality in a new way. It also shows another fact that helps people see the situation differently. The unsettling circumstances demand a solution. Thus, other events, of similar nature, occur that help people bring about and give shape to the required solution.

9. Notice how, in spite of personalization of social phenomena, this student is characterizing the historical situation as one in which events, common to various countries, occur at the same time because they live under similar conditions. It is a first appearance of the notion of a global system and historical period in which events are considered particular to that period. It does not mean this student has yet attained a proper concept of system or epoch, but we do think it is an indication of first steps being taken.

10. This person is pointing out that, in spite of the fact that there is a common ideal – the search for independence – local interests have a very strong bearing on possible decisions or on their reasons to become or not part of the process. This breaks with broad stereotypical generalizations and prejudgements caused by a lack of understanding historical agents' specific interests and their true contexts.

11. Jacott and Carretero, 'Historia'; Carretero, Jacott and López-Manjón, 'Perspectivas actuales', and 'La explicación'; Hallden, 'Learning history', and 'On the paradox.

12. Shemilt, 'Beauty'; Ashby and Lee, 'Children's concepts'; Portal, 'Empathy' and J. Dominguez, 'Enseñar a comprender el pasado histórico: conceptos y empatía', *Infancia y Aprendizaje,* 34 (1986), pp. 1–21.

13. In particular M. Booth, 'Ages and concepts: A critique of the Piagetian approach to history teaching', in Portal (ed.), *History Curriculum*; and Gardner, *Frames*.

14. See L. Kohlberg, *The Philosophy of Moral Development,* vol. 1; *The Psychology of Moral Development,* vol. 2 (New York: Harper & Row, 1985).

15. Very interesting ideas have been advanced in regard to this matter in the Comparative

European Survey on History Consciousness and Political Attitudes. See Magne Angvik and Bodo von Borries (eds), *Youth and History* (Hamburg: Koerber-Stiftung, 1997).

16. See Kohlberg, *The Philosophy.*
17. P.J. Rogers, 'History: The past as a frame of reference', in Portal (ed.), *History Curriculum.*
18. See P.J. Lee, 'Historical knowledge and the National Curriculum', in R. Aldrich (ed.), *History in the National Curriculum* (London: Kogan Page, 1991), pp. 39–65.
19. Ricoeur, *Time.*

9

The Development of History Teaching Curricula in China

YANG BIAO

The Evolution of History Teaching Curricula in China before the 1990s

1903–49

In a strict sense, history did not gain the status of a formal course in schools in China until a new educational system was adopted by the government in the last years of the Qing Dynasty. In modern times, the curricula in history teaching have developed in accordance with changes in the education system in China.

In 1903 the Qing government decreed 'the Imperial curricula of junior primary schools', 'the Imperial curricula of senior primary schools' and 'the Imperial curricula of high schools'. According to these decrees, the length of junior primary school education was four years, for senior primary school education it was also four years, and for high school education it was five years. History was listed as a compulsory course for the five years of high school education. The content of the course and the hours of teaching per week were as indicated in Table 9.1.

TABLE 9.1: HISTORY IN THE IMPERIAL CURRICULA DECREED BY THE QING GOVERNMENT IN 1903

Grade	1	2	3	4	5
Course content	Chinese history	Chinese history and Asian history	History of Qing Dynasty and Asian history	History of Japan and Western countries	History of Japan and Western countries
Hours per week	3	2	2	2	2

168

After the revolution of 1911 which overthrew the Qing Dynasty, the Ministry of Education of the Nationalist government summoned what it termed a 'conference on the school system' in 1922. As a result, the American school system was copied, and the length of high school education was modified to six years which were divided into two periods, junior high school and senior high school. History was listed as one of the compulsory courses. In 1932 the Nationalist government decreed 'the high school law' and 'the curricula for high schools' in which all optional courses were cancelled, the length of junior and senior high school education was set at three years for each, and all the courses were made compulsory. The curriculum in history teaching was as indicated in Table 9.2.

TABLE 9.2: THE HISTORY CURRICULUM DECREED BY THE NATIONALIST GOVERNMENT IN 1932

Level	Junior high school			Senior high school		
Grade	1	2	3	1	2	3
Course content	Chinese history	Chinese history	Chinese history and world history	Chinese history	Chinese history and world history	World history
Hours per week	2	2	2	2	2	2

The main content of the Chinese history course was the chronicle of Chinese dynasties and famous emperors. The world history course focused mainly on the history of western Europe, America and Japan. The overall curricula were revised twice, in 1936 and 1940; the curriculum in history teaching remained almost intact up to 1949.

1950–60
In 1950 the Ministry of Education of the People's Republic of China decreed 'a provisional teaching programme for high schools' which required that history be included in the teaching programme for each of the junior and senior school years, and that the teaching time should be three hours per week. The curriculum for each grade was as indicated in Table 9.3.

TABLE 9.3: THE HISTORY CURRICULUM DECREED BY THE MINISTRY OF
EDUCATION OF THE PEOPLE'S REPUBLIC OF CHINA IN 1950

Level	Junior high school			Senior high school		
Grade	1	2	3	1	2	3
Course content	Chinese ancient history	Chinese modern history	World history	Chinese ancient history	Chinese modern history	World history
Hours per week	3	3	3	3	3	3

The curriculum was required to progress from ancient Chinese history to modern Chinese history and then to world history, in both the junior high school and secondary high school years. Emphasis was laid on teaching the law of development of human society. However, in 1953 the Ministry of Education decreed that the teaching programme for high schools be revised. The new, revised history programme for high schools is summarized in Table 9.4.

TABLE 9.4: THE HISTORY TEACHING PROGRAMME DECREED BY THE
MINISTRY OF EDUCATION IN 1953

Level	Junior high school			Senior high school		
Grade	1	2	3	1	2	3
Course content	World ancient history	World ancient history	Chinese modern history	World modern history	Soviet modern history	Chinese modern and contemporary history
		Chinese ancient history			Chinese modern and contemporary history	
Hours per week	3	3	3	3	3	3

As shown in Table 9.4, the revised programme began with ancient history (ancient world and then ancient Chinese history), followed by modern history (Chinese, world and then Soviet modern history) and finally modern Chinese and contemporary history. The earlier 'double rotation' arrangement was replaced by a 'single rotation' with ancient world and Chinese history plus modern Chinese history taught in the junior high school years, and modern world and Soviet history, followed by modern Chinese and contemporary history, taught in the senior high school years. The reason for these changes was to follow Soviet patterns as the People's Republic of China and the USSR were close political allies at that time.

In 1955 the Ministry of Education decreed further revisions to the content of the history programme in high schools, and a set of uniform history textbooks and teaching references was edited and published together with the new programme. The 'double rotation' system for history content was resumed, though in a somewhat different form, with the purpose of enabling students to achieve knowledge of Chinese and world history in both the junior and senior high schools years. The revised course content is summarized in Table 9.5.

TABLE 9.5: THE HISTORY TEACHING PROGRAMME DECREED BY THE MINISTRY OF EDUCATION IN 1955

Level	Junior high school			Senior high school		
Grade	1	2	3	1	2	3
Course content	Chinese ancient history	Chinese modern history	World history	World modern history	Chinese ancient history	Chinese modern history
		Chinese contemporary history		World contemporary history		Chinese contemporary history
Hours per week	3	3	3	3	3	3

The teaching sequence decreed here had several merits. For example, the content of the history course in the junior high school years, which was quite integrated, could satisfy the needs of graduates whether they wanted to seek employment or admission to high school. The history course in the senior high school period could enable students to expand and deepen the knowledge they had gained in junior high school, and the Chinese history teaching in this period could benefit from the co-ordination with other courses, including world history, geography and Chinese language courses. Furthermore, the ancient history, contemporary events, Chinese history and world history syllabi were integrated into a whole with appropriate proportions, and a uniform set of textbooks was adopted nationwide for these syllabi after 1956.

1960–76

In 1963 the teaching programmes for primary schools and high schools were again revised by the Ministry of Education. Because of the ultra-left trend of thought which dominated China's society at that time and emphasized the present rather than the past, course content and teaching time for history were considerably reduced. Table 9.6 shows this, and the actual content and teaching time decreed at that time.

TABLE 9.6: THE HISTORY TEACHING PROGRAMME DECREED BY THE MINISTRY OF EDUCATION IN 1963

Level	Junior high school			Senior high school		
Grade	1	2	3	1	2	3
Course content		Chinese ancient history	Chinese modern history and Chinese contemporary events			World history
Hours per week		2	2			2–3

The Cultural Revolution from 1966 to 1976 dealt a heavy blow to education, not least history education. The reduction in time allocated to history teaching in the high school period was conspicuous. In the early years of the Cultural Revolution, all history courses were cancelled. Later, history began to regain its place in high schools, but overall the time allocated to history was considerably less than earlier in the century.

1976–90

After 1976 history, which at one stage had been obliterated from the curriculum during the Cultural Revolution, was restored as a formal course. In 1978 the Ministry of Education decreed the 'teaching programme for ten-year full-time primary and secondary schooling'; it also decreed a new teaching programme for history in high schools. This programme is summarized in Table 9.7.

TABLE 9.7: THE HISTORY TEACHING PROGRAMME DECREED BY THE MINISTRY OF EDUCATION IN 1978

Level	Junior high school			Senior high school		
Grade	1	2	3	1	2	3
Course content		Chinese ancient history	Chinese modern history Chinese contemporary events	World history		
Hours per week		2	2	2–3		

Later, in 1986, nine years of compulsory education nationwide were enforced by the 'compulsory education law of the People's Republic of China'.[1] The teaching programmes and curricula of all primary and secondary schools were to be revised in accordance with this new law. A transitional overall teaching programme was drawn up and enforced after 1987. The new history teaching programme for high schools was as shown in Table 9.8.

TABLE 9.8: THE HISTORY TEACHING PROGRAMME DECREED IN 1986

Level	Junior high school			Senior high school		
Grade	1	2	3	1	2	3
Course content	Chinese ancient history	Chinese contemporary events		World history		
	Chinese contemporary events	World history				
Hours per week	2	2		2–3		

A survey of the various history teaching programmes in China this century prior to the 1990s reveals a common basic framework underlying school history in China. Furthermore, the main features of school history in China can be said to be:

173

- The curricula were uniform nationwide, which means that the history curriculum in every part of the country was standardized.
- All courses were compulsory, and marked by uniformity.
- The structure of the course was fixed. The system of general history was adopted which emphasized the systematic nature of historical research and the integrity of historical knowledge. Teaching proceeded in an orderly way, step by step from ancient times to modern times and then the contemporary period. From Asia, Europe, the Americas to Africa, every part of the world was covered.

This mode of curricula helped to popularize historical knowledge, but in the fast developing society it gradually failed to satisfy the needs of the modernization process. Therefore, further reforms in history teaching in the People's Republic of China have been introduced in the 1990s.

The Transformation of the History Teaching Curricula in China since 1990

Great changes have taken place in history teaching in the People's Republic of China since 1990. Three different sets of teaching programmes have replaced the uniform curriculum which was formerly carried out nationwide. One of these new programmes – the teaching programme for nine-year compulsory education schools and senior high schools in China, designed by the National Education Committee, guides history teaching in most areas of the People's Republic of China.[2] The second programme, the reform programme for curricula in primary and secondary schools in Shanghai, designed by the local authority of Shanghai – guides history teaching in Shanghai and other economically developed regions. A third programme – the provisional teaching programme for compulsory education, designed by Zhejiang Province – guides history teaching in local rural and mountainous areas.

The curricula for history teaching in these three programmes embody the result of recent developments in history courses. They also show concern for the different requirements of schools of different levels and in different regions. In addition, they possess the features which allow students to develop their individual personalities.

The curriculum in history teaching suitable for most regions in China
Table 9.9 summarizes the main features of this programme for the primary and junior high school years.

174

TABLE 9.9: THE NATIONWIDE CURRICULUM IN HISTORY TEACHING IN THE PRIMARY AND JUNIOR HIGH SCHOOLS DECREED BY THE NATIONAL EDUCATION COMMITTEE IN 1991

Level	Primary school						Junior high school		
Grade	1	2	3	4	5	6	1	2	3
Courses arranged nationwide				Basic social knowledge			Chinese ancient history	Chinese modern history and contemporary events	World history
Hours per week				2	2	2	2	3	2
Course arranged by local authorities									
Hours per week									6
Extra-curricular activities									
Hours per week	5	5	5	5	5	5	2	3	3

History teaching in the senior high school years is divided into two parts: a compulsory course and an optional course. The curriculum is summarized in Table 9.10.[3] The hours of extra-curricular activities are planned by each school.

TABLE 9.10: THE 1991 NATIONWIDE CURRICULUM IN HISTORY TEACHING IN THE SENIOR HIGH SCHOOL YEARS

Grade	Senior 1	Senior 2	Senior 3
Compulsory course	World modern history and contemporary events	Chinese modern history and contemporary events	
Hours per week	2	2	
Optional course			Chinese ancient history
Hours per week		6	
Extra-curricular activities			

The new curriculum in history teaching for primary, junior high and senior high schools in most regions of China differs from the old curriculum in a number of ways. In the new nationwide curriculum both classroom teaching and extra-curricular activities are included. The extra-curricular activities – including group activities, social investigation and visiting historical sites – aim at promoting students' interest and ability in historical learning. A second major change is that a 'basic social knowledge' course has been included in the primary school curriculum. This course, integrating basic knowledge of history, geography and society, enables students to gain an overall, basic understanding of historical and geographical knowledge and social life of the local area, the whole country and the world. Another change is that an optional course, generally arranged in the last year of senior high school, has been introduced for the first time. This course is available to those students who are interested in learning history or who are trying to take relevant majors in colleges and universities. A fourth change is that the content of all the courses relevant to historical knowledge is no longer repeated only for repetition's sake but for sound educational reasons. Thus, in the primary school years students are taught basic and comprehensive knowledge in the 'basic social knowledge' course. In the junior high school years, systematic history teaching provides students with the necessary knowledge that each citizen should have acquired. After that, in the senior high schools, history teachers no longer repeat what students have been taught earlier, but teach the modern history and contemporary events of China and the world, which have great relevance to the world today.

In China's history education circles, it is considered that the regular pattern of cognitive ability development of the young people is in the following sequence: normally primary school students are in the perceptual stage of cognition and engage in intuitive thinking; junior high school students are in the aesthetical stage of cognition, often thinking in terms of images; senior high school students are in the rational stage of cognition and capable of logical thinking. The new curriculum, it is believed, complies better with young people's cognition development pattern through the arrangement of teaching basic knowledge in primary schools, teaching general history in junior high schools, and teaching important modern historic events in the senior high schools.[4]

The curriculum for the economically developed regions
In 1990 Shanghai put into effect a reform programme for curricula in primary and secondary schools in Shanghai. This was the first local teaching programme in the educational history of China. The curriculum has been adopted mainly in Shanghai and other economically and culturally developed regions.

TABLE 9.11: THE HISTORY CURRICULUM IN SHANGHAI (FROM 1990)

Level	Nine-year compulsory education									Senior high school		
Grade	1	2	3	4	5	6	7	8	9	1	2	3
Compulsory courses	Social knowledge						Chinese ancient history	Chinese modern and contemporary events	World history	China and the world in modern and contemporary times		
Hours per week		2	2	2			2	2	2	2	2	
Optional courses										Chinese cultural history	Chinese cultural history	Chinese ancient history
Hours per week										3	3	3
Extra-curricular activities Hours per week	6	6	8	8	8	8	8	5	5	6	6	6–8

The history curriculum designed and implemented in Shanghai has three outstanding features. First, a combined mode of curriculum has been established. History teaching in junior and senior high schools is made up of three parts: a compulsory course, an optional course and activities. The compulsory course equips students with essential historical knowledge and theory; the optional course emphasizes the formation of students' individual personalities; and students can acquire some necessary historical abilities and skills through activities.

A second distinctive feature is that the various elements of the history curriculum (the general history introduction, comprehensive social knowledge course, cultural history course on specific topics, and history course blending Chinese and world history) all contribute to the variegation of the curriculum structure. This new structure better satisfies the needs of students to enhance their knowledge, skill and personalities.

A third feature is that the content has been enriched at each level. In the past the content of history teaching was simply repeated three times – in primary schools, junior high schools and senior high schools. This led to redundant repetition of content and some waste of time. According to the new Shanghai teaching programme, junior high school students learn the basic knowledge of Chinese and world history, and Chinese modern history and contemporary events are combined with world modern contemporary history in senior high school teaching, abandoning the old style which separated Chinese history and world history. In addition, the new history textbook for Shanghai's senior high schools has been edited to support this way of teaching. With world history from the fifteenth century as the leading thread, the textbook combines Chinese history with the history of other nations; introducing Chinese history against the background of world events; enabling students to grasp the changes in the relationship between China and other countries; and promoting students' understanding of multiple cultures in the world and also of the future tendency of world development. The curriculum strengthens the comparative study of Chinese history with world history and ways of teaching by which students can be enabled to analyse domestic and world historical events from a global point of view. Students are expected to understand and accept multiple cultural phenomena, and gain understanding of the development and changes that China has experienced against the macro-background of the world situation.[5]

The history curriculum for rural and mountainous areas
Zhejiang Province designed the curricula for the local rural and mountainous areas in 1991. The curriculum for history is as shown in Table 9.12.

TABLE 9.12: THE HISTORY CURRICULUM IN ZHEJIANG PROVINCE

Level	Primary school						Junior high school		
Grade	1	2	3	4	5	6	1	2	3
Compulsory course	Basic knowledge						Social knowledge		
Hours per week	1	1	2	2	4	4	3	4	3
Optional course Hours per week									1
Extra-curricular activities Hours per week	2	2	2	2	2	2	3	3	2

Considering the large number of students and the current situation of schools and teaching staff in rural areas, this curriculum moved away from specific history courses. Instead, courses in basic knowledge and social knowledge were adopted. Historical knowledge was merged into the basic knowledge course in primary schools and the social knowledge course in junior high schools. In this way, the hours of teaching have been reduced, the burden on students relaxed and, at the same time, students' skills and abilities nurtured. With the interrelationship between individual human beings and society as the theme, the basic knowledge of politics, economy, culture, population and folk custom is blended into the content of the social knowledge course. Students are enabled to take the first step towards knowing the social environment in which human beings exist. Also, students' understanding of human history and society is promoted.

Conclusion

The three new curricula embody the development tendency of the scientific curricula setting in China. The design process of the three programmes saw a departure from the traditional programme structure for history teaching. The new structure of curricula was built upon consideration of three factors. The first of these factors was a view on the regular pattern of the development of students' cognition. The pattern considered in China assumes that generally students of primary schools, junior high schools and senior high schools are, respectively, in the perceptual stage of cognition, aesthetical stage of cognition and rational stage of cognition. The new curricula, therefore, are designed to comply with this pattern and correspondingly teaching focuses on basic knowledge, general history and important events for different stages.

A second factor is the rational structure of the course. It is thought that the former unified structure of history courses should be changed. The structures of new curricula try to co-ordinate compulsory courses, optional courses and extra-curricular activities, aiming at promoting students' interest and ability in historical learning.

A third factor concerns the needs of the developing society. Having ceased to be an agro-centred society in the late 1980s and having experienced an industrialization era until the beginning of the 1990s, China is undergoing a dramatic transformation toward a new society which will share more common interests with the world. Therefore, there is an attempt in the curricula to combine Chinese history with world history in order to enable students to grasp historical knowledge from a global point of view, and so meet the needs of the development of society.

The People's Republic of China contains approximately one-fifth of the population of the world. In terms of numbers of students taught, China's school history curricula have the most extensive and practical effects in the world. It can be argued, therefore, that international history education circles should be hugely interested in future reform and development of history curricula in this vast country.

NOTES

1. For details of this curriculum plan and another view of history teaching developments in the People's Republic of China, see Manling Chau, 'Change and continuity: History teaching in the People's Republic of China', in A. Dickinson, P. Gordon, P. Lee and J. Slater (eds), *International Yearbook of History Education* (London: Woburn Press, 1995), pp. 124–42.

2. For details of this programme see National Ministry of Education, *The Curricula Standards for Full-Time Nine-Year Compulsory Education: History Teaching* (Beijing: National Ministry of Education, 1996).

3. For further details of the standards for the senior high schools see National Ministry of Education *The Curricula Standards for Full-Time Senior High Schools: History Teaching* (Beijing: National Ministry of Education, 1996).

4. For further details see Higher Education Publishing House, *The Methodology of History Teaching in High Schools* (Beijing: Higher Education Publishing House, 1988); and Anhui Education Publishing House, *The Methodology of History Teaching: An Introduction* (Beijing: Anhui Education Publishing House, 1988).

5. For further details of these and other aspects of history education in the People's Republic of China see Shanghai Education Publishing House, *History Education* (Shanghai: Shanghai Institute of Social Sciences Press, 1989); Shanghai Institute of Social Sciences, *Comparative History of Education* (Shanghai: Shanghai Education Publishing House, 1995); and People's Education Publishing House, *The Study of History Teaching* (Beijing: People's Education Publishing House, 1999).

10

The Future of the Past:
A Brief Account of the Australian National
Inquiry into School History, 1999–2000

TONY TAYLOR

In September 1999 the Commonwealth Minister of Education, Dr David Kemp, announced a national inquiry into school history. The setting up of such an inquiry for history was not only unprecedented but also something of a surprise; in Adelaide, in the same year, a declaration issued by the Federal Minister and his state counterparts had outlined a national focus on curriculum development initiatives in very different areas, for example science, technology and vocational education. In the Adelaide declaration, history had not been mentioned. However, in launching the national inquiry into school history, Dr Kemp had stressed a perceived link between an exploration of the teaching and learning of history and recent federal initiatives in civics and citizenship education. It was this view of that relationship that had provided the political will to produce the funding for the national inquiry into school history.

Background to the Inquiry

Although the national inquiry into school history might have come as a surprise to many Australian educators, it came as no surprise to many history teachers and academic historians who felt that their subject had been under siege for the past 20 years. Opinions on this issue had been expressed by academic historians and other public commentators with growing vehemence during the decade preceding the announcement of the national inquiry.

Some commentators attacked uncaring educators,[1] others blamed the influence of rival disciplines,[2] but, more frequently, the blame was laid at the door of a generic approach to secondary school social studies known as studies of society and the environment.[3]

181

Studies of society and the environment (SOSE) originated in the new social studies approach of the 1960s and 1970s at a time when history was regarded by many curriculum developers as an elitist, backward-looking and irrelevant school subject.[4] The proto-SOSE movement gathered strength in the 1980s and, in 1989, following a federal and state ministerial council meeting on a national curriculum at Hobart, all states and territories agreed to adopt SOSE (one of eight key learning areas) as the main curricular vehicle for the integrated teaching of history, geography and commerce. As the decade developed, however, individual jurisdictions began to vary their approach to the SOSE key learning area (KLA).

In particular, New South Wales, led the charge in breaking out of the national curriculum framework. In 1992 New South Wales introduced an unabashed history/geography 7–10 syllabus approach. This new syllabus had 100 hours each of mandated historical/geographical study to be taught as separate disciplines, or under the umbrella of Australian studies.

Looking back, it is quite clear that New South Wales had decided as early as the late 1980s not to follow a SOSE approach in secondary schools and, in 1999, Australia's premier state diverged even further from that original Hobart statement on the SOSE KLA with new history syllabi for the junior secondary and senior secondary school curriculum.

Other states and territories did attempt to follow the SOSE approach in their early 1990s curriculum policies. However, because of state opposition to any attempt at Commonwealth centralism in education policy at state level, variations across the curriculum were so prevalent by 1996 that the national curriculum approach in all KLAs was considered to have disintegrated.

In Victoria, for example, many secondary school teachers continued to teach history and geography lessons in a locally adapted, school-based curriculum instead of following the state's curriculum and standards framework (launched in 1994 for introduction in 1995).

On the other hand, Queensland history teachers, having been deprived of the opportunity to teach any form of generic social studies under a repressively conservative government in the 1970s and 1980s, developed a strong and healthy relationship with SOSE; so much so that the Queensland History Teachers' Association (QHTA) is currently the major organizer of SOSE professional development conferences in that state.

Despite this patchy provision of SOSE, it was nevertheless blamed for the alleged collapse of school history. It was stated that SOSE lacked focus and that the particular skills required for the successful teaching and learning of history went begging in a generic social studies curriculum that was ill-regarded in the hierarchy of school subjects. In Western Australia and in South Australia, for example, the low status of SOSE had resulted in many teachers and students referring to it as 'social slops'.

It certainly seemed that history in the senior school had been in decline in the 1990s. The worst affected state was South Australia where the proportion of year 12 students taking history dropped by 16 per cent in the period 1993–98. In most other states and territories the picture was slightly less gloomy, but, from a history teacher's point of view, still depressing.

The Inquiry: Methodology

The Australian education system is a complex one. Indeed, it would be difficult to make many generalizations about education in Australia because of the control exercised over schools and schooling by the eight distinctly different states and territories. In these circumstances, a national inquiry into school history faced daunting challenges. The Monash University team who won the contract decided to mix a qualitative with a quantitative approach to the inquiry, with the accent on a rapid deployment of the former. This was because the team was working on a very tight timeline during the worst possible time of year, when the long summer break (December–January) accounted for at least two months out of the inquiry's six-month schedule, and the team needed a sharp focus on school-based trends and events rather than the sometimes more stilted, snapshot results to be gathered from survey sampling.

During the period November 1999 to March 2000, the team used, among others, the following data collection methods:

- the convening of focus group sessions in all states and territories with representative samples of primary and secondary school teachers;
- round table discussions with local history subject association executive members;
- interviews with local curriculum officials;
- a call for submissions from stakeholders and interest groups;

- a review of national and international research;
- a short review of university education departments' provision of history training;
- a review and analysis of curriculum documents and policies in all states and territories;
- a survey of history teachers in primary and secondary schools.

A Concise Summary of the Inquiry's Main Findings

Professional debate
There had been very little substantial Australian research in recent years on the teaching and learning of history. Nor was there any current text on the teaching and learning of history in Australia that might act as a handbook for teachers.

History and the primary curriculum
Many primary school teachers were inadequately trained in the teaching of history. Consequently, successful teaching and learning of history in primary schools frequently depended upon the enthusiasm and/or skill of individual teachers. In many primary schools, history appeared to be a marginalized part of the SOSE curriculum and many young students left their primary schools uncertain about the nature of history. However, primary school teachers, while keen for more professional development in history, were unanimous in their strong support for teaching the discipline within an integrated primary curriculum framework.

History and studies of society (SOSE) in the secondary school
In secondary schools where a SOSE-based curriculum framework had a clearly identified school history strand, the teaching and learning of history appeared to operate at a reasonably successful level, as in Queensland for example. Where there had been no clear identification of the subject within a SOSE framework, the study of history suffered.

Adverse consequences included a lack of student understanding of what constitutes historical study. Accordingly, students made poorly informed choices about senior school subjects, often rejecting history at years 10 and 11 because of its unfamiliarity. At the same time, there was a perception in many schools (in SOSE jurisdictions) of SOSE as a low-status, generalist key learning area (KLA). Accordingly, in the junior-middle secondary school, teachers who have little or no history background are frequently allocated to teach history-within-SOSE. This

184

'topping-up' exploitation of SOSE exacerbated the problem of poor subject identity and subject rejection, produced poor-quality learning outcomes, and added to the stresses and strains of qualified history teachers.

It was suggested that these factors explained in part the recent decline in the number of students studying history at senior school level in most jurisdictions. There were, however, other suggested factors in the decline of history in the senior school in different jurisdictions. These included competition from the growing number of business/management subjects on offer, the growing number of vocational education and training (VET) options open to senior secondary students, and the imposition of mandated history in the middle school. Opinions varied about the VET factor and the consequences of imposed middle school history.

History's relationship with civics and citizenship education

Teachers felt that school history provides an important, if not the most important, element in an integrated approach to civics and citizenship education (CCE). Many teachers also felt that CCE should be dealt with in a significant way in other school disciplines and should not be a separate, mandated part of the curriculum. On the other hand, if CCE is to be an integrated element in school history, teachers said that they needed an increased timetable allocation, additional curriculum resourcing and more sustained professional development.

Professional development and curriculum support

An apparent reduction in state-based curriculum support services, which had commenced during the late 1980s, had produced a widespread view that in-school professional development in history teaching was virtually non-existent. This phenomenon had particular implications for unconfident primary teachers and for non-historical secondary SOSE teachers as well as for bona fide history teachers who wanted to improve their skills.

Moreover, while an outcomes-based approach to the curriculum prevailed in all states and territories, in some jurisdictions there seemed to be a disparity between the setting of target outcomes and the provision of on-the-ground curriculum support and sustained professional development to achieve those outcomes. In this context, state/territory history teachers' associations (HTAs), which were generally managed and operated by enthusiastic and committed volunteers, continued to provide a key element in developing and maintaining strong history teaching in some schools; but HTAs had limited resources.

History and the prescribed curriculum
Experienced and enthusiastic teachers in all jurisdictions strongly rejected the idea that history should have a prescribed curriculum within a mandated framework that over-emphasized chronology at the expense of understanding. Furthermore, many teachers argued trenchantly against short tests of memorization. Teachers contended that they needed time to enable their students to achieve a well-developed understanding of historical skills, ideas and content. Teachers in SOSE jurisdictions preferred a minimum timetable allocation for history-based studies rather than a mandated series of prescriptive syllabuses.

Australian history and indigenous history
Teachers generally characterized Australian history in schools as suffering from lack of continuity, topic repetition and lack of coherence. It seemed to be unpopular with students in the middle secondary school and there was also evidence of a declining interest in Australian history at the senior school level. Regarding indigenous history, there were strong concerns about perceived inadequacies in teacher preparation and professional development for dealing with the content and the sensitivities of indigenous history, especially in the secondary school.

Pre-service issues and professional collaboration
Evidence emerged of widespread concern about the quality of many recently trained graduate teachers who were applauded for their enthusiasm but were a source of anxiety because of an apparently deficient knowledge base in historical studies. This anxiety applied both to primary and secondary trainees. Moreover, it was suggested that there should be more active and productive collaboration between history teachers and heritage-based professional historians including museum staff, heritage site staff, local historians and freelance history writers.

Political, administrative, teaching relationships
Bearing in mind the sensitive, and often politically fraught nature of history, the management of school history curriculum design and implementation seemed to work best in jurisdictions where there was strong collaboration and mutual respect. There were, however, fundamental and worrying problems regarding curriculum design, curriculum implementation and curriculum support for school history in jurisdictions where one or more of the following factors have applied, or currently apply:

- relations between stakeholders, interest groups and officials have broken down;
- curriculum design appears to have been undertaken without authentic consultation;
- curriculum implementation appears to have taken place hastily;
- curriculum officials have excessive workloads in a variety of curriculum areas;
- curriculum officials have little or no background in school history;
- curriculum officials have little or no direct contact with schools because of workload problems.

The inquiry team found that a disproportionate amount of responsibility was sometimes placed upon the shoulders of small numbers of overworked curriculum officials in several jurisdictions.

Recommendations

The following recommendations were part of the final 200-page report, submitted to the minister's Department of Education Training and Youth Affairs (DETYA) in May 2000. The report recommended that the minister fund a proposed Centenary of Federation Commonwealth Government National History Project to be implemented in two phases, with seeding grants and pilot projects introduced in 2000–2001 – and more substantial projects in 2001–2003. The project should comprise:

A national seminar
A national seminar should be convened to develop a coherent approach to the teaching and learning of Australian history in schools. Participants should comprise selected academic historians, leading history teachers, history educators and curriculum officials from the Commonwealth and state/territory departments and boards of studies.

A national centre for history education and a national association for history and civics and citizenship education
A national centre for history education should be established and initially supported by Commonwealth funding for three years. Thereafter, it should be self-sustaining. The proposed centre should initially be sited in one university or two (a collaborative effort), with possibly even more sites as a virtual national centre.

A primary history project and a secondary history project
Following the national seminar and the establishment of the national centre, a primary history project (grades 5/6/7) and a secondary history project (years 8/9) should be funded, modelled on the Schools History Project (SHP) in England. Each project should be relevant to local syllabus needs, would emphasize both skills and content and should be of one term's duration.

The creation of locally based professional development consortia and direct Commonwealth support for subject associations
Pilot schemes should be established in each state and territory, to be based on local professional development (PD) consortia of subject associations, faculties of education, university history departments and employers. Each pilot consortium should bid for Commonwealth funding for specific, locally based PD and curriculum development projects which should be aimed at primary and/or secondary schools and prioritize the use of IT in school history.

A nationally offered postgraduate programme in history education
DETYA should support the establishment of a PD-based, nationally offered postgraduate programme (graduate certificate/graduate diploma) in history education and/or CCE to allow participants to follow these pathway options:

- half the programme could be undertaken through consortium-auspiced PD programmes which involve assessment for credit;
- one-quarter (or one-half maximum) of the programme could be undertaken through studying history subjects in a history department;
- one-quarter (or one-half maximum) of the programme could be undertaken through studying history education subjects in a faculty of education.

The programme could be credited to further postgraduate studies, if applicable.

An Australian handbook on the teaching and learning of history
DETYA should commission a text to act as a handbook on the teaching and learning of school history and CCE in Australia. The book should cover primary and secondary teaching issues, should be practical and should have a national and international research/best practice background.

At the time of writing (May 2000), the report is due to be launched by the Federal Minister in June.

NOTES

1. S. Macintyre, 'A black armband for teaching history', *Sunday Age* (5 July 1998).
2. See D. Watson, 'Back to the past', *Australian Review of Books* (20 December 1997), pp. 6–7.
3. P. Price, 'History in schools – part of the problem, part of the solution', *Australian Historical Association Bulletin*, 88 (June 1999), pp. 30–5; P. Wagg, 'Response to Alan Ryan', *Australian Historical Association Bulletin*, 88 (June 1999), pp. 36–8.
4. See M. Skilbeck, 'The nature of history and its place in the curriculum', *Australian History Teacher*, 6 (1979), pp. 2–9; and R. Smith, 'Social studies education: The need for reappraisal', *Unicorn* 12, 3 (1986), pp. 147–53.

11

Signs of the Times:
The State of History Education in the UK

Review of *Issues in History Teaching*,
Edited by J. Arthur and R. Phillips

PETER LEE, ROSALYN ASHBY
AND ALARIC DICKINSON

Issues in History Teaching[1] is a collection of papers that, in the words of the publisher's blurb, 'attempts to incorporate every relevant major issue' relating to history education. No one will be surprised to find that the book does not quite manage to meet this claim, but it does give an interesting snapshot of the current state of health of history education in England and Wales. Its intended audience seems to be mainly teacher educators, and perhaps their charges – beginner and newly qualified teachers.

This review will not attempt to evaluate each chapter in the book, or to discuss all the 'issues' it does raise. Instead it will consider the collection as evidence of the current agenda in history education and of the kinds of thinking that young teachers will meet, and hence as one indication of the condition of history education in part of the UK. (England, Wales, Scotland and Northern Ireland have their own versions of the National Curriculum, so making generalizations is difficult. *Issues in History Teaching* has contributors only from England and Wales.)

James Arthur's introduction might be expected to give a clue as to what the 'issues' are, but unfortunately confines itself to a standard editor's summary of the contents. It affords no overview or specific insights into the issues for history education beyond the obvious worries about history's place in the curriculum (an issue that is not directly addressed in the book, although several papers touch on it in passing). Arthur's reminder that, if government action has fixed history in the curriculum for 11 to 14-year-olds, government decisions can as easily remove it, is a salutary one. Regrettably, he has nothing helpful to say about this, except to offer history teachers the unhappily formulated choice between giving 'greater priority to the value of history teaching, as part of the general aims of the school curriculum as a whole' or focusing 'their attention on improving history learning itself' (p. 3). This is an editorial opportunity, perhaps an obligation, missed.

On a more positive note, Arthur provides a valuable and well-judged summary of the workings of the History Task Group that revised the history National Curriculum, skilful in what it says by leaving some things unsaid (pp. 2–4). He claims that the book 'rightly focuses on the teaching issues arising out of the history classroom', a judgement that highlights a genuine strength of the book, one that is significant for history education in the UK, and therefore also for the purposes of this review (p. 5).

Some Peculiarities of History Education in the UK

Two features of the book stand out as indicators of the state of history education in England and Wales. First, it is strikingly different from any discussion of history education likely to be found in most of the world. There is little concern with battles over which story should be taught, or who owns the story, because disciplinary issues predominate: the assumed agenda is that students need to understand *history*, not to learn one particular story. Second, the matters under discussion tend to be directly related to the business of teaching and learning history; that is to say, they are not generic speculations or injunctions. The much loved distinction between 'theory' and 'practice' – so often used to berate anyone who dares to think about education – has no place here. Where individual papers are weaker on implications for practice, it tends to be because they are chronicling changes in instructions from government that set the framework for practice.

These two characteristics of *Issues in History Teaching* might seem mundane to history teachers in the UK, but they are the result of hard won political battles, long processes of innovative curriculum development in which teachers played a major role, research stemming from practical learning and teaching problems, and advanced assessment practices. In addition, UK history teachers owe a great deal to a few unnamed individuals in the relevant governmental and quasi-governmental organizations who fought to preserve the disciplinary focus of history in the National Curriculum through the 'key elements' (for example, 'interpretations of history', 'historical enquiry').

This concern to teach students about the nature and status of history, as well as about passages of the past, makes UK history education highly distinctive, even in comparison with other English-speaking parts of the world, or with other European countries. Hilary Cooper's chapter 'Primary school history in Europe', discussing a small-scale research project carried out in England, Finland, Greece and the Netherlands, recognizes this difference in a judiciously cautious way (p. 172). As it happens, there is some evidence that the difference may be more than skin deep. Factor analysis of responses from the sample of more than 30,000 in the Youth and History Project show that the 868 English and Welsh students see the use of sources and visits to historical sites as part of historical explanation and enquiry. In contrast, European students (taken together) tend to see them as part of an apparatus by which teachers try to enliven lessons. It may be that the disciplinary focus of UK history is showing up here.[2] Such a conclusion has to be treated with caution, since comparison of factors derived from one country with those for the whole data-set may be misleading. However, the data for this component of the Youth and History survey is better structured than for most other components (see next paragraph). Curiously, the chapter 'History in Europe', one section of which purports to report the Youth and History Project on the basis of a dissemination conference, makes no reference to this.

Research

Research is frequently cited in *Issues in History Teaching*, and some chapters focus directly on aspects of research. Ruth Watts' chapter on history in Europe (largely discussing the Youth and History Project) is an odd hybrid. Many of her comments relate more to opinions expressed in a dissemination conference than to the research. The chapter is a revealing example of the way in which research is sometimes poorly understood in the book. Watts gets her facts wrong: the 868 students in the sample were not English but Welsh and English, and many of them were 14, not 15-years-old (pp. 181 and 179). She claims that the 868 'is hardly a representative sample of a country', appearing to think that 'representative sample' means 'very large sample' (p. 181). She remains oblivious to the real methodological problems apparent in the questionnaire and responses. (For example, the modal response on a five-point scale was often the central point, that is, 'undecided' or its equivalents. Some double-barrelled items made it hard to interpret responses. Structure within item-blocks, as indexed by intercorrelations between responses, was often weak.) She quotes conference delegates' views about 'empathetic understanding' without reference to the now considerable research evidence from Europe (including the UK) and the USA (p. 180).[3] Confidence is further reduced by inaccurate references.

Watts makes frequent comments about the need for dissemination of work on Europe, and complains that not enough has been done. This is an important point to make, but, given that she does not explain that the Youth and History data is on a publicly available CD-ROM, there is a slight irony in her exhortations.[4]

The uncertain handling of research is not confined to 'History in Europe'. One of the problems about the book is that promiscuous citation in some chapters makes it difficult to judge what weight the quoted research will actually bear, since there is generally little indication of the scale or methodologies of the work cited. Such explanations cannot always be given, of course, since such treatment would reduce the argument to fragments. But where tiny surveys are generalized (implicitly or explicitly) to the school population at large, we need to know. Methodologies also sometimes require at least brief clarification. Stow and Haydn, for example, discussing 'Issues in the teaching of chronology', are clearly well read in this area, and make some useful points, but seldom give clues as to whether the research cited could support the claims that the text is making. Take the example of the paragraph on visual evidence and understanding of time (p. 91) in which four pieces of research are cited, characterized simply as having 'all used pictures as a stimulus for discussion about time'. Are these large- or small-scale studies? Can we generalize from them, or are they quoted as suggestive? What link is being made between these studies and the assertions that follow in the text?

Some of the research-based discussions are more sure-footed. Hilary Coopers' chapter (already mentioned) explores what young children in a range of European countries know about the past before they begin formal school history. It is careful in its claims, thoughtfully presented, and promises important further developments. Chris Husbands and Anna Pendry use aspects of a small-scale piece of research to argue a case with judicious caution. There is no attempt to make exaggerated claims, or to caricature other positions in order to appear to say something new.

Husbands and Pendry examine a few examples of students' responses in some detail (albeit without quite giving the precise wording of the task), and make some perceptive points. In particular, they raise three interesting issues. First, they emphasise the importance of pupils' talk for developing understanding. Second, they discuss the importance of the affective in students' attempts to come to grips with the strangeness of people's behaviour in the past. Finally, they insist that there are two chasms to be bridged here, not just one, arguing that we must recognize that it is youngsters who are being asked to make sense of this strange behaviour, while the behaviour in question is that of adults.

These are all worthwhile reminders. Pupil talk is plainly important at several levels. Social interaction can force students to recognize different standpoints and bring them up against weaknesses in their own assumptions.[5] It offers teachers a chance to listen in on students' thinking, in a way that even informal writing tasks cannot match. Above all it shows how students with reading and writing problems can nevertheless think to startling effect. In returning to the importance of talk, Husbands and Pendry are making a particularly timely intervention, since loose thinking about 'extended writing' (perhaps coupled with equally imprecise ideas about the necessity of a 'holistic' approach to history) seems increasingly common in UK history. The danger is that advocacy of extended writing in history is seldom clearly related to objectives. Understanding history does not require the ability to write well. Good writing may be an essential attribute of a professional historian, but the creation of professional historians is not a central goal of school history. We want students to understand the workings of the discipline, and use this understanding to good effect in also understanding how and why things happened as they did in particular passages of the past. Writing exercises may help develop understanding, but they need not be 'extended'. Indeed much work in the 1970s and 1980s demonstrated how it was possible to move students on and to assess their understanding (for diagnostic, formative or summative purposes) without reliance on extended writing. In assessment especially, the dangers of confusing writing ability with historical understanding are legion. None of this is to argue that students should not learn to write well, but simply to insist that this should not be confused with learning history.

The other two issues picked out by Husbands and Pendry both bear on a narrower sense of historical understanding, which has in the UK often – perhaps confusingly – been called 'empathy'. They rightly stress that prior understandings are crucial to learning (this is now backed by an immense weight of research in all areas of learning).[6] They couple this with a cautious speculation. 'Work in history education may have underestimated the extent to which children's capacity to respond to historical tasks is affected by issues of emotional and affective maturation, and not just by the level of their cognitive development'(p. 132).

Do students' own motives and emotional commitments make a difference? Almost certainly they do. There were signs of this in the CHATA Project (Concepts of History and Teaching Approaches, 7–14) where, for example, some of the younger children showed strong indications of wanting the story of King Arthur to be true, and moral revulsion at Roman treatment of slaves may have precluded certain lines of thinking.[7] However, we must be careful here. We cannot say how far, or in what circumstances, emotions necessarily override learnt 'rational passions' (for example, respect for evidence, and for people in the past) if and when they have been taught. And perhaps this is a big 'if': it is not clear how far there is any attempt to foster these dispositions as the 'ethics of thinking', rather than means of getting good grades, in schools. We need to be even more careful of notions like 'emotional and affective maturation', which will need a good deal of clarification before they are useful concepts in history. Husbands and Pendry do not make grand claims in the small space allotted them, sensibly confining themselves to beginning to raise the right questions.

Alongside the sensitive discussion of many aspects of students' historical understanding (in the sense of empathy) provided by Husbands and Pendry, Christine Counsell's chapter touches on this area. Counsell raises the interesting issue of the relation between substantive knowledge and second-order concepts (pp. 59–60).[8] She asks an important question – 'What kind of interactive effect takes place in history between [students'] general second-order ideas and their substantive knowledge?' – but then weakens the point when looking at explorations of 'empathy', by misunderstanding the research. She notes that higher level responses took account of the temporal context, and remarks: 'it is possible that pupils' ideas were shaped, to some extent, by their period knowledge'. This fails to take into account the fact that in research of this kind all the students have 'period' knowledge available, but only some think to use it. Whether they use it or not is a matter of the assumptions they make about doing history, not specific knowledge of one period. Some students behave as though they first ask the question 'Can we assume that people in the past are the same as us?'. The issue is one of whether students see fit to *cash* the information they are given (not even whether they cash it 'correctly', but whether they try at all). In recent research, some primary school students did this better than most year 9s: they did not know more about the period, but understood the activity of history better.[9] Wider knowledge (including substantive knowledge) comes in here, of course, in that increasing experience of history may make (indeed should make) students more wary of assuming that people in the past thought as we do. But this is not the same thing as specific contextual knowledge.

One possible moral is that as well as being in constant touch, research and teaching may sometimes need to be distinguished: they have different goals. In *teaching* history, detailed contextual knowledge and a deep grasp of substantive concepts is central, and students' work is partly judged on these. But in research (and tight diagnostic assessment) the criteria are rather different. For 'empathy' the issue is how far, and in what ways, students assume that people in the past were the same as us. Tasks must give them the possibility of going beyond our present ideas and values, and indeed make it hard to explain anything without going beyond them. Take the case of one of the tasks mentioned by Husbands and Pendry, where students have to make sense of Elizabeth's treatment of Mary Queen of Scots. The materials do not have to be comprehensive, for the question is not whether the students can reach the right answer, but what moves they make or do not make with what they do have available. So somewhere in the materials there must be ideas that cause difficulties for students who assume Elizabeth will think as they do. These might include some indication that Elizabeth did not always put her friends and relations first, or treat kindly even those with whom she had had very close relationships. There must be reference (however simple) to the fact that kings and queens tended to assume that they were chosen by God, and that it was not right for people to overthrow them or to kill them. Other ideas and circumstances must be available to give Elizabeth reasons for wanting to do the unthinkable. These might include the Spanish threat, and connected worries about the return of Roman Catholicism, together with Mary's potential role as a focus for plots, and the actual plots that occurred. (Note that deep understanding of Catholicism is not essential to the research task, but only a simplified sense of the perceived threat.) It is then possible to face students with a paradox, asking why Elizabeth delayed Mary's execution for so very long when many of her advisers and subjects thought the execution essential.

The categories used to analyze responses to this task will not be based on the degree to which students exhibit wider contextual knowledge than is provided in the task, but on how the provided material is used and the assumptions made about what needs to be done to explain Elizabeth's

196

delay. Holism in history education is a laudable goal, but valid holism has to be earned. It is where we get when we have sorted out the complexities, made the distinctions, and remembered the purposes of our tasks. (This is very clear in the chapters of Hunt and especially McAleavy, who have to break down the ideas of 'significance' and 'interpretation' in order to make any progress in thinking about teaching them. See below.)

Conceptual Matters

Conceptual problems still abound, even among teacher educators. It is worrying, for example, still to meet assertions like 'SCHP advocated that pupils "do" history in the same way as historians' (p. 114). Some early claims by some Schools Council History Project personnel did indeed say this sort of thing, but it is essential to point out that the project became much more circumspect in its claims.[10] Clarity matters here, because the press and public, let alone young teachers, need to grasp the difference between doing history in the same way as historians, and understanding something of how historical enquiry works, and the basis on which its explanations and accounts are given. Careless grand claims do not help.

Skills and concepts

Throughout the book there is a tendency to talk in general terms about 'skills' in an unfortunately unexamined way, as if everyone knows what one of those is. There are many cases of slithering between 'skills' and 'concepts', as if they were the same thing. Fortunately, Christine Counsell deals explicitly with this issue, and it would have been useful if some of the other contributors had read her comment complaining of:

> The absence of common distinction between those aspects of the subject that relate to understanding of the big ideas that history generates, such as causation, consequence, change, continuity and so forth. Although the latter is sometimes thought of as 'conceptual understanding', it is just as often characterized as a set of 'skills' (suggesting a process), such as the ability to construct multi-causal explanations.' (p. 57)

Counsell is absolutely right to make this crucial point; it is extraordinary that confusions persist about it after nearly three decades. There are complex issues here that cannot be considered in a review, but three crude points might be in order. First, 'skill' is generally used of single-track activities that can be improved by practice (for example, riding bicycles), so it does not satisfactorily describe the complex activities of history. Second, concepts cannot in themselves be developed or improved just by practice, but involve understanding and reflection. Third, the relation between understanding and doing is complex, more particularly when we group learning goals under broad headings like 'evidence' or 'source work'. For example, a low-ability student can acquire an understanding of a concept like 'evidence', but may still not be able to perform tasks that are arguably more appropriately thought of as skills, like cross-referencing. Conversely, able pupils who can cross-reference sources with ease may still think of them as information, and thus be unable to use them as evidence at all. On the other hand, it is very often what students do that tells us what they understand. The fact that Counsell has to make her point, and that some contributors to the book have clearly not begun to grasp what is at issue here, is a sad reflection on at least one rather basic aspect of history education in England and Wales at the turn of the century.

Specific concepts
Significance One sign of the vitality of the agenda of history education in the UK is that *Issues in History Teaching* includes some chapters setting out to clarify particular concepts. This is absolutely central to any serious development of history education, for, without a clear sense of what it is that we want pupils to learn, we are unlikely to get far with our teaching. And if research in the past 30 years has shown anything, it is the danger of underestimating the ideas of students, some of whom already operate with a highly sophisticated conceptual apparatus (well in advance of normal GCSE assessment demands) by year 9.[11]

Martin Hunt tackles the notion of 'historical significance'. His chapter is a welcome sally into a very complex area, and he makes some excellent points. He suggests that with more room for manoeuvre in the revised National Curriculum teachers should be 'sensitive to the implications of the chosen content and to the various ways the significance of events, people and changes can be interpreted'. He enunciates an important principle: 'Pupils need to be encouraged to understand how and why perceptions change, and why with time a topic could be seen as more or less significant.' In this connection he gives the useful example of how current constitutional reform 'could alter views about the significance of events in the past, including the presentation of content under the title of the National Curriculum study, 'The making of the United Kingdom' (p. 42).

Some of Hunt's remarks are reminiscent of battles fought in the 1970s and 1980s, which may suggest that they are still not won. 'When a pupil's recall of specific detail diminishes, it is the understanding that comes from conclusions about the significance of events, people and changes that creates the educational value' (p. 40). (Some ambiguities lurking in this kind of claim are discussed below.) It is particularly good to see his emphasis on the importance of long-run themes (p. 42). Sadly, however, he does not take the opportunity to comment on the utter failure of the National Curriculum to sort out a proper nesting structure, so that existing study units can fit into a long-run framework of history. Nor does he mention the abandonment even of the half-hearted moves in this direction made (and often misunderstood) in the first version of the curriculum. If 'significance' is to be properly tackled, this structural issue has to be addressed.[12]

Hunt makes reference to something that is an important aspect of, and a necessary condition for, progression. 'There will be times when pupils can only understand the real significance of what they have covered in earlier years after they have studied some of the more recent history usually taught in Year 9' (p. 42). This is in some ways an excellent point, but put this way there is an unfortunate suggestion that the 'real significance' is whatever it seems to be now. The principle is wider: the significance of events changes with the passing of time and with different timescales, so year 6 pupils can come to understand the significance of what they studied in year 4 in more complex ways, and year 8 pupils can do the same in relation to year 7. As Hunt says later, 'Often the significance of an event can only be seen in the light of subsequent events' (p. 47). The point is not that *recent* history is necessary.

The problem with Hunt's chapter is that it needs a sounder conceptual foundation than he offers us. Partington's list of content criteria is about as much as we get in the way of systematic elucidation (p. 41). The discussion under the heading 'practical' is helpful, but slips into talk about 'turning points' as if the latter were a synonym for other words like 'significance', 'important' or 'influence' (p. 47). The inductive categorizations of researchers can take us further than this. Lis Cercadillo's research, extending CHATA work on accounts into the specific area of students' ideas about historical significance in England.

and Spain, finds them operating with a wide range of notions (see Chapter 7 by Cercadillo in this volume).

The conceptual weakness leads to two major problems: (i) confusion between significance *within* accounts on the one hand, and the importance of historical knowledge in general on the other; (ii) the assumption that significance is a characteristic built into agents, events or processes. The second difficulty surfaces most painfully in the examples of practical exercises, which fall far short of the principles Hunt himself mentions earlier in his discussion, but somehow never quite manages to hang on to.

One exercise is headed 'Explanations of why the Great Fire of London is a significant event in history', and asks students to 'choose the three best explanations of the importance of the Great Fire in history'. The choices offered students are fine, but the task is absurd because the Great Fire has no fixed significance *in history* (p. 49). Does it have equal importance, or the same kind of importance, in the history of town planning as it has in the history of London? Is it as important in a general history of England as in a history of England in the seventeenth century? Does it have the same kind of importance for economic development as it has for living conditions? Hunt makes here the same sort of mistake as evidence exercises that ask about the reliability of sources without reference to a question. Significance has to be relativized to (at the very least) a theme and a timescale. Many 14 year-olds are well past this point already, and exercises like this can disastrously limit responses to low levels, while actively misleading other students.

A further exercise on the Second World War asks which of a list of events was the most significant, without any indication of parameters. If the task is to work, there should be some indication whether it is intended to be approached in terms of contemporary perceptions, of the outcome of the war or of subsequent events. It may be that the question is designed to raise questions about parameters, but there is no indication of this despite very detailed treatment, and taken with the previous example it is likely to be desperately damaging for some beginner teachers as well as their students.

The opening and the conclusion of the chapter both confirm the impression that there are deep-seated confusions here. Hunt rightly wants to point out that in some ways school history is again 'in danger', so it is important that students understand that it matters: 'A fundamental strategy is to try to ensure that pupils are very clear about the importance or significance of what they study in history and how this contributes to their general education, in the same way that a core curriculum subject does' (p. 40). At the end of the chapter he sums up:

> The emphasis on significance will help [pupils] understand the physical world they see around them ... They will learn why certain parts of the world speak English, and about those factors that have contributed to today's multicultural society ... The consideration of significance promotes not only the ability to explain and support a case, but also encourages teenagers to consider where they stand on some of the significant and enduring issues that arise from the study of people in the past (p. 52).

One can only applaud Hunt's general position here: his heart is clearly in the right place. But there are several matters at issue, and he slips uneasily between them throughout the chapter.

It may be useful to set out a rough and ready typology for thinking about significance in history before trying to disentangle some of the issues. (See Figure 11.1. Note that this schema would need more work before it could do the job required in history education, but it will serve to make some points in the context of a review.)

FIGURE 11.1:
A TENTATIVE SCHEMA FOR THINKING ABOUT HISTORICAL SIGNIFICANCE

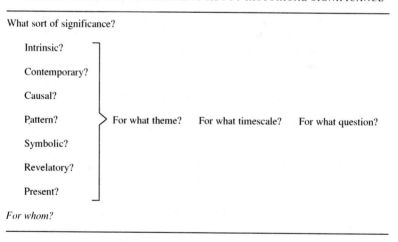

Any candidate for intrinsic significance is likely to need argument, but most of us tend to assume there are some, and some students certainly do.[13] Some actions, events or processes are given significance by people at the time, and this judgement by contemporaries may be very different from that of later historians. Many events cause further events, and these causal chains may be more or less wide-ranging, and have traceable ramifications more or less far into the future. Patterns of change in developmental accounts are picked out by concepts like 'trend' or 'turning-point', and in these patterns of events may acquire significance as anticipations, beginnings or endings. Some actions or events are recognized as symbols of something else (for example, enduring characteristics of a person, an institution or a nation). Some are held to reveal something about human beings or the nature of society. Others are important to our present interests. Note that this typology is not at the substantive level (using notions like political, ethical or social), that the same action, event or process may have different significance in different themes and timescales, and that this will be sensitive to the questions asked. It is perfectly possible for events to be significant in several ways at once and, equally, different attributions of significance may signal different kinds of clash between accounts, or none at all.

Hunt insists that students should be 'very clear about the importance or significance of what they study in history and how this contributes to their general education' (p. 40). There are (at least) two issues here. One is the claim that students need to know that the passages of the past they have to study are important. The other is the claim that they need to know why an understanding of historical significance is important to them. Stated as Hunt puts it, the first claim is defensible but misleading and possibly dangerous. If we teach students that the past they study is important for us because it made the world what it is, it may come across as having a fixed, given importance for which the present becomes the touchstone. (Whose present? Which version?) And what of the events or processes students do not study? Are these of less, or even no importance? Given the eccentricities of the National Curriculum, the consequences of this scarcely bear thinking about.

In any case being told that certain events are important in this sense will not carry conviction unless the students understand some other, rather difficult ideas. (For example, they will have to understand, at some level, how the past closes and opens options for the future.) Hunt needs to distinguish here between the past and history. It is the discipline of history that provides students with ways of understanding the exhortations that Hunt wants teachers to inflict on them. The central matter, as Hunt recognizes intermittently in his chapter, is that students understand how and why things can be important in the past. This means not just learning that certain events or processes *were* important, but also *how* notions like significance and importance work in the discipline of history. It is understanding of the latter that allows students to take on board and internalize the former. Understanding history makes it possible to attribute significance to elements of the past.

Interpretations Tony McAleavy deals with 'interpretations', a concept closely related to 'significance' (although there is no cross-referencing with Martin Hunt's ideas). The chapter offers an interesting summary of how 'interpretation' found its way into the National Curriculum, and there are lots of practical suggestions. The impact of these is often weakened by the absence of any rationale. For instance, McAleavy offers examples of 'debates that are perfectly accessible to 11 to 14-year-olds' (p. 75). These include 'how the Anglo-Saxons took control of Britain [*sic*] in the decades after the departure of the Roman army', and 'whether there was a blitz spirit in wartime Britain'. We are not given any clues as to what it is that makes these examples particularly accessible to 11- to 14- year-olds.

The main difficulty with the chapter is that it does not suggest any apparatus for the students to acquire, an omission which may have something to do with the distinction McAleavy makes between 'explaining to students how disagreements come about' and 'expecting them to arbitrate on the disagreement'. It is a helpful distinction, but to shift the focus onto the first and effectively duck the second is to leave students helplessly shrugging their shoulders in the face of disagreement. (CHATA responses suggest that this is precisely what many do.)

McAleavy gives us the NCC's extraordinary list of 'types of interpretation' (books, museums, TV documentaries, theme parks and so on) which is actually a list of locations or situations in which interpretations of the past are likely to occur, and only in a weak sense a list of *types of interpretation* (p. 74).[14] More promisingly, there is a list of opportunities for 'coverage of a range of modern interpretations', which, despite the last misleading phrase, seems to go beyond students learning about particular substantive interpretations ('modern' or not), to suggest useful methodological understandings (p. 76).

Unfortunately there is no systematic development of this crucial area. What is needed is discussion of the kind of intellectual toolkit students need for making sense of differing interpretations. We might start with sorting out the different possible relationships between interpretations. They can, among other things, complement one another, compete, conflict and contradict. These relationships are very different, and have important consequences for how we deal with them. We need to help students understand that interpretations relate to historical questions as well as human interests (in both senses). McAleavy rightly mentions 'purpose' as a central idea; interpretations have different jobs, not just different audiences. Students need to be introduced to differences between validity and truth, and be given tasks that face them with the impossibility of the idea that stories can be copies of the past. This in turn is likely to mean tackling other workable everyday but historically misleading ideas underlying students' conceptions, for example that history could in general have been 'eye-witnessed'.

McAleavy helpfully prints the 1991 and 1995 National Curriculum level statements on interpretation side by side, but makes no comment on the startlingly arbitrary nature of the progressions enshrined in each (p. 78). For example, evaluation of interpretations in 1995 is only 'beginning' (whatever that means) at level 8, whereas in 1991 it was clearly already happening at level 7. In 1991 students are aware by level 2 that different stories can give different versions of what happened, but in 1995 this does not seem to enter the picture until level 4. Much turns on the notion of 'representation' here, but, if the 1995 statements are to make any sense, it seems a rather concrete matter (see below).

Both sets of levels are appalling, but (as just one example) the transitions between levels 3, 4 and 5 in the 1995 set surely deserve some comment in a chapter intended for young teachers. Between levels 3 and 4 we get the sudden introduction of 'interpretation', where hitherto we had only 'ways in which the past is represented'. ('Representation' here is presumably used in much the same way as in the NCC 'types of interpretation', namely, concrete types of past-referencing artefacts or situations that students can list. Any more complex reading would make complete nonsense of progression.) Suddenly, at level 4, the students 'can *show how* some aspects of the past have been represented *and interpreted* in different ways' (emphasis added). Level 5 moves them on only in that they can 'suggest possible reasons' for the existence of different interpretations. (This is something most pupils can do only too easily by use of the Mandy Rice Davis argument, 'He would say that wouldn't he?') The notions of 'representation', 'interpretation' and 'reasons' for differing explanations have to be properly unpacked if there is to be any hope of making sense of this, or deciding whether it is justified by experience, assessment or research. It would be unfair to complain that McAleavy does not take on the task of sorting out the official levels statements (who in their right mind would?), but it is reasonable to be surprised that he is silent about the problems.

McAleavy justly comments on the lack of research in 1991, but does not recognize that by 1995 the situation was different (p. 77). American and British work was well under way, and some of it was accessible, either formally or informally.[15] In any case, regardless of the state of empirical work, the conceptual poverty of both sets of levels cannot be excused by lack of research. The Schools History Project already had a more powerful apparatus, and the Cambridge History Project had gone well beyond that, as indeed had many teachers of traditional A-level courses.

Knowledge Christine Counsell discusses substantive historical knowledge in her chapter, drawing on Rogers' work, and makes important points about analogy and what she calls 'resonance': 'Transfer implies the ability to practise an old skill in a new context. Resonance, at its simplest, simply suggests unconscious recognition – the hidden familiar tag that keeps motivation up for a few seconds longer before the pupil rebels or falls asleep' (p. 69). Perhaps the formulation begs questions, but the context makes it evident that this is a useful notion. Here some of the American research is relevant, particularly Gaea Leinhardt's detailed qualitative exploration of 'ikat' explanations (running ideas like threads woven into lessons), which would have given support and substance to Counsell's reference to teachers' practice (p. 68–70).[16] This whole area of exploring and understanding students' substantive knowledge, and how it can be made active and usable, is of immense importance and has been relatively neglected. Counsell's contribution here is timely and interesting.

Counsell rightly denies that choice of 'content' is unimportant, and at the same time makes some appropriately cutting remarks about both 'relevance' and 'neutral' curricula (p. 61). Here there is again a sense of battles being refought, but the confidence of her argument is evidence that they are getting easier each time. She sees salvation in the face of content problems in the 'astonishing innovation' of the appearance of 'interpretations' as an attainment target in the National Curriculum (p. 62). (Older teachers may feel that 'astonishing' is appropriate enough, given the political origins of the National Curriculum, but be rather surprised to find this target described as a startling 'innovation'!)[17] However, Counsell treats interpretation as if it solves content issues simply by switching focus from the 'reliability' of an interpretation to 'how it came to be' (p. 62). Leaving aside the question as to whether 'reliability' is a helpful notion here, experience and research combine to suggest that giving students multiple interpretations and examining 'how they came to be' is not likely to be sufficient. Students need an apparatus for understanding historical accounts. They need to begin to understand the status of accounts as compared with, for example, singular factual statements, and to grasp that accounts are not copies of the past. It will help if we can develop a better apparatus ourselves, so that, as teachers, we begin to make elementary distinctions (for example, in the relations between accounts, as suggested earlier). If, instead of collapsing disagreement between rival accounts immediately and helplessly into postmodern appeals to power, we begin to take seriously the complexity of historical accounts emphasized by the linguistic turn in philosophy of history, we can begin to construct a clearer picture of what we want students to learn. We will also need more sophisticated models of progression: what prior conceptions about rival accounts are students likely to hold?[18]

Much of what is at stake is illustrated by Counsell's uncertain handling of the notion of the 'status' of accounts:

> Most history lessons relate to one of two issues. The emphasis is either upon the *status* of accounts (whose side is it on? is it reliable? in what setting was this written/painted? what kind of account is this? how would this person have told the story differently? let's try to see this from her point of view...) or their *structure* (which factors were the most important? what *were* the key factors? how shall we summarize the main issues? does this example fit into this account? are these issues political or social? is this label any good or is it more confusing?)... The distinction here is between two types of history teaching *emphasis*:
>
> 1. Who is saying/writing this and what difference does that make? (status);
> 2. How do (or might, or should, or don't) these things fit together and what shall we call them? (structure). (pp. 63–4)

Counsell admits that the distinction obscures relationships between the two types of emphasis, but the problem is deeper. The notion of 'status' here is seriously impoverished: the status of historical claims is not just a matter of who is speaking or writing, of side-taking, reliability or even perspective. Different kinds of historical claims – singular factual statements, explanations, narratives, attributions of causal significance, developmental patterns – have different status in that they have different relationships to evidence, and are justified or refuted in different ways. Towards the end of her chapter, Counsell gets close to putting this right:

> To teach any discipline is to help pupils to see more clearly the common interpretive devices that allow it to make sense: to identify the conceptual devices that unify [sic]. To do history is to 'see' its information in a certain way. We have become familiar with its validation claims, the organizational shapes and patterns of its discourse structures. Whether these are left as implicit or explicit, as routine procedures or meta-cognitive reflection, depends on the emphasis a teacher is trying to achieve at any point. (p. 69)

The claim to familiarity here is arguably either premature or ironic, but if this passage is taken as one measure of the state of history education in the UK, there are grounds for arguing that it is in good shape.

Progression

Another feature of UK history education that stands out in this book is its concern with progression. This is not just because the notion is built into the National Curriculum, but because it is part of the way in which history education is thought about and disputed.

Christine Counsell again has important points to make here, although she confuses difficulties arising through oversimplification with the inherent problems of thinking in terms of progression (pp.58–9).[19] Of course, the idea of progression is not exhausted by the consideration of second-order concepts. But if this view of progression has taken root, it is a problem similar to that of 'skills', namely one of professional understanding, not something inherent in progression models. We need more models of progression in a wider range of second-order concepts, including understanding of 'generalization' and 'particular' which, curiously, Counsell seems to think both belong in some other category realm. We also need to look again at the development of substantive concepts, where research tended to die out with the (sometimes over-zealous) reaction to Piagetian work.[20] (There is more going on here now, in the UK and other parts of Europe.)[21] And of course there is progression in other areas too, like dispositions (respect for evidence, for people in the past and so on) and frameworks of knowledge. (This is a crucial area for future work. The most radical ideas are still those of Denis Shemilt and John Hamer, with some – marginal – developments by Lee.)[22]

Counsell seems to confuse progression models with the specification of individual student learning paths (p. 67). (There are similarities here with the example used early in her chapter, in which her student confused generalizations and particulars.) Progression models are generalizations about what students' prior ideas are likely to be, and as such are one consideration to be taken into account in setting goals. If progression is thought of as 'journeys' that students make, a progression model suggests several points where students' journeys might begin, and provides a map of some of the terrain (including landmarks and obstacles) that they may pass through to reach a cluster of possible destinations. The same cluster of destinations may be reached via different regions, so a model does not say if it is best to go by the east or west coast route, or even by train in the first place. Even less are such models to be construed as ladder-like, where one step must be mounted before the next, or as stages through which it is necessary to pass (p. 70).

History in the Curriculum

Rob Phillips and Penelope Harnett both discuss the development of the National Curriculum for history. Phillips considers it in its political context, and Harnett concentrates on the primary curriculum; both provide useful summaries. Harnett rightly points out at the beginning of her chapter that official sources 'cannot take into account the many other ways outside of school in which teachers and children encounter history and that influence their views of the past' (p. 25).[23] The strength of Harnett's approach is its sensitivity to unintended consequences of policy; throughout she implicitly reminds us of the way in which the actual operation of a centralized curriculum may differ from the predictions of its designers.

Anyone wanting to investigate the politics of the National Curriculum should read Phillips' outstanding, book-length treatment, but he raises some important matters in this briefer survey.[24] In particular, quoting Hargreaves and Evans, he argues the 'fundamental need ... to "bring teachers back in" to debates over policy and reform', and that 'history teachers and policy advisers need to regain confidence in the importance and relevance of the subject for the twenty-first century' (p. 22).

This last theme runs through the book, indicating a considerable degree of uncertainty about the future of history in the UK. McAleavy refers to history teachers' 'feeling that their subject is often marginalized'(p. 81). He also refers to 'the perception of difficulty that so bedevils secondary school history' (p. 80). Hunt talks about history being 'downgraded' in the National Curriculum, and worries about it losing its relevance (pp. 40–1). He quotes Ben Walsh (referring to Tim Lomas' research) to the effect that 'pupils are put off history less by its conceptual difficulty than by the amount of work they have to do, and the impression that much of it is simply grinding through material' (p. 47). This is a suggestive finding, making a melancholy contrast with the findings of Shemilt's *Evaluation Study* of 20 years ago, where the perception of conceptual difficulty went with a recognition of personal relevance.[25] Do we have to keep relearning the lesson that history can be difficult *and* popular, if it empowers students in ways they recognize? We need detailed research on a reasonably large scale to explore students' perceptions of difficulty and relevance, but only if both these notions are given some serious analytical attention; 'relevance' in particular has an appalling history of conceptual confusion in education. It would also be interesting to discover how far the prevalence of heavy writing demands in assessment at most levels (often with purposes only indirectly connected to understanding history) plays a part in perceptions of difficulty.[26]

Ian Grosvenor and Ian Davies treat specific contemporary concerns in, or linked with, history education. Grosvenor deals sensitively with multiculturalism and history teaching. His chapter gets off to a very bad start, when he asks 'what should be included in the narrative of the nation with which pupils engage in schools' (p. 148). They should not, of course, be engaging with 'the' narrative of anything, let alone of the nation. However, by the middle of the chapter things improve greatly, and he begins to make important points. He is spot on target in insisting that 'a concern for a pedagogy' that 'attends to historical skills, linked to appropriate content, will not necessarily produce rational thinking or greater toleration and understanding in pupils' (pp. 156–7). This is a central problem of history education, and one that demands attention from the advocates of citizenship. It may nonetheless be true that without historical understanding there is little hope of tolerance of the kind Grosvenor seeks.

Davies looks at current citizenship initiatives, which may take time from history in schools, but might possibly offer some compensatory opportunities to history teachers. He hints at, without ever quite following up, distinctions between 'action outcomes' (what students are able to do, and what they actually do, after a citizenship course) and 'history cognition' (which may systematically develop abilities, but cannot guarantee improvement – however understood – in behaviour). The old problem of which takes precedence, understanding history or approved-of citizenship aims, receives little attention. Historical understanding may be a necessary condition of citizenship, as of multiculturalism, and teachers should be confident in pursuing genuine opportunities offered by proposals to introduce citizenship education into schools. But this does not mean that history education should be subordinated to citizenship education, or that history teachers should desperately cast around to find chinks and interstices into which history can – by dint of some distortion – timorously squeeze itself. Davies' understandable wish to be helpful to worried teachers leads him uncomfortably close to such a strategy.

Between them, Grosvenor's and Davies' chapters suggest that it is important for history education to recognize its limitations in changing students' behaviour in any specified direction, without thereby in any way weakening its claim to be absolutely central to human understanding, which is necessarily past-referenced. We cannot avoid the past, so we had better equip students as well as we possibly can to address it rationally. This may be a necessary condition for certain kinds of desired behaviour (including sophisticated political behaviour and intolerance of racism), but it will not of itself achieve those ends. But then, it is not at all clear that anything that goes on in school can guarantee those, whatever politicians or OFSTED may think.[27]

Inspections

Three chapters in the book are provided by the HMI (Her Majesty's Inspectorate) History team, who were engaged in what they identified as 'the most complete and detailed investigation ever undertaken by HMI of how secondary history teachers are trained in England'. They inform us that this process 'produced a mass of information about what is actually happening in history courses, as well as judgements about the quality of the training process, upon which to reflect and try to identify some of the current major issues in the training of history teachers' (p. 191).

These chapters provide a welcome insight into inspectors' thinking and provide excellent examples of good practice. The writers take us behind the formal documentation and reporting framework to the front-line concerns of providers, helping to some extent to give meaning to the set of grades that are so inadequately described in the inspection framework. Although it is still not clear from this work where the grade boundaries are drawn, the reflections set out in these chapters are clearly a contribution to giving those standards substance, suggesting that standards tend to be set by practice rather than through government circulars.

Teacher trainers, like teachers, welcome the sharing of good practice, but there can be a downside to such sharing. The outstanding features of particular courses get collapsed into a set of qualities that describe the ideal course. While this may support excellence and raise standards in teacher training, it is important to be vigilant. The inspection process could push trainers into designing courses where short-term measurable goals that are easy for the inspection process to identify, replace the kind of teaching that can produce long-term understandings that will outlive fads and fashions. Trainees have very little time to come to terms with what is a major intellectual, physical and emotional challenge. Continuous monitoring and the setting of targets, of the kind necessary to provide evidence for inspection of the current standards, can be completely overwhelming for trainees, and often counter-productive.

The team found trainers reluctant to focus on the shortcomings of trainees, and remark that trainers' 'comments lack that critical edge that extends trainees and leads to improvements'. The claim that this critical commentary does not take place raises questions about the evidence base available for inspection. It ought to be evident why evidence of this kind of commentary is likely to be unavailable or compromised by the professional ethics of the situation and ordinary personal loyalties. Sharp criticism in front of a third party or in high-stakes documentation or dialogue simply breaches professional and human rules of conduct.

The inspectors identify trainees' limited questioning techniques as an area that might benefit from more direct critical commentary. While this process may support improvement it will not guarantee it. It is difficult to be sure what inspectors are arguing here, as space is obviously limited. If they are saying that *trainees'* thinking in history will be promoted through 'improvement of trainees' and teachers' questioning skills' then they may be putting the cart before the horse. If they are saying that improvements in trainees' questioning skills will support higher-level thinking in *pupils*, it is important to remember that good questioning skills depend on trainees' intellectual grasp of the learning goals of history, an understanding of their pupils' working assumptions and a knowledge of the kind of scaffolding that might support pupil progress.

Criticism of questioning is tinkering with symptoms. The increase in bureaucracy and the narrow monitoring of individual targets generated by the Standards has left little time for the kind of learning and reflection needed to support the effective development of these skills.

There is also an issue here about the relationship between Qualified Teacher Status (QTS) and the Post-Graduate Certificate of Education (PGCE) qualifications. A postgraduate qualification needs space for the demands set by the university. A PGCE is not equivalent to QTS. In addition to QTS it requires academic standards that have been set over many years in relation to subject teaching and wider issues of education as areas of study. It is important that space is reserved on any training course to ensure that subject teaching is understood beyond what is required for QTS. It may well be that the requirements for the PGCE will in the longer term support better teaching and a more educated teaching profession than can be delivered by simply meeting the standards. Faith in HMI's interpretation of the evidence and the standards, and in their ability to recognize ephemeral evidence, may be crucial in ensuring higher education courses can maintain their intellectual rigour. The kind of dialogue produced in these chapters, in going beyond the production of individual inspection reports, may be an important way forward.

A central matter for inspection is the relationship between subject knowledge and its application. It is clear from the discussion in these chapters that the evidence base used for the assessment of trainees' subject knowledge is not confined to an examination of the audit or record that purports to show how trainees have overcome 'gaps' in their knowledge. If recognition is to be given to the way in which providers enhance subject knowledge beyond that of any individual trainee's degree knowledge, then it will be important for inspection purposes that providers make this more explicit. However, this kind of 'value added' may be difficult to identify, particularly where benefits take longer to come to fruition than are recognizable in the training year. The chapter on subject knowledge quotes from Circular 4/98, Annex A, A1(i) where the standards for QTS demand that trainees need to demonstrate that they have a 'secure knowledge and understanding of the concepts and skills in their specialist subject(s) at a standard equivalent to degree level to enable them to teach it (them) confidently and accurately' (p. 211).

The standard equivalent to degree level ought to be demonstrated by the acquisition of the qualification itself, and it is this qualification that is required for entry to the course. However, this is clearly problematic in two ways. A degree in history is not something uniform in terms of the historical content students cover, or the range, depth and breadth of this content. Further, some degree courses do not make explicit a study of the nature and status of the knowledge being acquired, while others make it an integral and recognizable part of the course of study. This particular inspection team recognizes the resulting problems faced in recruitment. 'While ideally candidates would enter training with an overview of British, European and world history as well as a detailed knowledge of the content areas included in the school curriculum, inspectors are well aware that most lack both' (p. 212). It is reassuring to learn that the inspectorate sees expertise as more complex than the matching of historical content, and that inspectors:

> look carefully to see whether entrants have a clear understanding of the nature of the subject and its guiding principles; and whether they have sufficient experience of learning history to enable them to make good gaps in specific aspects of subject knowledge and, at the same time, acquire a 'mind' map of the past. (p. 212)

It must also be recognized that schoolteaching requirements cannot influence the nature and content of history degrees, and should not therefore restrict entry into teaching. Teaching needs people who have an excellent understanding of their subject in a more rigorous sense than the matching of historical content to the National Curriculum.

History training providers are therefore reconciled to the fact that they have to be able to use trainees' degree knowledge and experience to develop both a more explicit understanding of the nature of the discipline and to introduce new areas of historical content and argument. In the long run the teaching process itself may have a greater impact on the development of trainees' understanding of the concepts and skills of their subject than the acquisition of any collection of historical particulars. Many trainees report that they never really understood their subject until they came to teach it, and here they are clearly not talking about historical particulars. It is the way in which history teachers are able to apply their knowledge in the classroom and to monitor and assess their pupils' understandings that is important. Training provision usually pulls historical knowledge into the framework behind other targets in more sophisticated ways than is possible through any form of direct instruction. Over-concentration on the audit and monitoring of the acquisition of historical particulars – the concept of gap filling – may well be a distraction that cannot be afforded in the time available.

It is difficult to cultivate a climate in which genuine understanding of a subject is not severely undermined by continuous targeting of minor failings in the recall or acquisition of historical detail, and it is good to see that when inspectors ask themselves how well trainees cope with unexpected questions they find that 'those with high levels of subject knowledge either respond accurately to complex queries ... or are confident enough to acknowledge ignorance in dealing with unexpected and eccentric questions' (p. 218). Subject knowledge must not be perceived as a never-ending struggle to answer every conceivable question about everything that ever was or ever happened. It may be that the best access to trainees' understandings of their subject is through their ability to make explicit and express particular understandings, to identify impediments to learning history and to assess their pupils diagnostically.

Conclusion

Issues in History Teaching addresses practical matters in reflective ways. As such, it is a good indicator of the strength in depth of history education in the UK, despite the problems it faces. UK history education has benefited greatly in the past three decades from the work of practical teachers, teacher educators and trainers, examiners, inspectors, textbook writers and curriculum developers; so much so that it is often hard for researchers from outside the UK to grasp just how closely research and all the multifarious aspects of practice have gone hand-in-hand. The question 'What has been the influence of research on practice in the UK, is unanswerable in that form; research has been just one part of a complex matrix of change, not an independent variable. Much of the value of the small-scale research reported in the book is that it is 'use inspired'.[28] The contributors to this book continue a worthwhile tradition.

When it comes to conceptual analysis, however, much of *Issues in History Teaching* lacks subtlety or sophistication. Given the standing of the book's contributors, it is surprising to find in it almost no reference to the journal *History and Theory*, and indeed few signs of other works exploring aspects of philosophy of history. Even Keith Jenkins, who has become nearly as ubiquitous as Elton and Carr, is cited only as author of *Rethinking History*.[29] There is no hint of his more substantial pieces, although Richard Evans' *In Defence of History* does appear in the bibliography.[30] Important distinctions tend to be blurred, and otherwise interesting arguments weakened by failure to examine the ideas deployed in them. This has been a recurrent problem for at least the past few decades, but, if this book is evidence of the present state of history education, it has to be said that in this respect much remains to be done.

One more matter needs comment, especially for readers not versed in the recent vagaries of UK education. By its very existence the book gives insight into an aspect of education in the UK that affects history education along with almost every other area of education in the universities. The questionable influence of the Research Assessment Exercise (RAE) – a system of measuring academic research and publication that imposes on university teachers and researchers a desperation to publish to an arbitrary timetable – seems all too evident for the book contains errors of all kinds. They range from minor typographical errors – always difficult to eradicate completely – to the appearance in the bibliography of the item 'Got to get the title of forthcoming book for this reference' (p. 227). Papers are attributed to people who did not write them and references are given ambiguously, so that they might apply to two different publications (pp. 132, 228 and 234). Since errors occur in chapters by scholarly academics, it seems likely that a schedule dictated by the RAE is the culprit. It is hard to see that the gains produced by the RAE justify authors and editors having to suffer in this way.

The effect of the RAE has been more serious because OFSTED inspections of history education training courses (see above) have imposed huge burdens on those concerned. Most of the contributors to this book will have suffered these hugely bureaucratic impositions and had to spend their time generating paperwork. The impact of these inspections on time available for research and scholarship (and indeed the productive tasks of teaching and training) has been serious.

For these reasons, the critique given in this review should be considered in a wider context. It is remarkable that a book of this kind has appeared at all, and that its contributors have found time to read, think and research. It may be that the most important inference about the state of history education in the UK that can be made from this book is that, despite everything and against all the odds, it is flourishing. Everyone involved in *Issues in History Teaching*, as editor or as author, is to be congratulated for producing anything at all in the difficult circumstances in which they now have to work, let alone something that addresses so many important matters and opens so many debates.

NOTES

1. James Arthur and Robert Philips (eds), *Issues in History Teaching* (London and New York: Routledge, 2000).
2. P.J. Lee, A.K. Dickinson, D. May and D. Shemilt, 'Youth and history: Some initial conceptualizations and analyses of the British and Scottish data', in M. Angvik and B. von Borries (eds), *Youth and History*, vol. A (Hamburg: Koerber-Stiftung, 1997) pp. 377–87.
3. Examples include: A.K. Dickinson and P.J. Lee, 'Understanding and research', in Dickinson and Lee (eds), *History Teaching and Historical Understanding* (London: Heinemann Educational, 1978), pp. 94–120; A.K. Dickinson and P.J. Lee, 'Making sense of history', in A.K. Dickinson, P.J. Lee and P.J. Rogers (eds), *Learning History* (London: Heinemann Educational, 1984), pp. 117–53; D. Shemilt, 'Beauty and the philosopher: Empathy in history and classroom', in Dickinson, Lee and Rogers, *Learning History*, pp. 39–84; R. Ashby and P.J. Lee, 'Children's concepts of empathy and understanding', in C. Portal (ed.), *The History Curriculum for Teachers* (Lewes: Falmer Press, 1987), pp. 62–88; C. Portal, 'Empathy as an objective for history teaching', in C. Portal, *The History Curriculum*, pp. 89–99; P. Knight, 'A study of teaching and children's understanding of people in the past', *Research in Education*, 44 (1990), pp. 39–53; M. Downey, 'Perspective taking in historical thinking: Doing history in a fifth-grade classroom', paper presented at AERA annual meeting, San Francisco, 1995; K. Barton, 'Narrative simplifications in elementary students' historical thinking', in J. Brophy, (ed.), *Advances in Research on Teaching: Vol. 6, Teaching and Learning History* (Greenwich: JAI Press, 1996), pp. 51–83; P. Lee, A. Dickinson and R. Ashby, 'Just another emperor: Understanding action in the past' *International Journal of Educational Research*, 27, 3 (1997), pp. 233–44; L. Jacott, A. López-Manjón and M. Carretero, 'Generating explanations in history', in J.E. Voss and M. Carretero (eds), *International Review of History Education: Vol. 2, Learning and Reasoning in History*, (London: Woburn Press, 1998), pp. 294–306.
4. See Angvik and von Borries (eds), *Youth and History*.
5. Paul Light produced a valuable pioneering summary nearly two decades ago, 'Social interaction and cognitive development: A review of post-Piagetian research', in Sara Meadows (ed.), *Developing Thinking: Approaches to Children's Cognitive Development* (London: Methuen, 1983), pp. 67–88. Our own work (research using videos of small groups, and curriculum development for the Cambridge History Project) produced copious evidence – formal and informal – congruent with many of the claims about the importance of talk in developing students' ideas. Only a small part has appeared in print. See Dickinson and Lee, 'Making sense of history'; R. Ashby and P.J. Lee 'Discussing the evidence', in *Teaching History*, 48 (June 1987), pp. 13–17.
6. J.D. Bransford, A.L. Brown and R.R. Cocking (eds), *How People Learn: Brain, Mind, Experience and School* (Washington, DC: National Academy Press, 1999).
7. R. Ashby and P.J Lee, 'Empathy, perspective taking and rational understanding', in O.L. Davis Jr, S. Foster and E. Yaeger (eds), *Historical Empathy and Perspective Taking* (Boulder, CO: Rowman & Littlefield, 2001).
8. Maria Melo's work in Portugal is a beginning here. See 'Adolescents' tacit substantive understandings of history', unpublished PhD dissertation, Institute of Education, University of London, 2000.
9. See Ashby and Lee, 'Empathy, perspective taking and rational understanding'.
10. SCHP became SHP (the Schools History Project) when its initial funding ended.
11. P.J. Lee, '"None of us was there": Children's ideas about why historical accounts differ', in S. Ahonen *et al. Historiedidaktik: Norden 6,* Nordisk Konferens om Historiedidaktik, Tampere 1996, (*History of Didactics: Sixth Nordic Conference on History Didactics, Tampere 1996*) (Copenhagen: Danmarks Laererhøjskole, 1996), pp. 23–58; P.J. Lee,

'Learning the right stories or learning history? Developments in history education in England', in Organization of American Historians, *Newsletter*, 27, 2 (May 1999), pp. 7–8.

12. Encouragingly, several authors in *Teaching History*, 99 (May 2000) make the case for planning National Curriculum delivery in such a way as to repair this weakness.

13. See his cercadillo, Chapter 7 of this volume.

14. NCC was the National Curriculum Council, one of a family of quasi-governmental bureaucratic organizations designed to make the National Curriculum work in the way that policy makers wanted.

15. See, as one example among several, P. Seixas, 'Popular film and young people's understanding of the history of native–white Relations', *History Teacher*, 26, 3 (May 1993), pp. 351–70 which investigates students' responses to different film treatments of the American Indians. (The CHATA project had informal findings which had been discussed in research seminars here and overseas, but did not publish work on historical accounts until 1997.)

16. G. Leinhardt, 'History: A time to be mindful', in G. Leinhardt, I.L. Beck and C. Stainton, *Teaching and Learning in History* (Hillsdale, NJ: Lawrence Erlbaum, 1994), pp. 209–55.

17. This is not the only instance of some curious beliefs about the history of history teaching. On p. 70 Counsell writes: 'Detaching the word "enquiry" from common professional assumptions about frighteningly open-ended investigations, Riley tamed the idea of "enquiry" and linked it directly to a pedagogic rationale for layers of knowledge.' Loyalty to the achievements of one's co-workers is one thing, but here the comment on 'enquiry' is made as though SHP had never existed. Enquiry has been 'tamed' on more than one occasion, and no doubt will have to be again! One gets the distinct impression that some of the writers in this collection have had little direct experience of SHP or the thinking out of which it grew. It is as though they have read about it in the papers, or encountered diluted versions so far down the 'cascade' as to have lost all impetus from the source. This may be an effect of large-scale political and bureaucratic governmental interference based on political posturing, hearsay and rumour. In this sense the National Curriculum may be thought of as producing 'chaotic' (that is, non-linear and unpredictable) change, in which understandings are randomly lost as well as gained.

18. CHATA work here is a beginning, but only that. (See P.J. Lee and R. Ashby, 'Progression in historical understanding 7–14', in P. Seixas, P. Stearns and S. Wineburg (eds), *Teaching, Learning and Knowing History* (New York: New York University Press, 2000); P.J. Lee, '"A lot of guess work goes on": Children's understanding of historical accounts', *Teaching History*, 92 (August 1998), pp. 29–36.

19. It is hard to know what to make of Counsell's slightly odd sub-heading 'Dangers of over-reliance on models of progression within discrete cognitive domains' (p. 58). Presumably she means by this the conceptual strands picked out by any attempt to map students' ideas. These are not cognitive domains as usually understood, but convenient (more or less conventional) concepts or groups of concepts within history. (These are sometimes treated as assessment domains within history.)

20. A note on substantive concepts is perhaps in order here. Substantive concepts in history are picked out, as with any concepts, by means of a rule. The peculiarity of historical concepts is that they tend to expand any rule: they shift their meaning with time. This is one reason why they are difficult to teach, and why progression in these concepts is complex. Perhaps because she is ambivalent towards progression models, Counsell never quite links her discussion in a coherent way to the idea of progression in substantive concepts. We need progression models here too. Counsell's references to the development of substantive concepts tend to be made in the context of giving students an apparatus for sorting (political, economic, social and so on). She makes a strong case for this (p. 64). However, if such sorting is not tied to clear learning goals, it can become algorithmic in the same way as 'bias' or pointless 'source work'. Such an apparatus

requires some sense of where students should be heading (beyond simply being able to sort) and, equally important, what tacit prior understandings they come with.

21. The work of Adrian Furnham in the UK is interesting here: A. Furnham, 'Young people's understanding of politics and economics', in M. Carretero and J. E. Voss (eds), *Cognitive and Instructional Processes in History and the Social Sciences* (Hillsdale, NJ: Lawrence Erlbaum, 1994), pp. 17–47. See also M. Melo, 'Adolescents' tacit substantive understandings'.

22. P.J. Lee, 'Historical knowledge and the National Curriculum', in R. Aldrich (ed.), *History in the National Curriculum* (London: Kogan Page, 1991), pp. 39–65. But see especially D. Shemilt, 'The caliph's coin: The currency of narrative frameworks in history teaching', in Seixas, Stearns and Wineburg (eds), *Teaching, Learning and Knowing History* for a more comprehensive and penetrating treatment.

23. This is especially well attested in the American research. See, for example, Seixas, 'Popular film and young people's understanding'; J.V. Wertsch and M. Rozin, 'The Russian revolution: Official and unofficial accounts', in Voss and Carretero (eds), *Learning and Reasoning in History*, pp. 39–60; S. Wineburg, 'Making historical sense', in Seixas, Stearns and Wineburg (eds), *Teaching, Learning and Knowing History*.

24. R. Phillips, *History Teaching, Nationhood and the State* (London: Cassell, 1998).

25. D. Shemilt, *History 13–16 Evaluation Study* (Edinburgh: Holmes McDougall, 1980), p. 25.

26. Ken Adey's very interesting work in progress at Nottingham on students' choice of options at 14 promises to shed more light on some of these matters.

27. Office for Standards in Education, the government body responsible for inspecting schools and training courses.

28. M.S. Donovan, J.D. Bransford and J. Pellegrino (eds), *How People Learn: Bridging Research and Practice* (Washington, DC: National Academy Press, 1999), p. 31.

29. K. Jenkins, *Rethinking History* (London: Routledge, 1991).

30. R. Evans, *In Defence of History* (London: Granta, 1997).

Notes on Contributors

Ros Ashby leads the MA and PGCE courses in History in Education in the Curriculum Studies Group at the London Institute of Education. Her research interests include assessment in history and students' understanding of history. She has worked as teacher, LEA adviser and research officer, and has strong academic links with researchers in the USA, Canada, Europe and Taiwan.

Angela Bermúdez and **Rosario Jaramillo** live in Bogotá, Colombia, where they have created Cabildo Abierto, a new research centre for the understanding and fostering of social intelligence. They are engaged in developing research on historical understanding and political consciousness, and work as consultants for local governmental projects on social and moral education. They also teach history and ethics at a secondary school as part of their research projects. They have worked together with their Harvard Project Zero colleagues in the advancement of projects for 'Teaching for Understanding' in Colombia.

Yang Biao is an Associate Professor in the History Department of the East China Normal University, Shanghai, People's Republic of China. He earned his BA in 1984, his MA in 1987, and his PhD in 1997 from the East China Normal University. Since 1987 he has been a lecturer and Associate Professor in the History Department of the Shanghai Education Institute.

Chara Haeussler Bohan earned a PhD in Curriculum and Instruction from the University of Texas at Austin, where she currently teaches an elementary social studies methods course. Her research interests include history education, social studies education and curriculum studies. Her PhD dissertation on Lucy Maynard Salmon and the teaching of history was completed in 1999 and her writings on Lucy Maynard Salmon will be published in a forthcoming book.

Veronica Boix-Mansilla has worked as a researcher, consultant and project co-ordinator at Project Zero, Harvard Graduate School of Education since 1992. Her research and writings focus on understanding as it takes place in (and between) disciplines like science, history and the arts. Particular interests include the implications of an education towards disciplinary understanding in curriculum design, teaching practices, assessment and professional development. She is currently conducting a comparative study of adolescents' beliefs about the nature of knowledge in science and history.

Lis Cercadillo is currently teaching history at the El Escorial Institute in Madrid and earned her doctorate from the University of London Institute of Education in 1999. She is a Marie Curie Fellow and her research has been funded by the European Union. Her main interests include students' and teachers' tacit understandings in history across countries.

Alaric Dickinson taught history in secondary schools before becoming a teacher trainer and head of history at the University of London Institute of Education. He has co-directed curriculum development and research projects (including Project CHATA with Peter Lee) and now works as a consultant, principally with the International Baccalaureate Organisation for whom he was chief examiner for history from 1995 to 2000.

Peter Lee has responsibility for research in the History Education Unit at the University of London Institute of Education. He has co-directed curriculum development and research projects (the Cambridge History Project and Project CHATA) and was UK co-ordinator for the Youth and History Project. His current research activities include links with Taiwan and with the How People Learn Project in the USA.

Irene Nakou lives in Athens, Greece. Her PhD thesis was conducted at the University of London Institute of Education. Her main research interest is history and museum education. She has written eight books for children and has been responsible for the editing of multicultural educational material in various forms (books, videos, CD ROMs). She has also written several articles on history and museum education, and the book *Children and History: Historical Knowledge, Thinking and Interpretation.*

Dan Porat received his PhD from Stanford University in 1999. He is currently a senior researcher at the Historical Sense Making Project at the University of Washington, Seattle, a three-year longitudinal study investigating everyday historical consciousness. His fields of research include history of education, history of curriculum and the teaching and learning of history.

Peter Seixas is Professor in the Department of Curriculum Studies at the University of British Columbia. He has taught in high schools, earned a PhD in history from the University of Los Angeles and has published articles and chapters on history education. He is co-editor of *Knowing, Teaching and Learning History: National and International Perspectives* (New York University Press, 2000).

Tony Taylor taught in secondary comprehensive schools in the United Kingdom for ten years before completing his doctorate in the history and politics of education at the University of Cambridge. During his time as school teacher he had worked on the Humanities Curriculum Project, the Schools History Project and the Cambridge Schools Classics Project. After Cambridge, he moved to James Cook University, Queensland, Australia, and is currently Associate Professor in the Faculty of Education at Monash University in Victoria. His research interests include the politics of educational change, higher education policy, and the teaching and learning of history.

References

Adar, L. and Fox, S., *Nituch Tochnit Limudiem be-Historyah u-Bitzuah be-Veit ha-Sefer* (*An Analysis of the Content and Use of a History Curriculum*) (Jerusalem: Hebrew University School of Education, 1978).

Ahiyah, B. and Harpaz, M., *Toldot am Yisrael* (*History of Israel*) (Tel Aviv: Sherchbek, 3rd edn, 1965).

Almog, S., *Zionism and History: The Rise of a New Jewish Consciousness* (New York: St Martin's Press, 1987).

Ambrose, T. (ed.), *Education in Museums: Museums in Education* (Edinburgh: Scottish Museums Council, HMSO, 1987).

American Historical Association, *The Study of History in Schools: Report to the American Historical Association by the Committee of Seven* (New York: Macmillan, 1899).

—— 'Is revision of the course of study in history desirable? Summary of the report of the Committee of Five to the American Historical Association', *History Teacher's Magazine*, 2 (April 1911).

—— *The Study of History in Secondary Schools: Report to the American Historical Association by the Committee of Five* (New York, 1911).

—— 'AHA statement on excellent classroom teaching of history', *Perspectives*, 36, 4 (1998).

Angelou, M., *Gather Together in My Name* (New York: Random House, 1974).

Angvik, M. and von Borries, B. (eds), *Youth and History* (Hamburg: Koerber-Stiftung, 1997).

Anhui Education Publishing House, *The Methodology of History Teaching: An Introduction* (Beijing: Anhui Education Publishing House, 1988).

222

Anyon, J., 'Ideology and United States history textbooks', *Harvard Educational Review*, 49, 3 (1979).

Apple, M.W., *Official Knowledge: Democratic Education in a Conservative Age* (London and New York: Routledge, 1993).

Arnheim, R., *Visual Thinking* (Berkeley, CA: University of California Press, 1969).

—— *Art and Visual Perception: A Psychology of the Creative Eye* (Berkeley, CA: University of California Press, 1974).

Aronoff, M.J., *The Frailty of Authority*, Political Anthropology Series, No. 5 (New Brunswick, NJ: Transaction, 1986).

Aronowitz, S. and Giroux, H., *Postmodern Education: Politics, Culture and Social Criticism* (Minneapolis, MN: University of Minnesota Press, 1991).

Arthur, James and Philips, Robert (eds), *Issues in History Teaching* (London and New York: Routledge, 2000).

Ashby R. and Lee, P.J., 'Discussing the evidence', *Teaching History*, 48 (June 1987).

—— 'Children's concepts of empathy and understanding in history', in C. Portal (ed.), *The History Curriculum for Teachers* (Lewes: Falmer Press, 1987).

—— 'Empathy, perspective taking and rational understanding', in O.L. Davis Jr, S. Foster and E. Yaeger (eds), *Historical Empathy and Perspective Taking* (Boulder, CO: Rowman & Littlefield, forthcoming).

Avivi, B. and Perski, N. *Toldot Yisrael* (*History of Israel*) (Tel Aviv: Yavenh, 1955).

Bailyn, B., Dallek, R., Davis, D.B., Donald, D.H., Thomas, J.L. and Wood, G.S., *The Great Republic: A History of the American People* (Lexington, MA: D.C. Heath, 1992).

Barca-Oliveira, I., 'Adolescent students' ideas about provisional historical explanation', PhD dissertation (Institute of Education, University of London, 1996).

Barthes, R., *Le Degré zéro de l' écriture* (Paris: Editions du Seuil, 1972).

Barton, K., 'Narrative simplifications in elementary students' historical thinking', in J. Brophy (ed.), *Advances in Research on Teaching: Vol. 6, Teaching and Learning History* (Greenwich: JAI Press, 1996).

Becher, T., *Academic Tribes and Territories: Intellectual Enquiry and the Culture of Disciplines* (Buckingham: Open University Press, 1989).

Beck, I. and McKeown, M., 'Outcomes of history instruction: Paste-up accounts', in M. Carretero and J. Voss (eds), *Cognitive and Instructional Processes in History and the Social Sciences* (Hillsdale,

NJ: Lawrence Erlbaum, 1994).

Ben Baruch, B., *Greeks, Romans, Jews* (Tel Aviv: Tel Aviv Books, 1996).

Ben-Gurion, D., *Netsah Yisrael* (Tel Aviv: Ayanot, 1964).

Bennett, T., 'Texts in history: The determinations of readings and their texts', in D. Attridge, G. Bennington and R. Young (eds), *Post-structuralism and the Question of History* (Cambridge: Cambridge University Press, 1987).

—— *Outside Literature* (London and New York: Routledge, 1990).

Block, M., *Introducción a la Historia* (1952; reprint Mexico: Breviarios del Fondo de Cultura Económica, 1987).

Bloom, B.S. (ed.), *The Taxonomy of Educational Objectives* (New York: Longman, 1956).

Bohan, C.H., 'Lucy Maynard Salmon: Progressive historian, teacher, and democrat', in Margaret Smith Crocco and O.L. Davis Jr (eds), *'Bending the Future to their Will': Civic Women, Social Education, and Democracy* (New York: Rowman & Littlefield, 1999).

—— 'Go to the sources: Lucy Maynard Salmon and the teaching of history', PhD dissertation (University of Texas at Austin, December 1999).

Boix-Mansilla, V. and Gardner, H., 'What are the qualities of deep disciplinary understanding?', in Stone Wiske (ed.), *Teaching for Understanding: A Practical Framework* (San Francisco, CA: Jossey Bass, 1998).

Booth, M., 'Inductive thinking in history: The 14–16 age group', in G. Jones and L. Ward (eds), *New History Old Problems: Studies in History Teaching* (Swansea: University College of Swansea Faculty of Education, 1978).

—— 'A recent research project into children's historical thinking and its implications for history teaching', in J. Nicol (ed.), *Developments in History Teaching,* Perspectives 4 (Exeter School of Education, University of Exeter, 1980).

—— 'Ages and concepts: A critique of the Piagetian approach to history teaching', in C. Portal (ed.), *The History Curriculum for Teachers* (Lewes: Falmer Press, 1987).

Boozer, H., 'The American Historical Association and the schools, 1884–1956', PhD dissertation (Washington University, 1960).

Borke, H., 'Piaget's view of social interaction and the theoretical construct of empathy', in L.S. Siegal and C.J. Brainerd (eds), *Alternatives to Piaget* (London: Academic Press, 1978).

Borries, B. von, 'Representation and understanding of history', in J.F.

Voss and M. Carretero (eds), *International Review of History Education: Vol. 2, Learning and Reasoning in History*, (London: Woburn Press, 1998).

Bourdieu, P. and Passeron, J.C., *Reproduction in Education, Society and Culture* (Bristol: J.W. Arrowsmith, 1990).

Boylan, J.P. (ed.), *Museums 2000 – Politics, People, Professionals and Profit* (London: Museums Association, Routledge, 1992).

Bransford, J.D., Brown, A.L. and Cocking, R.R. (eds), *How People Learn: Brain, Mind, Experience and School* (Washington, DC: National Academy Press, 1999).

Breisach, Ernst, *Historiography* (Chicago, IL: University of Chicago Press, 1983).

Britt, M.A., Rouet, J.F., Georgi, M.C. and Perfetti, C.A., 'Learning from history texts: From causal analysis to argument models', in G. Leinhardt, I. Beck and C. Stainton (eds), *Teaching and Learning in History* (Hillsdale, NJ: Lawrence Erlbaum, 1994).

Bruner, J., *The Process of Education* (Cambridge, MA: Harvard University Press, 1960).

California State Board of Education, *History–social science content standards: Grades K-12* (2000). http://www.cde.ca.gov/board/historya.html

Carey, S.R., Evans, M., Honda, E. Jay and Unger, C.M., '"An experiment is when you try it and see it works": A study of seven students' understanding of the construction of scientific knowledge', *International Journal of Science Education* 11 (1989).

Carr, E.H., *What is History?* (London: Penguin Books, 1991).

Carretero, M., 'Perspectivas disciplinares, cognitivas y didácticas en la enseñanza de las ciencias sociales y la historia', in M. Carretero (ed.) *Construir y Enseñar. Ciencias Sociales e Historia* (Buenos Aires: Aique, 1995).

Carretero M. and Jacott L., 'Reasoning and casual explanations in history', paper presented at the Conference on Psychological and Educational Foundations of Technology-based Learning Environments, Crete, 26 July – 3 August 1992.

Carretero, M. and Voss, J.F. (eds), *Cognitive and Instructional Processes in History and the Social Sciences* (Hillsdale, NJ: Lawrence Erlbaum, 1994).

Carretero, M., Pozo, J.I. and Asensio, M. (eds), *La Enseñanza de las Ciencias Sociales* (Madrid: Visor, 1989).

Carretero, M., Asensio, M. and Pozo, J.I., 'Cognitive development, historical time representation and causal explanations in adolescence', in M. Carretero, M. Pope, R.J. Simons and J.I. Pozo (eds), *Learning and Instruction: Vol. 3: European Research in an International Context* (Oxford: Pergamon Press, 1991).

Carretero, M., Jacott, L., Limón, M., López-Manjón, A. and Léon, J.A., 'Historical knowledge: Cognitive and instructional implications', in M. Carretero and J.F. Voss (eds), *Cognitive and Instructional Processes in History and the Social Sciences* (Hillsdale, NJ: Lawrence Erlbaum, 1994).

Carretero, M., Jacott, L. and López-Manjón, A., 'Perspectivas actuales en la comprensión y enseñanza de la causalidad histórica: El caso del descubrimiento de América', in M. Carretero (ed.), *Construir y Enseñar: Ciencias Sociales e Historia* (Buenos Aires: Aique, 1995).

—— 'La explicación causal de distintos hechos históricos', in M. Carretero (ed), *Construir y Enseñar: Ciencias Sociales e Historia* (Buenos Aires: Aique, 1995).

—— 'Explaining historical events', *International Journal of Educational Research*, 27, 3 (1997).

Chau, Manling, 'Change and continuity: History teaching in the People's Republic of China', in A. Dickinson, P. Gordon, P. Lee and J. Slater (eds), *International Yearbook of History Education* (London: Woburn Press, 1995).

Collingwood, R.G., *An Autobiography* (Oxford: Oxford University Press, 1939).

—— *The Idea of History* (Oxford: Oxford University Press, 1946).

Colmenares, G., 'Sobre fuentes, temporalidad y escritura de la historia', *Boletín Cultural*, 10, 24 (1989).

Cooper, H. 'Young children's understanding in history', PhD dissertation (Institute of Education University of London, 1991).

—— *The Teaching of History in Primary Schools* (London: David Fulton, 1997).

Cremin, Lawrence, *The Transformation of the School* (New York: Vintage Books, 1961).

—— *American Education: The Metropolitan Experience, 1876–1980* (New York: Harper & Row, 1988).

Crismore, A., 'The rhetoric of textbooks: Metadiscourse', *Journal of Curriculum Studies*, 16 (July–September 1984).

Cuban, L., 'History of teaching in social studies', in J.P. Shaver (ed.), *Handbook of Research on Social Studies Teaching and Learning* (New York: Macmillan, 1991), pp. 197–209.

Davis, N.Z. and Starn, R., 'Introduction: Memory and counter memory', *Representations*, 26, 2 (1989).

Deans and principals of academies and high schools affiliating or co-operating with the University of Chicago, 'The fifteenth educational conference of the academies and high schools affiliating or co-operating with the University of Chicago', *School Review* (January 1902).

Department for Education (DFE), *History in the National Curriculum* (London: HMSO, 1995).

Department for Education and Science (DES), *History in the National Curriculum* (London: HMSO, 1991).

Dewey, John, *Democracy and Education* (1916; reprint New York: Free Press, 1944).

Dickinson, A.K. and Lee, P.J. (eds), *History Teaching and Historical Understanding* (London: Heinemann Educational, 1978).

—— 'Understanding and research', in Dickinson and Lee (eds), *History Teaching and Historical Understanding* (London: Heinemann Educational, 1978).

—— 'Making sense of history', in A. K. Dickinson, P.J. Lee and P.J. Rogers (eds), *Learning History* (London: Heinemann Educational, 1984).

Dickinson, A.K., Gard, A. and Lee, P.J., 'Evidence in history and the classroom', in A.K. Dickinson and P.J. Lee (eds), *History Teaching and Historical Understanding* (London: Heinemann Educational, 1978).

Dickinson, A.K., Lee, P.J. and Rogers, P.J. (eds), *Learning History* (London: Heinemann Educational, 1984).

Dominguez, J., 'Enseñar a comprender el pasado histórico: conceptos y empatía', *Infancia y Aprendizaje*, 34 (1986).

Donaldson, Margaret, *Children's Minds* (Glasgow: Fontana Press, 1978).

Donovan, M.S., Bransford, J.D. and Pellegrino, J. (eds), *How People Learn: Bridging Research and Practice* (Washington, DC: National Academy Press, 1999).

Downey, M., 'Perspective-taking and historical thinking: Doing history in a fifth grade classroom', paper presented at the American Educational Research Association annual meeting, San Francisco, 1995.

Dray, W. H., '"Explaining What" in History', in P. Gardiner (ed.), *Theories of History* (Chicago, IL: Free Press, 1959).

Eban, Abba, *An Autobiography* (New York: Random House, 1977).

Eldad, Y., *Pulmus Ha-Hurban U-Lekahav: Ketsad Nityahes Le-Hurban Ha-Bayit U-Le-Mered Bar-Kokhva (Controversy: Our Perception of the Destruction of the Second Temple and Bar Kochba's Revolt*) (Jerusalem: Van Leer Foundation, 1982).

Epstein, T., 'Sociocultural approaches to young people's historical understanding', *Social Education*, 61, 1 (1997).

Evans, R.J., *In Defence of History* (London: Granta, 1997).

FitzGerald, F., *America Revised: History Schoolbooks in the Twentieth Century* (Boston, MA: Little Brown, 1979).

Flavell, J.H., 'The development of inferences about others', in T. Mischel (ed.), *Understanding Other Persons* (Oxford: Blackwell, 1974).

Florescana, E., 'La historia como explicación', in C. Pereyra (ed.), *Historia ¿Para Qué?* (1980; reprint Mexico: Siglo XXI, 1995).

Foster, S.J. and Padgett, C.S., 'Authentic historical inquiry in the social studies classroom', *The Clearing House*, 72, 6 (1999).

Fox, George, 'History in English secondary schools', in American Historical Association, *The Study of History in Schools: Report to the American Historical Association by the Committee of Seven* (New York: Macmillan, 1899).

Funkenstein, A., 'Collective memory and historical consciousness', *History and Memory*, 1, 1 (1989).

Furnham, A., 'Young people's understanding of politics and economics', in M. Carretero and J.E. Voss (eds), *Cognitive and Instructional Processes in History and the Social Sciences* (Hillsdale, NJ: Lawrence Erlbaum, 1994).

Gardiner, P. (ed.), *Theories of History* (Chicago, IL: Free Press, 1959).

—— *Philosophy of History* (Oxford: Oxford University Press, 1974).

Gardner, H., *Frames of Mind* (New York: Basic Books, 1983).

—— *The Unschooled Mind: How Children Think and How Schools Should Teach* (New York: Basic Books, 1991).

—— *The Disciplined Mind: What All Students Should Understand* (New York: Simon & Schuster, 1999).

Gardner, H. and Boix-Mansilla, V., 'Teaching for understanding in the disciplines and beyond', *Teachers College Record*, 96, 2 (1994).

Gay, Peter, *Style in History* (New York: Norton, 1974).

Gitlin, T., 'Rewriting history', *Teacher Magazine* (November–December 1995).

Gruber, Carol, *Mars and Minerva: World War One and the Uses of Higher Learning in America* (Baton Rouge, LA: Louisiana State University Press, 1975).

Halbwachs, M., *The Collective Memory* (1950; reprint New York: Harper & Row, 1980).

Hallam, R., 'Piaget and thinking in history', in M. Ballard (ed.), *New Movements in the Study and Teaching of History* (London: Temple Smith, 1970).

—— A study of the effect of teaching method on the growth of logical thought with special reference to the teaching of history PhD dissertation (University of Leeds, 1975).

Hallden, O., 'Learning history', *Oxford Review of Education*, 12, 1 (1986).

—— 'On the paradox of understanding history in an educational setting', in G. Leinhardt, I. Beck and C. Stainton (eds), *Teaching and Learning History* (Hillsdale, NJ: Lawrence Erlbaum, 1994).

Harkabi, Y., *The Bar Kokhba Syndrome* (Chappaqua, NY: Rossel Books, 1983).

Haskins, Charles H., 'History in French Lycées', in American Historical Association, *The Study of History in Schools: Report to the American Historical Association by the Committee of Seven* (New York: Macmillan, 1899).

Hempel, C.G., 'Reasons and covering laws in historical explanation', in P. Gardiner (ed.), *Philosophy of History* (Oxford University Press, 1974).

Higher Education Publishing House, *The Methodology of History Teaching in High Schools* (Beijing: Higher Education Publishing House, 1988).

History-Social Science Curriculum Framework and Criteria Committee, *History Social Science Framework* (Sacramento, CA: California State Department of Education, 1988).

Hobsbawm, E.J., 'The revival of narrative: Some comments', *Past and Present,* 86 (February 1980).

Hodder, I., *The Archaeology of Contextual Meanings* (Cambridge: Cambridge University Press, 1987).

—— (ed.), *The Meaning of Things* (London: Routledge, 1991).

Holt, T., *Thinking Historically: Narrative, Imagination, and Understanding* (New York: College Entrance Examination Board, 1995).

Hooper-Greenhill, E., 'Museums in education: Towards the end of the century', in T. Ambrose (ed.), *Education in Museums: Museums in Education* (Edinburgh: Scottish Museum Council, HMSO, 1987).

—— 'The Museum: The socio-historical articulations of knowledge and things', PhD dissertation (University of London, Institute of Education, 1988).

—— *Learning and Teaching with Objects: A Practical Skills Based Approach* (Leicester: Department of Museum Studies, University of Leicester, 1988).

—— *Museums and the Shaping of Knowledge* (London and New York: Routledge, 1992).

—— *Museums and their Visitors* (London and New York: Routledge, 1994).

—— (ed.), *The Educational Role of Museums* (London and New York: Routledge, 1994).

Hughes, M. 'Egocentricism in pre-school children', PhD dissertation (Edinburgh: Edinburgh University, 1975).

Issac, B. and Oppenheimer, A., 'The revolt of Bar Kokhba: Ideology and modern scholarship', *Journal of Jewish Studies*, 36 (1987).

Jacott, L. and Carretero, M., 'Historia', in M. Carretero (ed.), *Construir y Enseñar: Ciencias Sociales e Historia* (Buenos Aires: Aique, 1995).

—— 'Historia y relato. La comprensión de los agentes históricos en el Descubrimiento (Encuentro) de América', in M. Carretero (ed.), *Construir y Enseñar: Ciencias Sociales e Historia* (Buenos Aires: Aique, 1995).

Jacott, L., López-Manjón, A. and Carretero, M., 'Generating explanations in history', in J.F. Voss, and M. Carretero (eds), *International Review of Education: Vol. 2, Learning and Reasoning in History*, (London: Woburn Press, 1998).

Jenkins, K., *Re-thinking History* (London and New York: Routledge, 1991).

—— *On 'What is History?' From Carr and Elton to Rorty and White* (London and New York: Routledge, 1995).

Johnson, Henry, *Teaching of History in Elementary and Secondary Schools* (New York: Macmillan, 1917).

—— *Teaching of History in Elementary and Secondary Schools with Applications to Allied Studies* (New York: Macmillan, 1940).

Katz, J., 'Ha-Historia ha-Yisraeliet ke-Gorem Hinukhi' ('Israeli history as an educational factor'), *Molad Jerusalem* (1954).

—— *Yisrael ve-ha-Amim, Kerech 2* (*Israel and the Nations, Vol. 2*) (Jerusalem: Tarshis, 1957).

—— 'Le-Darco shel Sefer ha-Limud be-*Yisrael ve-ha-Amim*' ('The method of the textbook in *Israel and the Nations*'), in A. Morgenstein (ed.), *Three Articles on History Teaching* (1963; reprint Jerusalem: Ministry of Education, 1977).

—— *With My Own Eyes* (Hanover: Brandeis University Press, 1995).

Kawazoe, A., 'Historiography? What's that?', *Quarterly of the National Writing Project and Center for the Study of Writing and Literacy*, 16, 2–3 (1994).

Keohane, Robert E., 'The great debate over the source method', *Social Education* (May 1949).

Kingsbury, Professor, 'Modifications in the report of the Committee of Seven Recommended by the N.E. Association', *History Teacher's Magazine*, 1 (December 1909).

Kirst, Michael W., 'Who's in charge? Federal, state, and local control', in Diane Ravitch and Maris A. Vinovskis (eds), *Learning from the Past: What History Teaches us About School Reform* (Baltimore, MD: Johns Hopkins University Press, 1995).

Kliebard, Herbert M., *The Struggle for the American Curriculum: 1893–1958* (New York: Routledge & Kegan Paul, 1987).

Knight, P., 'A study of teaching and children's understanding of people in the past', *Research in Education*, 44 (1990).

Kohlberg, L., *The Philosophy of Moral Development* (vol. 1), *The Psychology of Moral Development* (vol. 2) (New York: Harper & Row, 1985).

Kriekouki-Nakou, I., 'Pupils' historical thinking within a museum environment', PhD dissertation (University of London, Institute of Education, 1996).

Krug, Edward, *The Shaping of the American High School* (New York: Harper & Row, 1964).

Kymlicka, B.B. and Matthews, J.V., *The Reagan Revolution?* (Chicago, IL: Dorsey Press, 1995).

Lee, P.J., 'Explanation and understanding in history', in A.K. Dickinson and P.J. Lee (eds), *History Teaching and Historical Understanding* (London: Heinemann Educational, 1978).

—— 'Historical imagination', in A.K. Dickinson, P.J. Lee and P.J. Rogers (eds), *Learning History* (London: Heinemann Educational, 1984).

—— 'Why learn history?', in A.K. Dickinson, P.J. Lee and P.J. Rogers (eds), *Learning History* (London: Heinemann Educational, 1984).

—— 'Historical knowledge and the National Curriculum', in R. Aldrich (ed.), *History in the National Curriculum* (London: Kogan Page, 1991).

—— 'Historical knowledge and the National Curriculum', in Hilary Bourdillon (ed.), *Teaching History* (New York and London: Routledge/The Open University, 1994).

—— '"None of us was there": Children's ideas about why historical accounts differ', in S. Ahonen , P. Arola, C. Karlegärd, A. Køhlert, S. Lorentzen and V.O. Nielsen, *Historiedidaktik*: Norden 6, Nordisk Konferens om Historiedidaktik, Tampere 1996 (*History of Didactics: Sixth Nordic Conference on History Didactics, Tampere 1996*) (Copenhagen: Danmarks Laererhøjskole, 1996).

—— '"A lot of guess work goes on": Children's understanding of historical accounts', *Teaching History*, 92 (August 1998).

—— 'Learning the right stories or learning history? Developments in history education in England', in Organization of American Historians, *Newsletter*, 27, 2 (May 1999).

Lee, P.J. and Ashby, R., 'Progression in historical understanding among students age 7–14', in P. Seixas, P. Stearns and S. Wineburg (eds), *Teaching, Learning and Knowing History* (New York: New York University Press, 2000).

Lee, P.J, Ashby, R. and Dickinson, A.K., 'Progression in children's ideas about history', in M. Hughes (ed.), *Progression in Learning*, BERA Dialogues, 11 (Clevedon: Multilingual Matters, 1996).

Lee, P.J, Dickinson, A.K and Ashby, R., '"There were no facts in those days": Children's ideas about historical explanation', in M. Hughes (ed.), *Teaching and Learning in Changing Times* (London: Blackwell, 1996).

—— 'Children making sense of history', *Education 3–13*, 24, 1 (1996).

—— '"Just another emperor": Understanding action in the past', *International Journal of Educational Research*, 27, 3 (1997).

Lee, P.J., Dickinson, A.K., May, D. and Shemilt, D., 'Youth and history: Some initial conceptualizations and analyses of the British and Scottish data', in M. Angvik and B. von Borries (eds), *Youth and History*, vol. A (Hamburg: Koerber-Stiftung, 1997).

Leinhardt, G., 'History: A time to be mindful', in G. Leinhardt, I.L. Beck and C. Stainton, *Teaching and Learning in History* (Hillsdale, NJ: Lawrence Erlbaum, 1994).

Levstik, L., 'Any history is someone's history: Listening to multiple voices in the past', *Social Education*, 61, 1 (1997).

Light, P., 'Social interaction and cognitive development: A review of post-Piagetian research', in Sara Meadows (ed.), *Developing Thinking: Approaches to Children's Cognitive Development* (London: Methuen, 1983).

Limón, M. and Carretero, M., 'Evidence, evaluation and reasoning abilities in the domain of history: An empirical study', in J.F. Voss, and M. Carretero (eds), *International Review of History Education: Vol. 2, Learning and Reasoning in History* (London: Woburn Press, 1998).

Lincoln, Y., 'From understanding to action: New imperatives, new criteria, new methods for interpretive researchers', *Theory and Research in Social Education*, 26, 1 (1998).

Little, J.W., 'District policy choices and teachers' professional development opportunities', *Educational Evaluation and Policy Analysis*, 11, 2 (1989).

Lowenthal, D., *The Past is a Foreign Country* (1985; reprint Cambridge: Cambridge University Press, 1993).

Macintyre, S., 'A black armband for teaching history', *Sunday Age* (5 July 1998).

McCullagh, C.B., *The Truth of History* (London: Routledge, 1998).

McKeown, M. and Beck, I., 'Making sense of accounts of history: Why young students don't and how they might', in G. Leinhardt, I. Beck and C. Stainton (eds), *Teaching and Learning in History* (Hillsdale, NJ: Lawrence Erlbaum, 1994).

McLean, M., *Educational Traditions Compared* (London: David Fulton, 1995).

MEC, *LOGSE (Ley Orgánica 1/1990, de 3 de octubre, de Ordenación General del Sistema Educativo)* BOE 4-10-90 (Madrid, 1990)

Meier, D., *The Power of Their Ideas* (Boston, MA: Beacon Press, 1995).

Melo, M., 'Adolescents' tacit substantive understandings of history', PhD dissertation (Institute of Education, University of London, 2000).

Ministry of Education, Israel; *Tochnit ha-Limudiem le-Veit ha-Sefer ha-Yesodi ha-Mamlachti ve-ha-Mamlachti ha-Dati (Curriculum for National and National-Religious Elementary Schools)* (Jerusalem, 1956).

—— *Horat ha-Shoah be-Veit ha-Sefer (Proceedings on Teaching the Holocaust in Schools)* (Jerusalem, 1961).

—— *Tochnit ha-Limudim be-Historiah le-Kitot Vav-Tet be-Veit ha-Sefer ha-Mamlachti ve-ha-Mamlachti-Dati (History Curriculum: Grades 6–9 in National and National-Religious Schools)* (Jerusalem, 1970).

—— *Chozer ha-Manchal (Director – General Newsletter)* (Jerusalem, 1 June 1982).

—— *Tochnit Limudiem: Historiah le-Kitot Vav-Tet ba-Chinuch ha-Mamlachti (History Curriculum: Grades 6–9 in National Education)* (Jerusalem, 1995).

Mor, M., *Mered Bar Kokhba Otsmato ve Hekefo* (*The Bar Kokhba Revolt, its Extent and Effect*) (Jerusalem: Yad Yitshak ben Tsevi, 1991).

Morris, B., *The Birth of the Palestinian Refugee Problem, 1947–1949* (Cambridge and New York: Cambridge University Press, 1987).

National Center for History in the Schools, *National Standards for United States History* (Los Angeles, 1994).

—— *National Standards for History* (Los Angeles CA, 1996).

National Ministry of Education (People's Republic of China), *The Curricula Standards for Full-Time Nine-Year Compulsory Education: History Teaching* (Beijing, 1996).

—— *The Curricula Standards for Full-Time Senior High Schools: History Teaching* (Beijing, 1996).

Nelson, B.S. and Hammerman, J.K., 'Reconceptualizing teaching: Moving toward the creation of intellectual communities of students, teachers, and teacher educators', in M.W. McLaughlin and I. Oberman (eds), *Teacher Learning: New Policies, New Practices* (New York: Teachers College Press, 1996).

Neusner, J. (trans.), *The Talmud of the Land of Israel*, vol. 18 of *Besah and Taanit*, (Chicago, IL: University of Chicago Press, 1987).

Nora, P., 'Between memory and history: Les lieux de mémoire', *Representations*, 26 (1998).

Novak, P., *That Noble Dream: The Objectivity Question* (Cambridge: Cambridge University Press, 1988).

Oakes, J., *Keeping Track of How Schools Structure Inequalities* (New Haven, CT: Yale University Press, 1985).

Oakland Unified School District, *Annual Report to the Community on Oakland Public Schools* (Oakland, CA, 1997).

Olson, D.R., 'Writing: The divorce of the author from the text', in Barry M. Kroll and Roberta J. Vann (eds), *Exploring Speaking–Writing Relations* (Urbana, IL: National Council of Teachers of English, 1981).

Orwell, G., *1984* (New York: Signet Classics, 1949).

Page, R., *Lower Track Classrooms: A Curricular and Cultural Perspective* (New York: Teachers College Press, 1991).

Paxton, R.J., '"Someone with like a life wrote it": The effects of a visible author on high school history students', *Journal of Educational Psychology*, 89, 2 (1997).

Pearce, S.M., 'Objects as meaning, or narrating the past', in S.M. Pearce (ed.), *Interpreting Objects and Collections* (London and New York:

Routledge, 1994).

People's Education Publishing House, *The Study of History Teaching* (Beijing: People's Education Publishing House, 1999).

Pereyra, C., *El Sujeto de la Historia* (Madrid: Alianza, 1984).

Perfetti, C., Britt, A., Rouet, J.F., Georgi, M. and Mason, R., 'How students use texts to learn and reason about historical uncertainty', in M. Carretero and J. Voss (eds), *Cognitive and Instructional Processes in History and the Social Sciences* (Hillsdale, NJ: Lawrence Erlbaum, 1994).

Perkins, D., *Smart Schools: From Training Memories to Educating Minds* (New York: Free Press, 1992).

Perry, T. and Delpit, L. (eds), *The Real Ebonics Debate: Special Issue of Rethinking Schools*, 12, 1 (1997).

Pesick, S., 'Reading, writing and history: Teaching for historical thinking and understanding', PhD dissertation (Stanford University, 1998).

Phillips, R., *History Teaching, Nationhood and the State* (London: Cassell, 1998).

Piaget, J., *The Child's Conception of Space* (London: Routledge & Kegan Paul, 1956).

Portal, C., 'Empathy as an objective for history teaching', in C. Portal (ed.), *The History Curriculum for Teachers* (Lewes: Falmer Press, 1987).

Pozo, J.I. and Carretero, M., 'El adolescente como historiador', *Infancia y Aprendizaje* (1983).

—— 'Las explicaciones causales de expertos y novatos en historia', in M. Carretero, J.I. Pozo and M. Asensio (eds), *La Enseñanza de las Ciencias Sociales* (Madrid: Visor, 1989).

Price, P., 'History in schools – part of the problem, part of the solution', *Australian Historical Association Bulletin*, 88 (June 1999).

Ram, U., 'Zionist historiography and the invention of modern Jewish nationhood: The case of Ben-Zion Dinur', *History and Memory*, 7, 1 (1995).

Ravitch, Diane, *The Schools We Deserve* (New York: Basic Books, 1985).

Resnick, L.B. and Klopfer, L.E. (eds), *Toward the Thinking Curriculum: Current Cognitive Research* (Washington, DC: ASCD, 1989).

Ricoeur, P., *Time and Narrative,* vol. 2 (Chicago, IL: University of Chicago Press, 1984).

—— *Oneself as Another* (Chicago, IL: University of Chicago Press, 1992).

Rodrigo, M.J., 'Promoting narrative literacy and historical literacy', in M. Carretero and J.F. Voss (eds), *Cognitive and Instructional Processes in History and the Social Sciences* (Hillsdale, NJ: Lawrence Erlbaum, 1994).

Rogers, P.J., 'Why teach history?', in A.K. Dickinson, P.J. Lee and P.J. Rogers (eds) *Learning History* (London: Heinemann Educational, 1984).

Ross, Dorothy, *The Origins of American Social Science* (Cambridge: Cambridge University Press, 1991).

Salmon, Lucy, 'History in the German gymnasia', in American Historical Association, *The Study of History in Schools: Report to the American Historical Association by Committee of Seven* (New York: Macmillan, 1899).

Saxe, David Warren, *Social Studies in Schools: A History of the Early Years* (Albany, NY: State University of New York Press, 1991).

Schaff, A., *Historia y Verdad* (Mexico: Grijalbo, 1974).

Schrag, P., 'The emasculated voice of the textbook', *Saturday Review* (21 January 1967).

Schwab, J., *Science Curriculum and Liberal Education: Selected Essays* (Chicago, IL: University of Chicago Press, 1978).

Seixias, P., 'Parallel crises: history and social studies curriculum in the USA', *Journal of Curriculum Studies*, 25, 3 (1993).

—— 'Historical understanding among adolescents in a multicultural setting', *Curriculum Enquiry*, 23, 3 (1993).

—— 'Popular film and young people's understanding of the history of native–white relations', *History Teacher*, 26, 3 (May 1993).

—— 'Conceptualizing growth in historical understanding', in D. Olson and N. Torrance (eds), *The Handbook of Education and Human Development* (Cambridge, MA and London: Blackwell, 1996).

—— 'Mapping the terrain of historical significance', *Social Education*, 61, 1 (1997).

—— 'The place of the disciplines within social studies: The case of history', in I. Wright and A. Sears (eds), *Trends and Issues in Canadian Social Studies* (Vancouver, BC: Pacific Educational Press, 1997).

Shanghai Education Publishing House, *Comparative History of Education* (Shanghai: Shanghai Education Publishing House, 1995).

Shanghai Institute of Social Sciences, *History Education* (Shanghai: Shanghai Institute of Social Sciences Press, 1989).

Shavit, S. (ed.), *Shiuriem be-Historia, Kerech 2* (*History Lessons, Vol. 2*)

(Jerusalem: Ministry of Education, 1987).

—— *Toldot Yisrael ve-ha-Amim, Kerech 2* (*History of Israel and the Nations, Vol. 2*) (Jerusalem: Ministry of Education, 1987).

Shemilt, D., *History 13–16 Evaluation Study* (Edinburgh: Holmes McDougall, 1980).

—— 'The devil's locomotive', *History and Theory*, 22, 4 (1983).

—— 'Beauty and the philosopher: Empathy in history and the classroom', in A.K. Dickinson, P.J. Lee and P.J. Rogers (eds), *Learning History* (London: Heinemann Educational, 1984).

—— 'Adolescent ideas about evidence and methodology in history', in C. Portal (ed.), *The History Curriculum for Teachers* (Lewes: Falmer Press, 1987).

—— 'Review essay' on L. Kramer, D. Reid and W. Barney, *Learning History in America: Schools, Cultures and Politics* (Minneapolis, MN: University of Minnesota Press, 1994), in *History and Theory*, 35, 2 (1996).

—— 'The caliph's coin: The currency of narrative frameworks in history teaching', in P. Seixas, P. Stearns and S. Wineburg (eds), *Teaching, Learning and Knowing History* (New York: New York University Press, 2000).

Shmueli, M., *Korot Amenu* (Jerusalem: Tarbut ve-Chinuch, 1958).

Sizer, T., *Horace's Compromise: The Dilemma of the American High School* (Boston, MA: Houghton Mifflin, 1992).

—— *Horace's Hope: What Works for the American High School* (Boston, MA: Houghton Mifflin, 1996).

Skilbeck, M., 'The nature of history and its place in the curriculum', *Australian History Teacher*, 6 (1979).

Smallwood, M.E., *The Jews under Roman Rule* (Leiden: E.J. Brill, 1976).

Smith, R., ' Social studies education: The need for reappraisal', *Unicorn*, 12, 3 (1986).

Stearns, P., Seixas, P. and Wineburg, S. (eds), *Teaching, Learning and Knowing History: National and International Perspectives* (New York: New York University Press, 2000).

Stern, M., *Greek and Latin Authors on Jews and Judaism*, 2 (Jerusalem: Israel Academy of Sciences and Humanities, 1980).

Steward, S. and Praetzellis, M. (eds), *Sights and Sounds: Essays in Celebration of West Oakland* (Oakland, CA: CALTRANS, District 4, 1997).

Stone, L., 'The revival of narrative', *Past and Present* 85 (1981).

Sullivan, James, 'Suggested changes in course of study in history', *History Teacher's Magazine*, 2 (January 1911).

Thompson, D., 'Understanding the past: Procedures and content', in A.K. Dickinson, P.J. Lee and P.J. Rogers (eds), *Learning History* (London: Heinemann Educational, 1984).

Topolski, J., 'Towards an integrated model of historical explanation', *History and Theory* (1991).

Trabasso, T. and Sperry, L., 'Causal relatedness and importance of story events', *Memory and Language*, 24 (1985).

Van Maanen, J., *Tales of the Field : On Writing Ethnography* (Chicago, IL: University of Chicago Press, 1988).

Van Tassel, D., 'From learned society to professional organization: The American Historical Association, 1884-1900', *American Historical Review*, 89 (October 1984).

Veyne, P. *Cómo se Escribe la Historia: Foucault Revoluciona la Historia* (Madrid: Alianza Editorial, 1984).

Veysey, Laurence R., *The Emergence of the American University* (Chicago, IL: University of Chicago Press, 1965).

Voss, J.F., Carretero, M., Kennet, J. and Silfies, L.N., 'The collapse of the Soviet Union: A case study in causal reasoning', in M. Carretero and J.F. Voss (eds), *Cognitive and Instructional Processes in History and the Social Sciences* (Hillsdale, NJ: Lawrence Erlbaum, 1994).

Vygotsky, L., *Thought and Language* (1934; revised edn by Alex Kozulin, Cambridge, MA: Massachusetts Institute of Technology, 1989).

Wagg, P., 'Response to Alan Ryan', *Australian Historical Association Bulletin*, 88 (June 1999).

Walker, Linda Robinson, 'John Dewey at Michigan', *Michigan Today* (Fall 1997).

Walsh, W.H., *An Introduction to Philosophy of History* (1951; reprint London: Hutchinson, 1967).

Watson, D., 'Back to the past', *Australian Review of Books* (20 December 1997).

Webster's New Biographical Dictionary (Springfield, MA: Merriam-Webster, 1983).

Wertsch, J.V. and Rozin, M., 'The Russian revolution: Official and unofficial accounts', in J.F. Voss and M. Carretero (eds), *International Review of History Education: Vol. 2, Learning and Reasoning in History* (London: Woburn Press, 1998).

Whelan, Michael, 'Albert Bushnell Hart and the origins of social studies education', *Theory and Research in Social Education*, 22 (Fall 1994).

—— 'A particularly lucid lens: The Committee of Ten and the Social Studies Committee in Historical Context', *Curriculum and Supervision*, 12 (Spring 1997).

White, H. *Metahistory: The Historical Imagination of Nineteenth-Century Europe* (Baltimore, MD: Johns Hopkins University Press, 1973).

—— *The Content of the Form: Narrative Discourse and Historical Representation* (Baltimore, MD: Johns Hopkins University Press, 1987).

White, J.J., 'Searching for substantial knowledge in social studies texts', *Theory and Research in Social Education*, 16, 2 (Spring 1988).

White, R., *Remembering Ahanagran* (New York: Hill & Wang, 1998).

Wineburg, S., 'Historical problem solving: A study of the cognitive processes in the evaluation of documentary and pictorial evidence', *Educational Psychology*, 83, 1 (1991).

—— 'On the reading of historical texts: Notes on the breach between school and academy', *American Educational Research Journal*, 28, 3 (1991).

—— 'The psychology of learning and teaching history', in D.C. Berliner and R.C. Calfee (eds), *Handbook of Educational Psychology* (New York and London: Macmillan, 1996).

—— 'Making historical sense', in P. Seixas, P. Stearns and S. Wineburg (eds), *Teaching, Learning and Knowing History* (New York: New York University Press, 2000).

Wineburg, S. and Fournier, J., 'Contextualized thinking in history', in M. Carretero and J.F. Voss (eds), *Cognitive and Instructional Processes in History and the Social Sciences* (Hillsdale, NJ: Lawrence Erlbaum, 1994).

Wiske, M.S. (ed.), *Teaching for Understanding: A Practical Framework* (San Francisco, CA: Jossey-Bass, 1998).

Wrong, George M., 'History in Canadian schools', in American Historical Association, *The Study of History in Schools: Report to the American Historical Association by the Committee of Seven* (New York: Macmillan, 1899).

Yerushalmi, Y.H., *Zakhor: Jewish History and Jewish Memory* (Seattle, WA: University of Washington Press, 1982).

Zerubavel, Y., *Recovered Roots: Collective Memory and the Making of Israeli National Tradition* (Chicago, IL: University of Chicago Press, 1995).

Index

241